NEWCASTLE-UNDER-LYME
ITS RAILWAY AND CANAL HISTORY

BY

ALLAN C. BAKER & MIKE G. FELL

Newcastle station in 1952 looking south towards Stoke and the single line tunnel. Notice the platform mounted signal box to the right and the covered walkway from road level to the left hand, up platform. The bridge carries King Street over the railway and the booking office, which was at street level, is to the right above and behind the signal box. The Borough Hotel, which was on the opposite side of King Street, provides the backcloth.

IRWELL PRESS Ltd.

ACKNOWLEDGEMENTS

Bev Stringer, mentioned in the Preface, has kindly assisted in the description of Newcastle station and goods warehouse from an architectural viewpoint and has provided copies of drawings and maps. Thanks are also due to Delyth Copp, Manager of the Newcastle-under-Lyme Museum, Phil Atkins, formerly Research Centre Manager at the National Railway Museum at York, and Jean Milton, formerly of the Museum of Science and Industry in Manchester, who have all kindly made available photographs and records in their care. We need to record our thanks to those responsible for the National Archives at Kew where Allan has spent many hundreds of hours searching the records of the North Staffordshire Railway and its successors for information relevant to this work; without Allan's dedication to this primary research it would be much the poorer. Other depositories consulted include the General Register Office, the House of Lords Record Office, the Staffordshire County Record Office at Stafford, the Stoke-on-Trent City Archives (housed in the Central Reference Library at Hanley), Keele University Library and Sheffield Archives where the records of the Yorkshire Engine Company are kept.

A special word of thanks for Martin Connop-Price who so diligently recorded the railways of newcastle when he lived in the area. One of the authors was extremely pleased to acquire his negatives some years ago via the good offices of Basil Jeuda.

Basil Jeuda has been very helpful in providing useful information and we are most appreciative to Roger Hateley for his excellent cartographic skills. We have also drawn on the writings and observations undertaken by the following who are sadly no longer with us: Dr. J R (Jack) Hollick, William (Bill) Jack, Robert Keys, Harry Minshall and Jack Riley. All photographs are either individually credited or are from the authors' collections.

We would like to mention our membership of the North Staffordshire Railway Study Group which is devoted to recording the history of the former North Staffordshire Railway. For those wishing to learn more about *The Knotty*, membership of this Group is highly recommended. Please log into the website www.lnw1.demon.co.uk/nsrsg.htm or contact David Moore, 6 Pennine Way, Biddulph, Staffs. ST8 7EJ.

ABBREVIATIONS and MEASUREMENTS

BR	British Railways
BRB	British Railways Board
BWB	British Waterways Board
GJR	Grand Junction Railway
GWR	Great Western Railway
L&MR	Liverpool & Manchester Railway
LMR	London Midland Region
LMS	London Midland & Scottish Railway
LNWR	London & North Western Railway
MCCI	Midland Coal Coke & Iron Company Limited
NSR	North Staffordshire Railway
PET	Potteries Electric Traction Company Limited
PMT	Potteries Motor Traction Company Limited
SNuLR	Silverdale & Newcastle-under-Lyme Railway

Note. The NSR Traffic Committee existed until 1867 when it was superseded by the Traffic & Finance Committee.

Used in the text: One furlong = 220 yards; one chain = 22 yards; one link = 7.92 inches; there are 100 links in a chain.

First published in the United Kingdom in 2009
by Irwell Press Limited, 59A, High Street, Clophill,
Bedfordshire MK45 4BE
Printed by Konway Printhouse

CONTENTS

Apedale Junction on 25 April 1964 looking towards Silverdale with the Apedale branch curving away to the right. The line on the extreme right is the siding to serve the British Thomson Houston Company factory which connected with the main line behind the photographer.

PREFACE

This is the story of canal and railway activity in and around Newcastle-under-Lyme in North Staffordshire. Both authors used to live within one mile of Newcastle railway station: Allan Baker at Basford and Mike Fell at Cross Heath. During our time in Newcastle the canals had long been derelict but we were very familiar with the local railways then operated by the nationalised British Railways (BR). When our fathers were born the railways were owned and operated by the North Staffordshire Railway (NSR) but they knew them best after ownership and control had passed to the London Midland & Scottish Railway Company (LMS) in 1923. They encouraged our interest, especially when we got together through a common bond – the history and operation of those railways and their predecessors, the canals. That bond was fired still further by our mentor Dr. Jack Hollick who at that time was a general medical practitioner and lived at 'The Grey House' in Ashbourne. As *the* authority on the NSR, he ensured that our quest for ever more information intensified as the years passed by. Stephen Allan Baker (1911-1997), Arthur James Fell (1916-1985) and John [Jack]

Reginald Hollick (1910-1991) would have been proud to have read this book. It is dedicated to their memory.

The initial inspiration came from Bev Stringer who lives in Newcastle and his late wife Joy. Bev is building a model of Newcastle Station and Goods Yard which encouraged Mike to produce an article describing those facilities for the North Staffordshire Railway Study Group. Following Mike's usual consultation with Allan, the article has blossomed to become this book which now includes not only our memories and extensive local knowledge of transportation in and around Newcastle but, more importantly, the fruits of Allan's exhaustive primary research in the National Archives and elsewhere, including a visit to Cheshire to study canal archives retrieved from their dusty hiding place in a former salt mine!

We apologise in advance for the lack of an index. To have included one would have occupied a lot of space and we felt most readers would prefer a larger illustrative content instead. However, we have sub-divided the Chapters, listing the sub-divisions on the Contents page, and hope that this will help compensate and allow readers to

find what they may be looking for reasonably easily. There is some duplication between the Chapters as although we have attempted to separate the canal history from the railway history, there is inevitably some overlap, as there is with the four Chapters dealing with the railways. Please note that some events, in the interests of clarity, are taken out of strict chronological sequence.

We obviously hope the book will appeal to those interested in railways and canals but we also anticipate that it will appeal to those interested in Newcastle's industrial history as well as those who simply like to know more about where they live and what happened in the past. The book can be read from cover to cover but each chapter is also designed around a particular topic that can readily stand alone. Moreover, the copious illustrations, maps and drawings have been carefully chosen and have long captions to encourage those who simply wish to browse. We hope that you will like what you see and enjoy the fruits of our research.

Allan C. Baker, High Halden, Kent
Mike G. Fell, Elloughton, East Riding of Yorkshire

Class K mixed pick-up freight, denoted by the headlamp positions, just breasting the grade from Knutton as it approaches Brampton Sidings on 15 January 1966. The engines is one of Stoke's numerous Stanier Class 5 4-6-0s 45422. The site of Liverpool Road Halt is lost in the smoke to the rear of the train. (Martin R Connop-Price - Authors Collection)

Stoke Newcastle Junction, situated a short distance north of Stoke, was where the Newcastle & Market Drayton branch left the NSR main line to Macclesfield & Crewe. The train seen here is a mixed class H hauled by one of Stoke's Fairburn Class 4 2-6-4 tank engines, 42674, on 12 April 1962. The train is on the down slow line, the fast line being on the other side of the signal box, which dates from the 1908 remodelling of the junction. (FW Shuttleworth)

Harts Hill, notice the signal box name board has it as two words, although it is more usually spelt as one, is where the single line section through the tunnels to Newcastle commenced. The train is a down one for Newcastle consisting of a light engine and brake van, the van being propelled and the crew having just collected the electric token for the single line section. The date is 14 January 1966, shortly before this section closed, and the engine one of Stoke's Stanier Class 5 4-6-0s, doubtless heading for either Holditch or Silverdale colliery to collect loaded wagons. The catch points on the left hand, up line, are unusual, as the grade is 1 in 102 falling towards Newcastle Junction in the distance. They are however, provided in view of the single line section, and to allow shunting to take place in the sidings to the left beyond the signal box. (Martin R Connop-Price - Authors Collection)

INTRODUCTION

In 1801, shortly after the last links in its canal system had been completed, Newcastle-under-Lyme supported a population of about 4,600. Fifty years later at the dawn of Newcastle's railway era this had grown to around 11,000 inhabitants. Traditional local trade comprised clay pipe making, pottery manufacture, hat making, shoe making and brewing. Industry on a larger scale included silk and cotton milling, fustian production and, in the outlying districts of Chesterton, Apedale and Silverdale, coal and ironstone mining and the manufacture of iron. It was primarily to meet the needs of the coal and iron industries that the canals and railways were built.

Newcastle has never been a part of The Potteries. The six pottery towns of Tunstall, Burslem, Hanley, Stoke, Fenton and Longton combined to form a single county borough of Stoke-on-Trent on 31 March 1910, later acquiring city status on 5 June 1925. In 1932 the urban district council of Wolstanton, covering the parishes of Chesterton, Silverdale and Wolstanton, happily amalgamated with the Newcastle-under-Lyme municipal borough thus increasing its population overnight from 24,000 to over 55,000 inhabitants. The amalgamation took place in order to keep the increasingly ambitious city of Stoke-on-Trent at bay.

Transport through Newcastle has experienced a fascinating but frustrating history. The town benefited marginally from the canal era, principally through access to cheap coal supplies and as a source of water for steam engines that drove the machinery of its silk and cotton mills, but it was disadvantaged by not being located on a major through waterway. The town's thriving stagecoach business was decimated on 4 July 1837 with the opening of Whitmore Station on the Grand Junction Railway (GJR) which formed part of the west coast main line running north to south some fives miles to the west of Newcastle. At this date over 40 horse drawn stagecoaches passed through Newcastle each day, with 10 coaches, including the Royal Mail, to London, four to Birmingham, six to Liverpool and four to Manchester. Goods transport was also well organised with scheduled wagon services to London (daily), Liverpool, Manchester, Oxford and Bristol. The GJR ended virtually all of this long distance road traffic, customers

preferring the more reliable and speedier service by rail. Whitmore was described by the GJR as a 'First Class Station' and it became the transhipment point for Newcastle and the Potteries. This situation did not improve even when the North Staffordshire Railway (NSR) arrived on the scene, as its main line from Crewe to Derby and Burton, opened in 1848, also by-passed the town to the east. Newcastle found itself sandwiched between two main lines which between them had wholly eclipsed the once thriving trade on its turnpike roads. This is why Newcastle's industrialists and landowners had earlier taken independent action in an endeavour to make things happen.

The frustration is summed up admirably by Arnold Bennett (1867-1931) on the first page of *CLAYHANGER*, published in 1910. With a scene set in 1872, Bennett, who always ignored Fenton, had this to say about the Borough of Newcastle-under-Lyme: *A hundred years earlier the canal* [i.e. the Trent & Mersey Canal] *had only been obtained after a vicious Parliamentary fight between industry and the fine ancient borough, which saw canals a menace to its importance as a centre of traffic. Fifty years earlier the fine and ancient borough had succeeded in forcing the greatest railway line in England* [i.e. the GJR] *to run through unpopulated country five miles off instead of through the Five Towns, because it loathed the mere conception of a railway. And now, people are enquiring why the Five Towns, with a railway system special to itself* [i.e. the NSR], *is characterised by a perhaps excessive provincialism. Oldcastle* [Bennett's pseudonym for Newcastle] *guessed not the vast influences of its sublime stupidity.*

Strong words indeed, but very true.

The first railway to arrive in the town of Newcastle was Ralph Sneyd's Silverdale & Newcastle-under-Lyme Railway which reached Pool Dam in November 1849. This was followed by the North Staffordshire Railway line through Newcastle Station which was opened on 6 September 1852. This line carried on westwards to meet Sneyd's line at Knutton. The branch railway to Apedale was opened in 1853 and in the following year the proprietors of the Newcastle-under-Lyme Canal opened a short railway from the canal basin at Brook Lane to make on end-on connection with Sneyd's railway at Pool Dam. To

complete the overall picture, in later years the railway to Silverdale was extended to Market Drayton under an Act of Parliament obtained in 1864 but did not open for goods and passenger traffic until 1 February 1870. The Audley line, authorised by a separate 1864 Act, was opened for goods traffic on 24 July 1870 but had to wait a further ten years for passenger trains which commenced running on 28 June 1880.

Newcastle's railways were branch lines but they served the community well until they too were eclipsed by electric trams, traction engines, steam lorries and motor vehicles. Somewhat ironically, the town's Liverpool and London Roads, formerly turnpikes, witnessed a revival of freight and passenger traffic after the passing of the Trunk Roads Act in 1936 when they became part of the A34. This situation prevailed until the opening of the M6 motorway in 1963. Once again, Newcastle's congested roads now carry only local traffic and the town has no canals, no trams and no railways. Such is the march of progress unfolded by our story.

A comparatively late view from the bridge taking Church Lane, which runs from Silverdale to Knutton, over the line and looking towards Silverdale. By the time this photograph was taken on 21 October 1989, the remaining single line was already out of use as Holditch Colliery had ceased coal winding the previous July. Note to the right the prominent remains of several colliery dirt tips. The gradient here is 1 in 82 raising towards Silverdale, and always a stiff proposition for loaded trains. This is part of the very first railway to serve Newcastle, Ralph Sneyd's Silverdale & Newcastle-under-Lyme Railway of 1849.

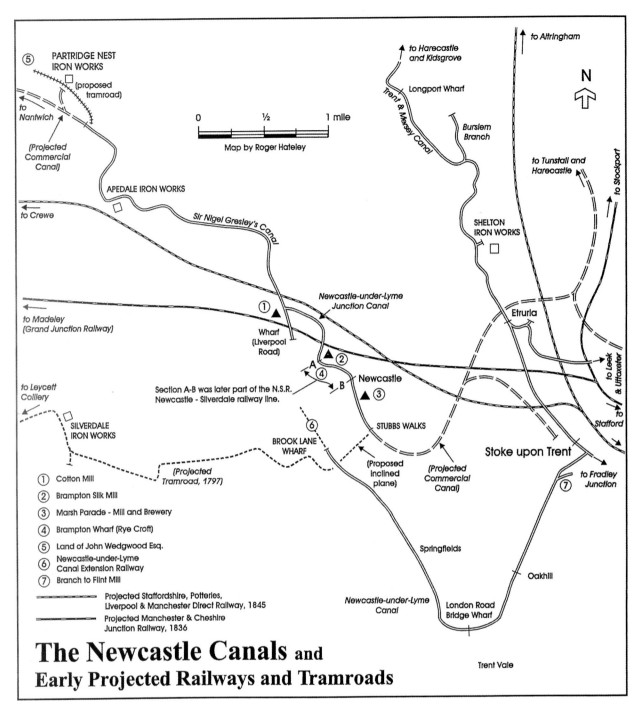

Map labels (top section)

⑤ PARTRIDGE NEST
IRON WORKS
□ (proposed tramroad)

to Nantwich

(Projected Commercial Canal)

to Crewe

APEDALE IRON WORKS
□

Sir Nigel Gresley's Canal

0   ½   1 mile

Map by Roger Hateley

to Harecastle and Kidsgrove

Longport Wharf

Trent & Mersey Canal

Burslem Branch

to Altringham

N

to Tunstall and Harecastle

to Stockport

SHELTON IRON WORKS
□

Newcastle-under-Lyme Junction Canal

① ▲

Wharf (Liverpool Road)

to Madeley (Grand Junction Railway)

Etruria

▲ ②

A
④
B

Newcastle

▲ ③

Section A-B was later part of the N.S.R. Newcastle - Silverdale railway line.

to Leycett Colliery

SILVERDALE IRON WORKS
□

(Projected Tramroad, 1797)

⑥

BROOK LANE WHARF

STUBBS WALKS

(Proposed inclined plane)

(Projected Commercial Canal)

to Leek & Uttoxeter

to Stafford

Stoke upon Trent

to Fradley Junction

⑦

Springfields

Oakhill

Newcastle-under-Lyme Canal

London Road Bridge Wharf

① Cotton Mill
② Brampton Silk Mill
③ Marsh Parade - Mill and Brewery
④ Brampton Wharf (Rye Croft)
⑤ Land of John Wedgwood Esq.
⑥ Newcastle-under-Lyme Canal Extension Railway
⑦ Branch to Flint Mill

—————— Projected Staffordshire, Potteries, Liverpool & Manchester Direct Railway, 1845
—————— Projected Manchester & Cheshire Junction Railway, 1836

The Newcastle Canals and
Early Projected Railways and Tramroads

Trent Vale

Loaded coal train on the Apedale branch approaching Apedale Junction on New Year's Day 1964; some years before it was a Bank Holiday in England. The engine is one of Stoke's Stanier Class 5s, in this case 45074 with a respectable load for the 1 in 190 gradient. (Martin R Connop-Price - Authors Collection)

CHAPTER ONE
THE NEWCASTLE-UNDER-LYME CANALS

Three Canals

There cannot have been many towns in this country the size of Newcastle-under-Lyme, that could boast no less then three independent canals, all of which (though two of them to a greater extent than the third) having a significant influence on the later development of railways to serve the town. The three canals were respectively: Sir Nigel Gresley's Canal which dated from 1776 or thereabouts; the Newcastle-under-Lyme Canal of about 1800 and lastly the Newcastle-under-Lyme Junction Canal of about 1801. Let us now examine them one by one, along with their relationships, not only between themselves, but also with other canal schemes and the later railways; those that were actually built, along with those that got no further than the planning stage.

The Gresley Canal

Sir Nigel Gresley (6th Bart 1726-1787) was a member of the Gresley family of Drakelow Park near Burton-on-Trent and a significant land owner in and around Newcastle and in particular to the north-west of the town at nearby Apedale and Chesterton. In and around Apedale there were extensive coal and ironstone mines as well as early iron making operations, 'situate at Apedale, by Chesterton and Holditch', as the Canal Act about to be described put it. To better serve the town of Newcastle with its need for coal, Sir Nigel and his son Nigel Bowyer Gresley (7th Bart 1753-1808) promoted a Bill through Parliament to 'make and maintain a navigable cut or canal from certain coal mines in Apedale to Newcastle-under-Lyme'. The canal was projected to be three miles long, level throughout with a terminus at a wharf alongside the Newcastle to Chesterton road – later the Liverpool Road – which became a Turnpike Road in 1714. The Act to build the canal received the Royal Assent on 13 April 1775 (15 Geo III ch xvi); the actual date of opening appears to have gone unrecorded, but would doubtless have been some time in the following year, 1776. Among its many clauses the Act, which runs to 37 pages, stipulated that the town of Newcastle, as well as those parts of Stoke-upon-Trent adjoining (this is the town of Stoke itself; not to be confused with the later Federation of Pottery towns which became Stoke-on-Trent), to be provided with land-sale of coal for a period of 21 years at 5/- (25p) per ton, and for a further 21 years at a rate of 5/6d (27½p)

per ton – pro-rata for lower quantities. There was also a clause allowing the latter figure to be increased to 6/- (30p) per ton under certain circumstances – one reason why Commissioners were appointed as described in the next paragraph – as well as a commitment under a financial penalty to maintain a stock of coal at the wharf, although the exact quantity was not stipulated.

The Act embodied powers to enter lands and make surveys, take land, alter roads and make towing paths. The land to be taken was not to exceed a width of 20 yards, including the towing paths, except where boats were to pass, in which case it could be 30 yards, while the depth of the cut was not to exceed

five feet. Despite the powers for the compulsory purchase of the land required, it appears that most, if not all of it already belonged to the Gresley estate. The water supply, which it seems was for ever a problem with this and the later Junction Canal, was planned to come from the coal mines and 'such springs as may be found when making the canal, streams and water courses, as well as may communicate with land cut or canal or be found within a distance of 1,000 yards'.

There were several clauses in the Act relating to potential disputes over land ownership (although in the event this does not appear to have been a problem) and how legal expenses in this

Sir Nigel Gresley Bt (1726-1787) who features prominently in our story; Lord of the Manor of Apedale and what a dapper chap he appears to be. (Portrait by Henry Pickering, courtesy National Museum of Wales)

Two views of the remains of the Gresley Canal, just short of the site of the Apedale Ironworks, 28 December 1966. The top looks towards Apedale and the bottom to Newcastle; the high ground to the rear in the top photograph is part of the former ironworks slag tip.

connection might be paid. Numerous influential people are listed in the Act to perform the duties of arbitrators (called Commissioners and including just about anybody who was anybody for miles around!) in the event of any disputes arising – almost 300 in the end. There were provisions as how the Commissioners were to act, how any expenses were to be paid, fees and penalties collected, along with how any legal proceedings might be progressed, should they become necessary. There was also a requirement for a clerk to be appointed to manage the day-to-day activities of the canal. Fences were to be provided and if any 'highways' were obstructed bridges had to be built first, and any adjacent landowners could make their own bridges if they so wished. Last but not least, any owner or occupier of adjacent land could use boats – presumably supplied by themselves – for carrying manure without paying any tolls. Obviously the movement of agricultural manure was important hereabouts!

The Gresley Canal as we shall hereafter call it, would appear to have been a reasonably successful undertaking, despite being completely isolated from the main inland waterway system which was rapidly developing in the country around the same time. In the words of Joseph Priestley, writing in his *Navigable Rivers & Canals* in 1831: 'There are few private works of more real utility to the public than Sir Nigel Gresley's Canal, which has added considerably to the interests of the inhabitants of Newcastle, by the regularity wherewith they are supplied with coal at a moderate charge'. The reference here to Sir Nigel Bower Gresley, inferring he was the owner of the canal, is incorrect, as by this time both father and son had passed on. Unfortunately no information appears to have come down to us as to exactly how the canal was used but the main traffic of coal would have been carried in boats belonging to Gresley or his successors; in other words whoever was working the Apedale mines at the time. No more do we know how much, or if any manure was actually transported and therefore, if any 'private' boats operated alongside those carrying the coal. Iron might also have been carried, as Newcastle had for many years a well established iron-market; one of the main thoroughfares in the town to this day is known as The Ironmarket.

In 1812 a second Act of Parliament was obtained in connection with the Gresley Canal, entitled 'An Act for better supplying with Coal the Town of Newcastle-under-Lyme, in the County of Stafford' (52 Geo III ch lxxvii); it received the Royal Assent on 5 May 1812. This Act concerned itself with a number of matters, not least the change in ownership of the canal since the Gresleys, father and son, had died. It would appear that disputes had arisen

among the new owners. Not just the canal, but the mines and other works at Apedale had passed to other members of the Gresley family, along with Thomas Levett and Richard Edensor Heathcote – we shall be better acquainted with Heathcote later. The earlier arbitration arrangements proved unwieldy; unsurprisingly perhaps, with almost 300 individual Commissioners potentially involved, so a much smaller group was constituted under this Act, twenty-four of them this time. The Act also provided for an increase in the charges for the land-sale of coal in Newcastle. The mines originally considered in the earlier Act having almost become exhausted, the increase allowed for the capital expenditure on developing new coal seams, as well as the intended erection of a fire-engine – a steam beam pumping engine to keep the workings from flooding. Coal from the seven and eight foot Nabs seams at Bignall Hill (this pit was actually at Partridge Nest) was to be sold at a price of 7/6d (37½p) per ton, and that from the eight and ten foot Hams mines at Apedale at 6/- (30p) per ton. In each case the price agreement was for a period of six years, from 20 July 1812, but thereafter it was possible for the proprietors to increase the price to 8/- (40p) and 6/6d (32½p) respectively, provided good reasons were advanced, for example increased capital expenditure or labour costs, the agreement of the Commissioners first being obtained. The minimum amount of coal to be offered for land-sale was not less than 100 tons per week, all of which had to come from the Hams seams; that is, the less expensive coal, although any quantity in excess of this could come from either of the mines. Provision was made for coal to be sold from wharfs on the Newcastle-under-Lyme Junction Canal (still to be described) in which case a further 4d (1½p) per ton could be charged to allow for the additional distance it had to be carried. Other earlier concerns involved the correct weighing of the coal, and there was a requirement to erect a public weighing machine at Red Lion Square in Newcastle – this is in the High Street, at the junction with Church Street, by St Giles Church. Additionally, a stock of not less than 1,000 tons of coal had to be maintained on at least one of the coal wharfs in the town, between 5 December and the end of January each year; in earlier years ice had made the canal un-navigable and stocks had been completely exhausted.

The Newcastle-under-Lyme Canal - The Lower Canal
We must now turn our attention to the Newcastle-under-Lyme Canal. But first of all it is opportune to mention that the original scheme for the Grand Trunk Canal (later renamed the Trent & Mersey) had envisaged a branch to Newcastle. The Grand Trunk had opened throughout from Preston Brook

in neighbouring Cheshire, where it joined the Duke of Bridgewater's Canal (which connected with the River Mersey) to Derwent Mouth at Wilden Ferry in Derbyshire in 1777; there it joined the River Trent, which was navigable at that point. In the event a branch was not built and it was left to a group of local industrialists to promote a Bill for a canal to serve the town. This canal, which like Gresley's was level throughout, was almost four miles long and ran from a junction with the Trent & Mersey at Stoke, to a wharf at Brook Lane south-west of the town. Lime kilns were later erected at the Brook Lane basin and one of the principal traffics was limestone from the Caldon Low quarries in the Staffordshire Moorlands, which came via the Caldon and Trent & Mersey canals. The route was surveyed by William Clowes and the plans are dated 13 September 1794; the Bill and plans were deposited with Parliament on 30 September 1794. The Act, The Newcastle-under-Lyme Canal Act 1795, received the Royal Assent on 2 June 1795 (35 Geo 111 ch lxxxvii) and the canal opened at some time between 1798 and 1800; the exact date appears to have gone unrecorded. From its junction with the Trent & Mersey at Stoke it headed south-west towards Trent Vale and Hanford, before turning more or less sharp right to head due north to follow the Lyme Brook (a tributary of the River Trent) to the town of Newcastle. This circuitous route was necessary to avoid the high ground otherwise separating Stoke from Newcastle. In stark contrast to this almost four miles of canal, when a railway was eventually built to serve Newcastle, the distance from Stoke was but two miles and three chains, albeit at the expense of two tunnels, 96 and 650yds in length, along with gradients as steep as 1 in 102 for over a mile. The Newcastle Canal had a short tunnel under part of Stoke town centre, and there was a short branch on its south side and immediately on the Newcastle side of the tunnel – it formed a trailing junction for boats heading towards Newcastle. The branch served the Gordon Flint Mill and was but 150 yards long and partly in a tunnel; it left the main line exactly three furlongs from its junction with the Trent & Mersey.

The Newcastle-under-Lyme Junction Canal - The Upper Canal
It was an attempt to join the two canals, the Gresley and the Newcastle, that the town's third and last canal was promoted, hence its name, the Newcastle-under-Lyme Junction Canal. Before describing it we have to introduce another 'landed' family into the story, the Heathcotes, briefly mentioned above. They too were originally from Derbyshire, but from 1777 were resident in Longton and, later, Apedale. Sir John Edensor Heathcote (1757-1822) married in 1780 Anne, the eldest daughter of Sir Nigel Gresley and thereby inherited a

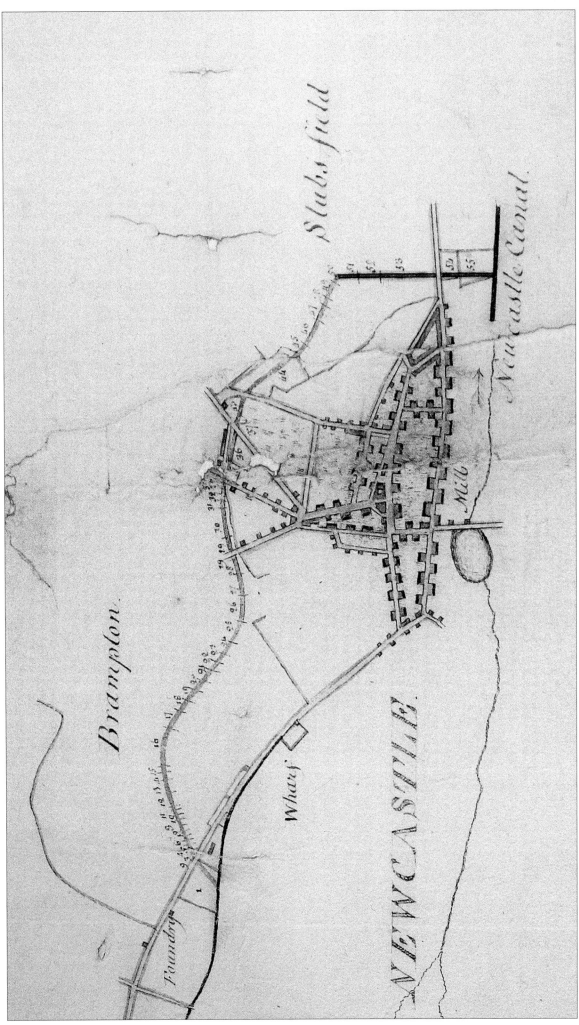

Plan of the Newcastle-under-Lyme Junction Canal taken from the 1797 survey by Charles Roberts which accompanied the Bill for an Act of Parliament to build the canal. The small numbers along the route were part of a key to indicate land ownership for which compulsory purchase powers were required. Note that the plan shows the proposed 'inclined plane or railway' from Stubs Field (the modern spelling is Stubbs) between numbers 50 and 55, connecting with the Newcastle-under-Lyme Canal, here described as the Newcastle Canal. Note too, the extreme eastern end of Gresley's Canal with its wharf alongside the London Road. The stream running along the bottom of the plan is the Lyme Brook. Unfortunately, in view of its age, this plan is in far from being in perfect condition; however, it is felt its inclusion is justified in the light of its historical value.

12

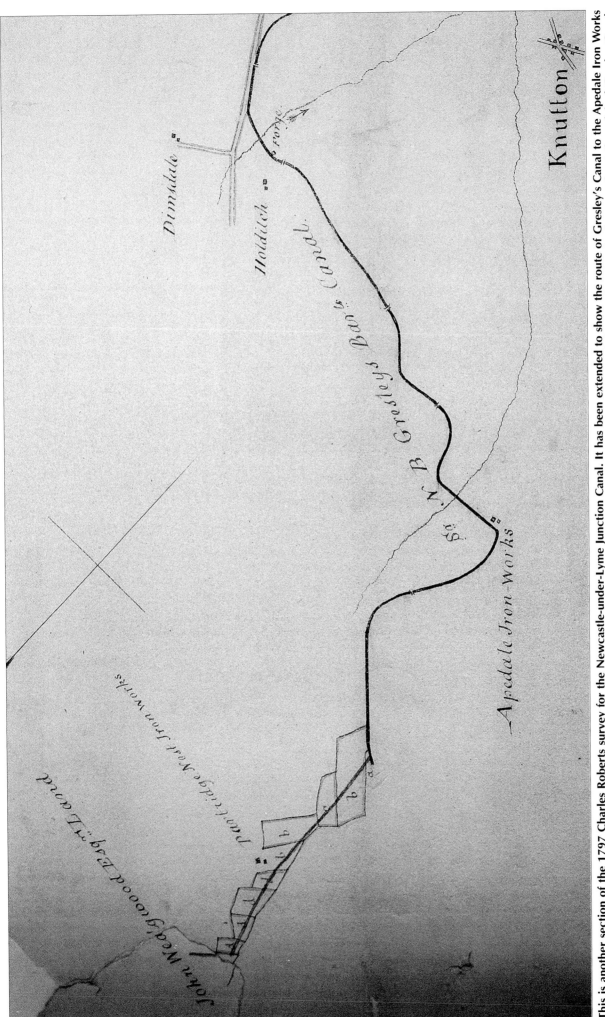

Dimsdale

Holditch

Forge

T. B Gresleys Bar's Canal.

is

Apedale Iron-Works

Partridge Nest Iron works

John Wedgwood Esqr.

Knutton

This is another section of the 1797 Charles Roberts survey for the Newcastle-under-Lyme Junction Canal. It has been extended to show the route of Gresley's Canal to the Apedale Iron Works and onwards to connect with a proposed 'railedway' to the Partridge Nest Iron Works and adjacent coal pits. This was part of the Junction Canal scheme and not the original Gresley Canal, although there is no evidence that a railway was in fact ever built, at least in the form shown here and at a contemporary date. The small letters on the line of the tramway are part of a key indicating land ownership.

Junction of the Trent & Mersey Canal in Stoke and the Newcastle-under-Lyme Canal; the towpath has been taken over the branch canal by the bridge. A small stub of the canal remained here until recent times, used as a base for local boats, but the recent widening of the A500 main road has obliterated any trace.

substantial part of the Apedale estate – one third. Although Sir Nigel Bowyer Gresley did not die until 1808, Heathcote, after his marriage, seems to have taken the leading role in the management of the Apedale estate. Together with his wife he took up residence at Apedale Hall, while Nigel Bower Gresley appears to have retreated to the family estate at Drakelow Park. Also in 1808, Sir John Edensor Heathcote's son, Richard Edensor Heathcote (1780-1850), married his younger cousin Emma Sophia Gresley, daughter of Nigel Bowyer Gresley and thereby the Heathcote family inherited another substantial portion of the Apedale estate – another third in fact. Sir Nigel Gresley and later his son Sir Nigel Bowyer Gresley were Lords of the Manor of Apedale, while another influential Newcastle family, the Kinnerslys, father and later a son, were Lords of the Manor of Chesterton. Thomas Kinnersly (1751-1819) and his son, who was also named Thomas (1782-1855), belonged to an old established and wealthy Newcastle family; they owned substantial land and property within the town itself as well as being its principal bankers. At this time the Kinnerslys also owned land north of Apedale at Partridge Nest, rich in coal and ironstone, along with the Clough Hall estate at Kidsgrove, at the extreme north of the county on the borders of Cheshire. This was another

area rich in mineral deposits where the family not only owned land, but also leased a large area of mineral rights. Thomas Kinnersly resided at Clough Hall, in the Hall itself, and there were extensive coal and ironstone workings together with an iron works and forge on the estate. Another son, William Shepherd Kinnersly (1780-1823) was for many years the Member of Parliament for Newcastle. Worth a note is the spelling of the Kinnersly name, as it is often quoted, in both official and unofficial sources, as Kinnersley. However, on the balance of evidence, including signatures, the spelling as used here is considered to be the correct one, at least at the period being discussed.

The Junction Canal had the purpose of connecting the Gresley Canal with the Newcastle Canal, but in view of a height difference of some 88 feet, a figure quoted in the plans, the proposal anticipated 'an inclined plane or railway' to connect the two. Once again the promoters of the Bill were local people with Sir Nigel Bowyer Gresley heading the list with 12 shares, while the other principal promoters were Sir John Edensor Heathcote and Thomas Kinnersly, each holding nine shares. As well as the canal and inclined plane, the Bill before Parliament proposed a 'railedway' from the end of the Gresley Canal at Apedale, to serve the 'coal and other works' of Thomas Kinnersly at Partridge Nest and John Wedgwood at

'Bignal' (the more common and later spelling is Bignall) End. John Wedgwood, who held seven shares, had extensive mining interests at Chesterton and Audley, and among the other subscribers were the famous pottery manufacturers Josiah Wedgwood (no direct relation to the John Wedgwood mentioned here) and Josiah Spode, each with three shares. The Wedgwood and Spode interests centred on getting Apedale coal to the Pottery towns where their operations were concentrated, both quicker and cheaper than the existing method of pack horses and carts on the primitive local roads. The canal was projected to be one mile three furlongs and a little over seven chains long, the railway extension to Partridge Nest from the Gresley Canal at Apedale would have been four furlongs one chain and 20 links long.

As well as the projected railway to Partridge Nest, the original plans, as surveyed by Charles Roberts, also proposed a series of 'railedways', to Silverdale Iron Works and Leycett Colliery. The line to Silverdale would have left the Newcastle Canal just short of its termination at Brook Lane (about two furlongs) to head in a general westerly direction via Knutton to Silverdale, a length of two miles seven furlongs six chains and 90 links. A second line, two furlongs seven chains and 70 links long, would have connected the village of Silverdale with the iron works, which lay north of the village. Lastly there was an extension of the main route south-west to Leycett Colliery, six furlongs three chains and 70 links long. In the event, while powers to build the Partridge Nest line were embodied in the Act, these other lines were not included, and had in fact been dropped from the Bill before it went before Parliament.

As mentioned in the proceeding paragraph both the canal and the railway routes were surveyed by Charles Roberts in 1797, and the estimated costs in a statement dated 23 November that year, which accompanied the Bill, amounted to £5,932. This figure included £360 for the railway to Partridge Nest, and £1,800 for the inclined plane, which included any machinery connected with it, although the papers are silent on exactly what machinery might have been necessary. The Bill was successful and the Newcastle-under-Lyme Junction Canal Act, received the Royal Assent on 26 May 1798 (38 Geo 111 ch xxviv). However, the powers did not take effect until 15 June that year, on which date the Newcastle-under-Lyme Junction Canal Company became a body-corporate. Unfortunately, like its two predecessors the actual date the canal opened has gone unrecorded, but as the inclined plane, which would have largely followed the course of the present Occupation Street and the Partridge Nest connecting railway were never built, construction of this short canal would not have taken very long. Like the other two canals it was level throughout but it did require a deep cutting between King Street in Newcastle and the Brampton, some 450 yards long and 65 feet deep at its greatest depth. The only other engineering feat of any magnitude was a substantial brick culvert taking the canal over the Lyme Brook at the Brampton. There were concerns about the provision of water for the canal and while the Act allowed water to be drawn down from the Gresley Canal, this was not to take place if it lowered the water in that canal below 'its highest present level'. Whatever this level was is not stated, but water was a constant source of concern to the proprietors for the entire operational life of this canal. The Company were not to 'interfere' with Sir Nigel Bowyer Gresley's rights to sell coal in Newcastle, but they could convey coal for other users and factories adjacent to the new canal. The Junction Canal with its lengthy title soon became colloquially known as the Upper Canal, while by definition the Newcastle Canal often took the sobriquet the Lower Canal, and we shall use these terms hereafter.

Before we leave the Upper Canal mention needs to be made of a late 1780s partnership between Sir John Edensor Heathcote and Thomas Kinnersly, to build an ironworks and to mine for coal and ironstone at Partridge Nest; hence the projected tramway. The works were not profitable, closing about 1800, and despite attempts to sell as a going concern, remained dormant until largely dismantled and sold off piece-meal in 1805. The sale included a Boulton & Watt beam engine used for furnace blowing; dating from 1790 this would have been one of the earliest rotative beam engines to be put to work in North Staffordshire. The remains of a furnace at Springwood were part of this operation and are now among the oldest physical traces of iron making anywhere in the world.

The Commercial Canal Scheme
Before discussing the later history of the three canals, it is perhaps worth mentioning another scheme for a canal that would have served Newcastle, the somewhat ambitious Commercial Canal Scheme of 1796. This was a very grandiose and widely embracing scheme, intended to counter, in part, what the promoters saw as the monopoly of the Trent & Mersey. Planned as a broad canal; that is, wider than the seven foot of the 'narrow canals' as adopted by the Trent & Mersey and the three Newcastle canals, it was intended to run from the Ashby-de-la-Zouch Canal in Leicestershire to the Chester Canal (later part of the Shropshire Union) at Nantwich. Its route took in Burton-on-Trent and its suburbs of Shobnall and Horninglow,

before following the general course of the River Dove in a westerly direction via Tutbury, Marchington to Uttoxeter. It was then intended to head north towards the Pottery town of Hanley, before turning due-west to Newcastle; the scheme also included a branch from Hanley to serve the Pottery towns of Burslem and Tunstall. At Newcastle it was planned to use the bulk of the length of the Upper Canal, along with all of the Gresley Canal and to continue via Apedale and Partridge Nest, westwards towards a junction with the Chester Canal at Nantwich. The plans also proposed a short branch two furlongs and six chains long to serve the Partridge Nest Iron Works, presumably as the authorised 'railedway' had not been built. At Burton-on-Trent communication was planned with the River Trent, which was navigable at that point, and at Shobnall with the Trent & Mersey Canal. A series of other branches were envisaged; for example to Lane End (Longton), Cheadle (Staffs), Ellestone, and from Burton-on-Trent to join the Coventry Canal at Fradley Heath. At what was termed a general public meeting held at the White Hart Star Inn in Uttoxeter on 26 July 1796, with Sir Nigel Bowyer Gresley in the Chair, this ambitious scheme was first launched. It would transform, it was considered, the transport of goods from London to the Potteries and the sea ports of north-west England. The plans and sections were deposited with the local authorities on 9 September 1796.

Gresley was supported in the promotion of the scheme by a whole range of like-minded folk, all generally annoyed at the way the Trent & Mersey treated its customers. Included among the promoters were of course the proprietors of the Chester and Ashby Canals, as well as numerous tradesman and industrialists along its projected route, not least of course, in the Potteries and other parts of North Staffordshire. Not surprisingly there was much opposition to the scheme, including the Trent & Mersey and the Grand Junction Canal Companies. However, their objections appear to have been largely concerned with the prospect of having to convert all or part of their systems to wide canals, if the scheme went ahead, rather than competition as such. They need have had no worries, because as a direct result of their and other opposition no powers were obtained and, indeed, there is no evidence in the Parliamentary records that a Bill was ever presented before Parliament. However, some good did result from the proceedings as the Trent & Mersey Canal Company was cajoled into extending the Caldon Canal southwards to Uttoxeter, powers being conferred by Act of Parliament (37 Geo111 ch lxxxi), which received the Royal Assent on 6 June 1797. This gave the sizeable Staffordshire market town access to the canal system, and there were powers to build a branch

to Leek, conferred by a second Act (37 Geo111 ch xxxvi), Royal Assent 24 March 1797. The inhabitants and business men of the Staffordshire Moorland market and mill town of Leek had for some time been anxious for better transport. Roads from the Pottery towns where a large proportion of their business was conducted were particularly poor. The branch was important to the canal company too, as the Act also gave powers to build a reservoir about two miles north-west of the town in a vale at Rudyard, and within the watershed of the River Dane, which ran to the north. This reservoir is more familiarly known these days as Rudyard Lake, and under the auspices of the North Staffordshire Railway became, and still is, a local beauty spot. The plan encompassed a feeder channel two and a half miles long to the terminal basin of the Leek Canal and, as might be expected, the Act stipulated various measures to protect the water of the nearby River Churnet. It was intended that the reservoir water would come from a series of nearby streams, as it lay in a small valley, but these proved inadequate for the needs of the canal and in 1809, and again in 1823, the company obtained powers to take water from the River Dane, north of Rudyard and a second feeder channel was built from the river at Wincle Weir, just below Dane Bridge, to feed the reservoir. By these means the water supply to the summit level of the Trent & Mersey Canal was improved, as the Caldon Canal ran into it; in fact the supply for the Trent & Mersey, and in consequence the Newcastle-under-Lyme Canal, had been a constant source of problems since it first opened. The two canals, Leek and Uttoxeter, were some consolation to the many otherwise disappointed advocates of the Commercial Canal scheme; but the powers were only obtained following considerable opposition from the Chester Canal Company, annoyed that it was not to be connected to the wider canal network due to abandonment of the Commercial Canal scheme. The Leek branch opened in 1802, but the inhabitants of Uttoxeter had to wait until 1811 before the extension of the Caldon Canal from Froghall to Uttoxeter was completed.

The Upper Canal in Difficulty
While the Gresley and Newcastle (Lower) Canals were reasonably profitable before the coming of the railways, the same cannot be said for the Junction, or Upper Canal. As financial constraints seem to have prevented the proposed connection between the Upper and Lower Canals ever being made, there was no through traffic as such. In fact there was almost no commercial traffic from a wharf adjacent to King Street in Newcastle and the canal's southern terminus at Stubbs Walks (referred to as Stubbs Field on the plans and in the papers). At Stubbs

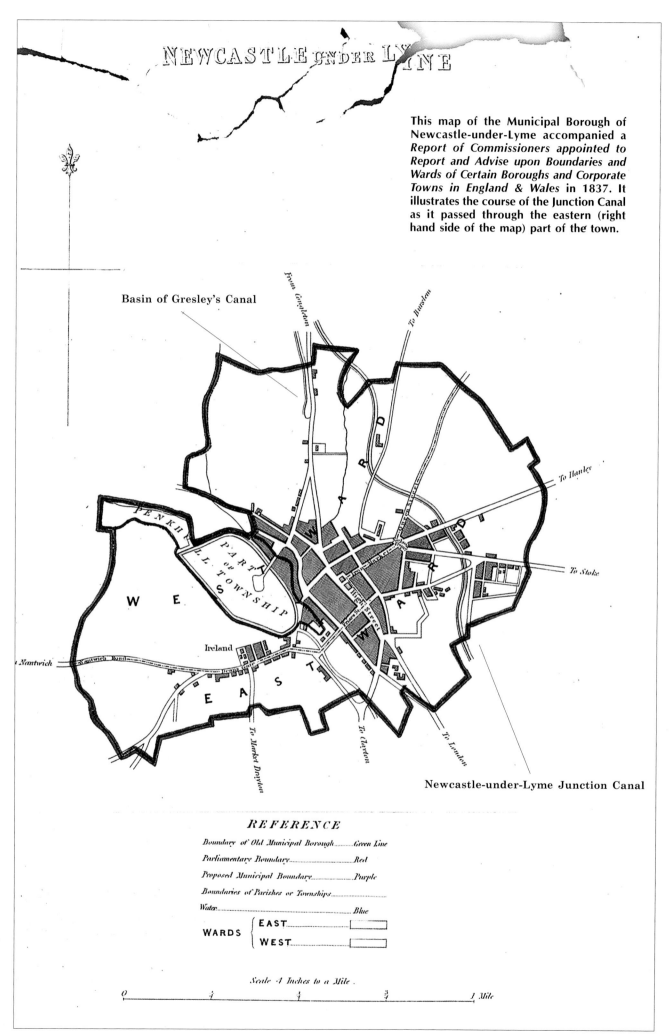

NEWCASTLE UNDER LYME

This map of the Municipal Borough of Newcastle-under-Lyme accompanied a *Report of Commissioners appointed to Report and Advise upon Boundaries and Wards of Certain Boroughs and Corporate Towns in England & Wales* in 1837. It illustrates the course of the Junction Canal as it passed through the eastern (right hand side of the map) part of the town.

Basin of Gresley's Canal

From Congleton

To Burslem

To Hanley

To Stoke

PENKHULL TOWNSHIP

PART OF

WEST

WARD

WARD

Ireland

Nantwich

Nantwich Road

Brook Lane

EAST

To Nantwich

To Market Drayton

To Clayton

To London

Newcastle-under-Lyme Junction Canal

REFERENCE

Boundary of Old Municipal Borough .... *Green Line*

Parliamentary Boundary .... *Red*

Proposed Municipal Boundary .... *Purple*

Boundaries of Parishes or Townships ....

Water .... *Blue*

WARDS { EAST ....

WEST ....

Scale 4 Inches to a Mile.

0 .... ¼ .... ½ .... ¾ .... 1 Mile

Walks those intrepid folk who navigated thus far, could only scan the Lyme valley some 90 feet below and wonder how they might transport boat loads of goods the half-mile between the two points! Added to this daunting prospect was, as we have already seen, the fact that the proprietors were not allowed to land-sell coal (although under the 1812 Gresley Canal Act, they could charge for its movement) and therefore, what traffic there was would appear to have been confined to serving a small number of mills and factories along the short length of the Upper Canal. With water supply being a constant headache, especially during the summer months, there is evidence that, at least in later days the section beyond the wharf at King Street was allowed to dry out and a stop-block was provided alongside Marsh Parade; there was a factory there that did need to be served. One source of profit was the supply of water to the mills and factories along the route, especially in later years for both feed water and condensing purposes, when some of them acquired steam engines. However, once again if the water flowing from the Gresley Canal was in short supply, there was little that could be done in this respect.

The Upper Canal proprietors appear to have eventually woken up in 1825, when five of them gave notice in *The Staffordshire Advertiser* (issue dated 25 March 1825) calling what became the first meeting of a Special General Assembly, to be held at the Public Office in Newcastle on `5 April. Six of the proprietors attended, or were represented at the ensuing meeting, consisting of Thomas Kinnersly, represented by Thomas Pearson who held his proxy and other local businessmen. These were Benjamin Eardly, James Smith, Samuel Mayer, William Holland and Thomas Fenton, most of whom were either original shareholders or descendents thereof. Fenton, a solicitor in the town, was also the Town Clerk and Manor Steward, as well as being one of the Commissioners appointed under the 1812 Act covering the Gresley Canal – as was Samuel Mayer. It appears that the construction of a silk mill at the Brampton galvanised the company into action, as the owners had requested permission to take water from the canal for 'the purpose of their steam engine at all times'. Sensing some much needed income, urgent action was necessary! The meeting elected Thomas Fenton as Clerk of the company and James Smith its Treasurer, along with a committee to support them consisting of no less than eleven shareholders. Included among the new committee members, notwithstanding their absence at the meeting, were Thomas Kinnersly (another of the Commissioners appointed under the 1812 Gresley Canal Act), Richard Edensor Heathcote, Josiah Wedgwood and Thomas Spode. As the company does not appear to have had

either a Clerk or a Treasurer prior to this meeting, its assets must have been pretty moribund.

The meeting also agreed on a charge for the water, assuming it was available of course. This amounted to five guineas per annum for a period of seven years, but if this was extended to 21 years the price was 10 guineas per annum (strange economics this, one would have expected it to be the opposite way round). There was also a condition that the water from the condensed steam should be returned to the canal. Some years elapsed before the committee saw fit to call another meeting – on 7 October 1831 in fact – at the Roebuck Hotel in High Street, Newcastle. Heathcote, who was in attendance in person, was appointed Chairman of the meeting and, as on earlier occasions, Thomas Kinnersly was represented by his solicitor Thomas Fenton, still holding his proxy. Four other shareholders attended, two of whom were the executors of William Holland, and in total 28 shares in the company were represented by those present out of the total of 107 that had been issued. Perhaps this meagre representation gives some indication of the lack of interest in the undertaking on the part of its proprietors.

The meeting seems to have been largely concerned in trying to sort out the finances of the company, doubtless brought about by the death of its Treasurer – John Smith – although his executors were not represented. The assembled company decided that Smith's executors should be required to pay interest on money belonging to the company and held by them, as there was a suggestion that Smith may have been using the company's cash for his own business purposes! There were debts outstanding for land taken, presumably in building the canal all those years earlier, totalling £40 14/4d (£40 72p). Creditors were the Rector of Newcastle who was owed £30, nearly thirty years rent of 'Glebe Land' which had been used by the canal up to Christmas 1831, and £17 to the Newcastle Marsh Trustees. The Marsh Trustees were responsible for some land in and around Newcastle. As a body corporate it came into existence following an Act of Parliament in 1782; there was a further Act in 1783 and a consolidating one to amend and extend the earlier Acts as late as 1861. These Trustees were concerned with 25 acres of waste land which as a result of its powers had been enclosed and divided up for a number of useful purposes, including building works and applying any profits in aid of the poor rates. We shall come across this body later in connection with Newcastle railway goods yard. There was also three years rent on land controlled by the Trustees and used by the canal and this too, covered the period up to Christmas 1831.

There were a number of other creditors including Samuel Henshall, the owner of another silk mill (the one alongside Marsh Parade mentioned earlier) and he too required water for his steam engine. Henshall, who was yet another of the Gresley Canal Commissioners under the 1812 Act, had to agree to pay the same annual rental 'as charged to the occupier of the mill in Brampton Field'. From this we can deduce that there were at least two mills at this time taking water from the canal. There is also a reference to a Mr (Richard) Faulkner having to pay rent for 'water used by his mill since his occupation of same', but whether this is one and the same as the mill in Brampton Field is not clear. However, as this is a separate reference in the minutes, perhaps not; in which case we have no less than three mills taking water, and presumably at least three steam engines operational in Newcastle at that time. The Henshall mill, incidentally, was the oldest silk mill in Newcastle, established in the early 1820s, and at one period operated by a partnership of Samuel Henshall and Thomas Lester. Newcastle had become well established nationally in the silk throwing industry by this date, and Lester was later in partnership with Richard Faulkner, at yet another mill in Blackfriars Road. This was adjacent to the Brook Lane basin of the Lower Canal, so it would not be for this mill that Faulkner would be taking water from the Upper Canal.

The same meeting elected a new committee to look after the business of the company consisting of Heathcote, Kinnersly, Josiah Wedgwood, Thomas Fenton and a few others. Last of all the meeting 'desired to have communication with the proprietors of the Newcastle-under-Lyme Canal and learn upon what terms they will admit coals and other articles to pass from this canal along the former'. This is an interesting statement perhaps confirming what has been inferred earlier, that even by means of road transhipment between the two, there was little or no through traffic between the Upper and Lower canals. From the foregoing it will be seen that the Upper Canal Company had not been very diligent in undertaking its obligations, to say the very least!

When the committee next met a summary of the financial position was presented. The company had creditors to the tune of £843, give or take a few shillings, with some sums outstanding from as far back as 1802, while it had debtors to the tune of £850 - again give or take a shilling or two. No less than £485 17/1d (£485 85p) in cash was still in the hands of the executors of its late Treasurer John Smith. Other interesting accounts illustrating that at least some traffic was passing along the canal are those of Sir Nigel Bower Gresley and Messrs Heathcote and Kinnersly (jointly); £132 11/4d (£132 57p) and £128 7/4½d (£128 37p) respectively. These

Remains of the Gresley Canal, looking towards the site of the Burley Colliery from what was known as the Burley Bridge, the parapet of which can just be seen in the foreground. This is about 1960, when the tile works (in the background) occupied part of the site of the former colliery. The bridge carried the un-metalled road from Chesterton to Alsagers Bank which passed, on its route, the site of Apedale Hall.

credited sums are listed as for 'tonnages', presumably meaning tonnages carried along the canal. There are a few other smaller 'tonnages' mentioned in the statements, while Messrs Birks & White are noted in bankruptcy and in debt for water used by their engine since 25 December 1825; presumably yet another owner of one of the mills. Richard Faulkner is mentioned again as the owner of a mill and owing a sum of money for water used, although the amount in question is not quoted, no more is the mill to which it referred. It does appear however, that he had financial interests in a mill or mills, in addition to the one in Blackfriars Road.

Upper and Lower Canals - A Revived Link
Realisation of the need to sort out the financial affairs promoted yet another meeting a couple of weeks later on 8 November 1831. Among the issues discussed on this occasion was that the Chairman (Heathcote) should be requested to 'procure for the information of the proprietors (with plans and sections) best method of opening communication by railway

between this canal and Newcastle-under-Lyme Canal (Lower Canal)'. Heathcote reported at a follow-up meeting held on 9 December, that the view was (not stated whose view this was) that it would be better to convert the Upper and Gresley Canals to a railway, as unless this was adopted 'opening a railway between Upper and Lower Canals was of little advantage'. This is an interesting statement, as the original statutory powers of the company envisaged exactly that, a railway between the two canals, but now it was seen to be 'of little advantage'. The meeting agreed to pay a one third share of the expense, in conjunction with Heathcote (who by this time was the proprietor of the Gresley Canal, along with the Lower Canal) 'of taking the opinion of Mr Stephenson on the subject of opening a railway as above'. It was further agreed that Mr Trubshaw (this is Charles Trubshaw, the Staffordshire County Surveyor) be appointed to meet Mr Stephenson at the time of the survey. One assumes that the agreement of the Lower Canal owners had already been sought regarding their contribution and that no less an engineer than George Stephenson had already been approached with the prospect of undertaking the work.

Whatever the case, no time was wasted and Stephenson's report, which was written in Liverpool, is dated 31 December 1831 and was discussed at a General Assembly Meeting of the proprietors held at the Roebuck Hotel in Newcastle on 6 January 1832. Stephenson was of the view that because of the curving nature of the Gresley and Upper Canals, which in the case of Gresley's Canal had been necessary to avoid any changes in levels, the course of the two canals was not suitable for conversion to a railway. Extensive 'deviations' would be necessary and this would make it a very expensive option. Stephenson went on to outline in the report that as the 'grand

object' was to establish a connection between Upper and Lower Canals, his recommendation was the construction of a railway between the termination of the Upper Canal and the commencement of the Lower Canal. He went on to declare that a lock should be established at the end of the Upper canal and provided with a sluice so as to draw off the water, a suitable railway wagon being constructed for the canal boats to sit on inside the lock, so that they could be traversed up and down an inclined railway between the two canals. He recommended that the operation be under the control of a steam engine and a powerful brake and estimated the cost, excluding the earthworks, at £2,206, of which £600 was for the engine, pumps and winding gear. The distance was one half-mile and the 40lb per yard rails he recommended were estimated to total 32 tons at a cost of £9 per ton, amounting to £288. This combined estimate of £2,806 which, note, was minus the earth-works, makes an interesting comparison with the £1,800 in the original estimates for the complete incline works. One seemingly important issue that does not appear to have been considered, was exactly how the proposed inclined railway was to carried over the main highway into Newcastle from the south; this was London Road, the later A34. Although this road, running from Darlaston south of Newcastle and near to Stone to Talke, had been made a Turnpike Road as far back as 1714, the particular area where the railway would have crossed was considerably improved in the period 1822-1823, as part of a better route through the town, along with improvements north of the town to by-pass Chesterton. Newcastle was one of the first towns in North Staffordshire to benefit from a Turnpike Road, and by 1818 about 40 stage coaches a day passed through the town, stopping for the passengers to take refreshments and for the horses to be changed. As the town was on part of the principal route between London, Birmingham, Manchester and Liverpool, an amicable arrangement of some sort would have been necessary with the Turnpike Trustees, before a crossing of any sort could have been made. It is strange that no mention is made of this.

The meeting agreed that Mr Heathcote be requested to make a proposal to the next meeting to outline on what terms he (Heathcote) would be 'willing to rent the tonnage of the canal and railway in the event of the communication being made; such proposal to embrace either the tonnages on the whole line of the canal and railway, or the additional tonnages only, which may be provided by the adoption of the plan of communication'. Clearly the proprietors did not feel able to take the financial risks associated with the scheme and the meeting was adjourned

Demise of the Gresley Canal

Despite the abandonment of the Upper Canal, the Gresley Canal continued to be navigable for its entire length, but its future became very much involved with the NSR branch to Apedale. However, despite an agreement with the NSR for ownership of this canal to pass to the railway company, in the event, and as explored in Chapter Three, it never did. Neither was any part of its course used in connection with the Apedale branch railway (apart perhaps, from a few yards at its Newcastle basin used for the line between Newcastle and Apedale Junction; see later). Therefore, while it remained as a navigable waterway in its entirety, it is doubtful if much traffic continued to use it once the railway line to Apedale was opened. There may have been some very local traffic between various parts of the Apedale ironworks and colliery complex; photographs would suggest that the section of the canal connecting the various parts of the works was kept in good weed-free condition until well into the last century. In addition to this, while the Staniers had the Apedale lease, two boat loads of coal were sent via the canal to the cotton factory at Cross Heath, one on the last day of each year and another on the first day of the following year, presumably to maintain navigable rights. This factory was owned by Richard Thompson and was

built in 1797. It closed as a cotton factory in the early 1970s, the building having subsequently been put to a variety of uses. Parts of it are still standing today.

In January 1890 a new company was established to operate the mines and other concerns on the Apedale estate, the Midland Coal, Coke & Iron Company Limited (MCCI). There is, however, no evidence that this company took over the Stanier lease of the canal. It actually took over from the Stanier interests on 1 April 1890, by which date the owner of the estate was Captain Justinian Heathcote Edwards-Heathcote (1843-1928), Richard Edensor Heathcote's grandson. He was the son of Richard's daughter Elizabeth Anne, who had married the Rev Edward Justinian Edwards, vicar of Trentham, assuming the additional surname of Heathcote in 1870. This was after the death of his uncle John Edensor Heathcote (1810-1869), son of Richard Edensor, when he inherited the estate. The Staniers involved here were Francis Stanier Broade (1838-1900), the son of Francis, who had died on 13 October 1856, and his mother Mary (née Wilkinson), Francis's wife. The additional surname of Broade was adopted between 1856 and 1876. Stanier had taken on the lease on 1 September 1866 for a period of 35 years, with powers to terminate on 1 April 1890; this duly took place, hence the new

company mentioned above. Francis Stanier was a Director of the NSR from 1863 until his death in 1900, and Deputy Chairman between 1887 and 1899. He is buried at Hodnet in Shropshire, near to where he lived at Peplow. Worthy of a note is the fact that his son, Sir Belville Stanier (1867-1921) was also an NSR Director, from 1909 until his death.

Whatever the case, this residual traffic would have ceased some time in the 1880s at the latest, and thereafter the Gresley Canal fell into complete decay. Notwithstanding this, parts of it held water for many years; indeed, at one time just after the end of the last war, a section of it at Apedale was used for testing amphibious vehicles. As with the Upper Canal, despite having been built under statutory powers, no specific powers were obtained for its abandonment even though there was a clause in the original Act, for the land to revert to the original owners, or their successors, should there be no traffic for a period exceeding five years. It would seem to have been by this clause, whether intentionally or not, that the land was gradually used for other purposes. True to form, despite the various negotiations and agreements with the Heathcotes, regarding ownership of the Gresley Canal and its potential use for all or part of the course of the Apedale branch railway, no statutory powers were ever conferred

In July 1976 this bridge taking Racecourse Road at Oakhill over the site of the Newcastle-under-Lyme Canal was still extant. The road served one of the entrance gates to the Michelin tyre factory, part of which can be seen to the right. Standing on the bridge is the late Clive Guthrie, with whom one of the authors spent many enjoyable hours exploring local industrial remains.

The bridge taking Clayton Lane over the Newcastle-under-Lyme Canal at Spring Fields, in the 1930s. This bridge was dismantled in 1941 when the road layout was altered.

chapters of this book, that the line from Newcastle to Silverdale might have caused the canal to lose a few yards at its terminal basin at the Newcastle end. This was certainly within the Parliamentary limits of deviation for the line, and later plans indicate that this may have been what took place.

The Newcastle-under-Lyme Canal Extension Railway

The later history of the Lower Canal is itself interesting; once the railway was opened to Newcastle traffic over the canal reduced enormously and in efforts to stem the losses, in May 1853 the canal company built a half-mile railway from its basin at Brook Lane to the termination of the Silverdale & Newcastle-under-Lyme Railway (SNuLR) at Pool Dam. The SNuLR was a private line, built by Ralph Sneyd and his partner Francis Stanier, to connect the Silverdale iron works and mines with the town of Newcastle. The new line, which went under the grandiose title of The Newcastle-under-Lyme Canal Extension Railway, cost the canal company £1,725, and the engineer was Charles Trubshaw. Despite the fact that this short railway, which opened some time in 1854, crossed three public roads on the level, no statutory powers were obtained to facilitate its construction. This is particularly interesting and not a little strange, as the three roads in question were also the principal thoroughfares serving the town from the west. Presumably some sort of agreement must have been entered into with the Borough, as it appears to have included clauses preventing the canal company from using any mechanical motive power on this short section of railway. Wagons, it must be presumed, were therefore hauled either by horse or manpower, or both.

Whatever effect this new railway had on the financial situation of the canal company, it cannot have amounted to very much, and once the NSR took a lease of the SNuLR in 1860 (Ralph Sneyd's 1859 Act to build this railway is fully described in Chapter Two) the canal company was in effect faced with competition by the NSR at both ends of its undertaking. The NSR lease of Sneyd's Railway, as if to add insult to injury, gave the NSR the powers which Sneyd already had, to use the Canal Extension Railway, though still without locomotives. The construction of the Canal Extension Railway had, however, been legalised as a part of Sneyd's 1859 Act, but it was not until the NSR Act of 1880 that the use of locomotives was allowed. The authors are of the view however, that a wager would probably be won on the fact that locomotives had been used on the railway prior to that date!

The Lower Canal under North Staffordshire Railway Control

At Stoke of course the NSR owned the

to do so. It would seem that in its initial enthusiasm, it might have appeared to the NSR Directors that financial savings may have accrued if the railway to Apedale had followed all or part of the course of the canal. However, when detailed surveys were undertaken later, it would have been clear that such was not the case. The railway did not have to maintain a level winding course and in the event was routed far more directly and well to the west of the canal. In a later agreement with R E Heathcote dated 28 August 1856, following a lot of negotiation from as far back as June 1854 with Heathcote attending in person the NSR Traffic Committee (TC) meetings on several occasions, the NSR expunged the obligations in earlier agreements regarding its potential ownership of the canal. At the same time, it removed the restriction on Heathcote, or whoever was operating the works and mines at Apedale at the time, regarding use of the canal in competition with the NSR. They were in fact able to use the canal in any way considered appropriate; the NSR, it would seem, had concluded that whatever competition it might present, it would be comparatively small and not worth the challenge. This and other agreements between the NSR and the Heathcotes are covered in more detail in the railway chapters of this book.

It is worth a short diversion here to visualise Richard Edensor Heathcote

setting out from Apedale Hall in all his finery, top hat and tails, and doubtless a stick, by coach and pair for Stoke station where the Traffic Committee met. Or of course, he may have asked his coachman to take him to Newcastle, taking a reserved first-class compartment for a train journey to Stoke, once the line opened. He was an important person hereabouts, and doubtless did not take too kindly to having to make frequent visits to Stoke, and may have preferred it if a deputation of Directors had come to Apedale! Be that as it may, one wonders if he was entertained to lunch on any of the occasions; perhaps he might have been once an agreement had been reached!

Some emphasis has been placed on the fact that the Gresley Canal did not pass into the ownership of the NSR, despite the oft-quoted theory that it did. As we have seen, the canal did feature in the deliberations of the NSR Directors but the railway company did not have statutory powers to acquire the canal in its Act of Parliament to build a railway to Apedale. It is therefore convenient to emphasise this point and mention that despite extensive research, absolutely no evidence has been found to support the theory that ownership of the Gresley Canal did in fact pass to the NSR. There is the possibility however, as related in the railway

Trent & Mersey Canal, which it had acquired as a part of its original Acts of Incorporation in 1846. Because of this rather untenable situation the Newcastle-under-Lyme Canal Company found itself in, negotiations were entered into with the NSR to sell or lease its undertaking to the railway. The NSR Directors discussed this at a meeting of 10 June 1863, when the Chairman, Lt Col Charles Pearson (1799-1885) stated that after 'mature consideration', he was of the view that the Company should acquire the canal if it could be done so on reasonable terms, and that he had instructed the Engineer, J C Forsyth, to investigate the issue. Forsyth's report, which is dated 6 June 1863, mentioned that the canal company had been empowered to raise by its Act of Incorporation £7,000 by the issue of 140 shares of £50 each, and further raise by mortgage a sum of £3,000. However, its proprietors had in fact raised £10,200 by a share issue, 204 shares at £50, plus £2,001 by mortgage, but just how it circumvented its Act has gone unrecorded. The average receipts per annum for the years 1859 to 1861 amounted to £682, against the average expenditure of £307 which, along with the mortgage interest of £100, gave a balance of £275. On the capital of £10,200, this equated to about 2¾ per cent. Forsyth's report concluded with the comment that if the canal could be leased at 4%, and if the traffic and receipts remained the same, there would be an annual loss of £133. Forsyth was actually partly wrong here, as although the canal company had exceeded its powers in raising additional capital, it was only to the tune of £200, as the authorised figure was £10,000. The sum raised by mortgage was a little over £2,000 and not the £3,000 he quoted. As might be imagined a lengthy discussion ensued, but there was general agreement that in view of the mineral wealth of the Silverdale, Apedale and Audley areas, it was better for the canal to be in the railway's hands rather than any other, and it was resolved that the Traffic Committee be authorised to negotiate with the canal company for the best possible terms.

The Traffic Committee reported on its activities at the next meeting, held on 8 July 1863, when the following terms were proposed. The NSR was to take a 999 year lease of the canal company at an annual rent of £520 payable half-yearly, along with the mortgage debt of £2,001 18/9d (£2,001 94p). All expenses connected with the resultant agreements and the parliamentary proceedings leading to the necessary Act of Parliament, were to be borne in equal shares by both companies, but the canal company share would be limited to a maximum of £300. The lease was to run from 1 July 1863, despite the fact that shareholder authority was considered necessary, and of course an Act of Parliament was also required. In the event shareholder authority was forthcoming, at the half-yearly meeting held on 7 August 1863, and the powers were conferred by the Newcastle-under-Lyme Canal (Lease) Act 1864 (27-8 Vic ch cxviii), which received the Royal Assent on 23 June 1864. The NSR had, as we have already seen, taken on the lease of the canal despite the Act not becoming law until the following year; the lease of course included the Canal Extension Railway. The terms of the lease as embodied in the Act were in perpetuity, the NSR acquiring a debt of £2,000, along with payment of an annual rent of £536 10/- (£536 50p), or 5% on the canal company share capital of £10,200 if greater, such payments were to rank before dividends on both preference and ordinary canal company shares. The Act also legalised the raising of the additional capital and, more importantly, the earlier construction of the Canal Extension Railway. Thereafter, the canal was in effect worked as an integral part of the Trent & Mersey system, and the railway as a part of the NSR. However, it will be seen that the proprietors of the canal company had driven a hard bargain, and one that was to benefit them for many years to come, the canal never proving to be very much of a financial asset to the NSR. Nevertheless, it was doubtless considered worth the effort in adding yet another string of protection to the tightly knit area of North Staffordshire which the railway company regarded as its own.

The Impact of Electric Street Tramways
In the Parliamentary session of 1899 the NSR submitted a Bill which, among other things, projected construction of a railway between Stoke and Newcastle. It was planned to run from a junction at Mount Pleasant, which is just south of Stoke on the NSR main line, to Colwich and Stafford, via Oak Hill, Trent Vale and then following the route of the Newcastle-under-Lyme Canal and the Lyme Brook to the Brook Lane Wharf at Newcastle. At its termination, referred to as the Pool Dam Wharf in the submission, it was intended to make an end-on connection with the Canal Extension Railway. The Bill also proposed abandonment of the Lower Canal between Oak Hill and Brook Lane, without prejudicing the rights of

Remaining bed of the Newcastle-under-Lyme Canal between Spring Fields and Newcastle, about 1955. The view looks towards Newcastle, about a quarter of a mile distant. On the opposite side of the road entrance to the City General Hospital, water can be seen in the bed of the old canal to this day.

The cotton mill at Cross Heath that features so prominently in the history of the Gresley and Newcastle-under-Lyme Junction Canals. Photograph taken about 1964 looking due north from the rear of the factory, the opposite side to the Liverpool Road. The Gresley Canal ran behind and parallel to the wall.

the canal company shareholders for their financial remuneration under the 1864 NSR Canal Lease Act. There was, however, a stipulation in the eventual Act for the provision of a wharf between the new railway and the canal at Oak Hill, so as to provide for the interchange of traffic between the two. The NSR Traffic & Finance Committee had discussed this scheme at its meeting on 16 August 1898, part of a plan to run passenger trains from Stoke to Newcastle via Pool Dam. The committee also discussed the possibility of an east-facing curve at Knutton Junction to allow through working from Pool Dam to Newcastle and Stoke – the existing connection was towards Silverdale. However, plans to build such a curve were not in the Bill or the subsequent Act, which received the Royal Assent of 9 August 1899 as the North Staffordshire Railway Act 1899 (62-63 Vic ch ccxxxi). Three years were allowed in the Act for the compulsory purchase of land, and two more for completion of the railway which was to be three miles, three furlongs, six chains and 40 links long.

The spur to this project was competition from the local street tramways which had recently abandoned steam in favour of electrification. Under new management, in addition to the conversion of the existing street tramways from steam to

electric traction, an extensive and ambitious enlargement of the system was underway. On 17 March 1900 the tramway from Hanley to Newcastle via Basford had opened, in direct competition with the NSR and in 1897 a further tramway had opened from the West End at Stoke – where the earlier steam system had terminated – via Oak Hill to Trent Vale. In 1902 the new tramway operator, the Potteries Electric Traction Company Limited (PET) obtained powers under the Light Railways Act 1896 (The Potteries Light Railways [Extensions] Order 1902) to both extend the Trent Vale tramway one furlong south to Hanford, as well as building an additional tramway one mile six furlongs six and a half chains long from Trent Vale to Newcastle. This second tramway would have been in direct competition with the proposed NSR railway for which powers were granted in the 1899 Act referred to above. Three years were allowed for the completion of these street tramway works. The Hanford extension opened in November 1905 while the powers to build the tramway to Newcastle, although extended to 1910, were never exercised and allowed to lapse. The NSR was, not surprisingly, a strong objector at the various public enquiries arranged by the Light Railway Commissioners in connection with almost all the local tramway proposals. It was however,

largely unsuccessful in preventing any tramways being built; moreover it allowed the powers to build its projected line from Mount Pleasant to Pool Dam (referred to above) to lapse, and so the line was never built. Neither was any part of the Lower Canal abandoned under the powers of the 1899 Act. Nevertheless some land was purchased and at a Traffic & Finance Committee meeting on 29 November 1904, the sum of £1,288 8/10d (£1,288 44p) was in effect written-off as a result of land bought and no longer required. One is left wondering what the NSR might have done if in fact the PET had constructed its authorised tramway. Presumably in such circumstances, it would have built the railway, abandoning the canal in the process.

In 1911 the NSR, this time in conjunction with Newcastle-under-Lyme Borough Council, following a request dated 8 June that year, again considered the possibility of a second passenger line to serve Newcastle. In this case the proposal was to extend the Trentham Park branch northwards alongside the course of the Lyme Brook, to make an end-on junction with the Pool Dam branch – actually the Canal Extension Railway – at Newcastle. The short branch from the main line at Trentham to Trentham Park was one mile and 14 chains long, and although authorised in an Act of 1907 (7 Ed VII ch cxlvii, Royal

Assent 21 August 1907) was not opened until 1 April 1910. Its primary purpose was to exploit the use of the newly introduced steam rail motors along with the recently opened gardens on the Duke of Sutherland's Trentham Estate, which were adjacent to its terminus. The plans involved obtaining a Light Railway Order and operating the line from Trentham to Knutton Junction, along with a connection to the Apedale branch, as light railways under the terms of the Light Railways Act of 1896. Connections were planned at Knutton to allow direct movements towards Stoke (as had been considered in the 1899 scheme) and similarly directly to Apedale, by a connecting line with the Apedale branch which would have passed under the main line between Apedale Junction and Silverdale. A rail motor type service would then have been provided from Stoke to Silverdale and Apedale via Trentham, serving as well the existing Newcastle station. The Borough Council was anxious to have the provision of public transport on the route from Trent Vale to Newcastle because the PET had not built its authorised tramway. The Council was also conscious of the increasing popularity of the gardens at Trentham as a local pleasure resort and there were also the needs of the workers at the iron works and collieries at Apedale. They lived locally and would benefit from the proposed line. A public golf course together with facilities for other sporting activities was planned at Trentham and there were schemes for a considerable expansion of housing in the area.

The original plans for the scheme, prepared by the NSR Engineer George J Crosbie Dawson (1841-1914) envisaged a double track line with the Pool Dam and Canal Extension Railways converted to double track at the same time. In addition it was proposed to divert the Lower Canal in two places, to avoid the need for two bridges at Trent Vale, and to allow better alignment for the railway between Trent Vale and Newcastle. Total cost of all the works including the canal diversions was estimated at £117,240. The proposal to divert the canal is intriguing; remember that, in the 1899 Act, the railway company had obtained powers (lapsed in 1904) to abandon completely the canal from Trent Vale to Newcastle and it is interesting to speculate what had prompted this change of mind. Maybe it was to avoid opposition, but as will be seen this came later following yet another change in the plans.

Following the application by the NSR to the Light Railway Commissioners dated 20 November 1911, a public Inquiry was held at the North Stafford Hotel in Stoke on Friday 1 March 1912, when a number of objections were raised. The Commission was represented by Hon A E Gathorne-Hardy as Chairman, accompanied by Colonel G F O Boughey RE., and Henry

Allan Steward. At this meeting Crosbie Dawson mentioned that while the bridges and so on would be constructed to allow for a double track railway, only a single track would initially be laid, allowing a reduction of £9,000 on the estimate of £117,240. Stations or halts were planned at Hanford, Trent Vale, Springfields (adjacent to Clayton Lane) and Pool Dam. Many of the objections were of a quite minor nature and were resolved at the Inquiry, the NSR agreeing to amend its plans accordingly. However, there were also a number of objections of a more serious nature. Wolstanton Urban Council was concerned about the dimensions of the two proposed road bridges over the Silverdale to Knutton Roads. These bridges were necessary for the connecting line from the Pool Dam branch to join the main Silverdale to Newcastle line in the direction of Newcastle. Apparently they were planned to have a height above road level of only 16 feet, and even this necessitated lowering the Knutton Road such that the road gradient would be much steeper, 1 in 20 instead of the 1 in 54 that was then the case. The Council gave evidence of the existing problems with the bridge taking the Pool Dam branch over the Silverdale Road, which also had a clearance of only 16 feet. In view of the proposed widening of the formation there to take a double line of railway, it considered that this bridge should be reconstructed to give better clearance for road traffic. The Council also requested that a bridge be built to take the Apedale branch under Milehouse Lane in substitution of the existing level crossing; it claimed considerable delays to road traffic occurred at this location. This crossing incidentally, remained an inconvenience to road users until rail traffic ceased when Holditch Colliery closed in July 1989. One of the authors recalls, it has to be said with great pleasure, long delays when travelling on the school bus to the playing fields at Knutton! The railway representatives pointed out that any significant alteration to the proposed bridges, or the existing one, would in effect make that part of the scheme uneconomic. The Commissioners considered that the NSR should not be required to substitute a bridge on the Apedale branch, while reserving judgement on the other bridges pending an inspection. The meeting was concluded on these lines, with an agreement to convene again after the inspection and further consideration by the Commissioners.

It is worth mentioning here that until 1932 Wolstanton was an Urban District Council in its own right, administered completely separately from Newcastle. It was in fact larger than Newcastle in both extent and population. In 1932, following a lot of discussion, a decision was made to join with Newcastle partly, if not completely, to assist in staving

off the increasing desire of the then quite new city of Stoke-on-Trent (its city status dates from 1925) to absorb much of the surrounding area within its boundaries. As events turned out this ploy has stood the test of time, and the Borough of Newcastle-under-Lyme remains administratively completely independent from the adjacent city.

The Inquiry was reconvened, but not until 7 February the following year, while in the meantime the NSR had, in November 1912, tabled a significant revision to the scheme following unrecorded discussions with the Commissioners. Instead of the two diversions of the Lower Canal it was now proposed to abandon a section of it, from Boothen to Newcastle; this was similar to the abandonment powers of the 1899 Act. It was inevitable that this change in the plans would result in additional opposition, which is exactly what happened. The second hearing, also held at the North Stafford Hotel and before the same Commissioners, considered the estimated saving of £9,261 if the section of canal was abandoned. Objections were lodged by George Neal (or rather his executors, for by the time the reconvened inquiry took place he had died) and the Trent Vale Tileries and Wheatly & Company of the Springfield Tileries. They were all concerned with the proposed 'stopping up' of the canal despite the fact that none of them was sending much if any traffic at all by canal. At best, it was suggested, Wheatly sent one or two boats a year along the canal. Mr W Allen, in evidence on behalf of the Newcastle-under-Lyme Canal Company, stated that 20 of its shareholders representing £9,150 of the total share capital, were in favour of the proposal, while the remaining two, representing shares to the value of £450, were neutral on the matter. He made the point however, that agreement to the proposal was on the understanding that the £520 a year rent payable by the NSR under the 1864 Lease Act remained an obligation on the railway company. The canal shareholders had no need to worry themselves, as the Light Railway Order, when it became law, did not release the NSR from any of its obligations under the 1864 Canal Lease Act in so far as their payments were concerned. The canal shareholders had done very well out of the original leasing arrangements and were to continue to do so. Evidence was presented indicating that the principal use of the canal at the time (1913) was in connection with Newcastle Gas Works, but that the Gas Works owners – Newcastle Borough Council – considered it a nuisance and wanted to move the traffic to rail. The gas works already enjoyed rail access by a connection to the Canal Extension Railway, but seems to have continued to use the canal for at least some of its traffic.

According to the evidence presented to the Commissioners, for the preceding few years the total annual takings for canal traffic were in the region of £60, of which £40 was on the stretch to be abandoned, against total expenses of between £70-80. Mr Boddington, Managing Director of canal carriers the Anderton Company, stated that while his firm carried a large quantity of goods to Newcastle, it preferred to take them to Etruria and then tranship to road. It was further stated that on average but one boat a day traversed the canal, presumably taking coal to the gas works. The General Manager of the NSR, W D Phillipps (1839-1932), mentioned that it was a 'wretched little canal 120 years ago and was now totally inadequate'! One wonders if the Directors would have shared this view when they agreed to take on the lease back in 1864. Nevertheless, the NSR agreed to cater for the concerns of the two brick and tile companies anxious not to lose the canal, by building a short spur from its existing Trentham Park branch to the Trent & Mersey Canal at Trentham. This spur would have been one furlong and 9.4 chains long with a wharf and transhipment facilities; estimated cost £1,691. It was also agreed to let the two brick and tile companies have sufficient land for private sidings adjacent to the proposed line, so that if at a later date it was decided to have such a facility, it could easily be provided. Quite perversely, it was also suggested that if the two companies still wanted to use canal boats, this would allow traffic to be loaded to rail at the respective tileries and then, if it was felt appropriate, transhipped to the Trent & Mersey Canal at the proposed new facilities at Trentham. This convoluted proposal did not make economic sense, and as we shall see came to nothing anyway; such, however, was the lengths the NSR went to in pacifying the opposition.

There were a number of other matters raised by various landowners adjacent to the canal, in the main concerned about drainage and other peripheral matters, but they did not amount to very much and need not detain us here. On the plus side Stoke-on-Trent Corporation was anxious to get rid of the bridge over the main London Road at Trent Vale, as it was a hump back bridge unsuited to the tramway lines passing over it and there was constant trouble with the road surface. Agreement was reached to convey to the Corporation the legal title to the bridge and adjoining land, free of any charges or other encumbrances. In so far as the vexed question of the bridges over the Silverdale and Knutton Roads was concerned, it was agreed that the minimum height above road level should indeed be 16 feet, as in the existing plans. Presumably, Wolstanton Urban Council had already been informed of this decision, for it did not

bother to be represented at the reconvened Inquiry. The PET was, as might be expected, represented at the Inquiry, and while a strong objector, the Commissioners took little heed of the competition concerns it raised.

The way was now clear for The North Staffordshire (Trentham Newcastle-under-Lyme & Silverdale Light Railways) Order 1914 to become law, which it did on 6 May 1914. The Order gave the NSR, along with much else, powers to raise additional capital not exceeding £100,000 to facilitate the works. Worth mentioning is the fact that this was not the first scheme for the Pool Dam and Apedale branch lines to be operated for passengers as light railways under the 1896 Act. There had been earlier proposals in 1905, together with a few other NSR branch lines, and powers for some of them to be operated as light railways were obtained under the North Staffordshire (Light Railway) Orders of 1905 and 1906 – the latter became law on 2 March 1906. These Orders did not, however, grant such powers for the Pool Dam branch (although it had been part of the application) but they did cover the Apedale branch – hence the 1914 Order did not need to include such powers for it. The Light Railway Commissioners took the view that as the NSR had obtained powers to build a line from Stoke to join the Pool Dam branch in its 1899 Act, as well as powers to operate passenger trains between Stoke, Newcastle and Silverdale by this route, and as it had allowed these powers to lapse, such a line should be built before they would allow the Pool Dam line to be operated as a light railway. Obviously for this to happen new powers would be necessary. In the event it was all rather academic, as none of the powers granted were ever exercised.

The NSR, once the Order became law, made considerable progress on the light railway including purchase of much of the necessary land at Knutton and Apedale, as well as between Trentham and Trent Vale. In conjunction with Newcastle-under-Lyme Council a Government guarantee was obtained to cover part of the construction costs; the Council in particular, was anxious to get the additional railway accommodation and seems to have used its influence in this respect. On 2 June 1914 the tender of Messrs Baldry, Yerburgh & Hutchinson was accepted a t £38,777/7/11d (£38,777 40p) for the earthworks.

This figure did not include the permanent way materials which the NSR was to supply, or the material for the bridge over the main road at Trentham. For these materials and works the NSR went to tender separately. It did however include the costs of 'stopping up' and draining the canal, as and where necessary. On 2 June 1914 agreement was reached on the notices to be posted regarding closure of the portion of the

canal and on 28 July the contract for the construction was formally signed. Work soon started and the bridge over the main road at Trentham was erected just before the start of the First World War. However, commencement of hostilities effectively caused work to stop and eventually a mutual agreement was reached to release the contractor from its obligations under the terms of the contract. A monetary settlement, agreed on 9 January 1917, completely discharged the NSR from any obligations under its contract with Baldry, Yerburgh & Hutchinson. However, the Light Railway Order was renewed in 1919 and discussions continued with both Newcastle Borough Council and Staffordshire County Council, regarding ways of financing the line. This the NSR was, understandably, no longer prepared to do by itself. Nothing came of this and the statutory powers to acquire the land, abandon portions of the canal and build the lines were allowed to expire on 5 June 1921.

A Lingering End for the Lower Canal
Following the lapse of the powers granted to the NSR under the Light Railway Orders, and as the canal from Trent Vale to Newcastle had not therefore been abandoned, the NSR included powers to do so in its 1921 Act. This was the North Staffordshire Railway Act 1921 (11-12 Geo V ch cxvii) which received the Royal Assent on 19 August 1921. Once again however, this Act did not release the NSR from its financial obligations to the canal shareholders. It would nevertheless appear that this portion of the canal had seen little use for some years and had to all intents and purposes already become almost un-navigable due to the growth of weeds and build up of silt. The Act gave the NSR powers to abandon and 'stop up' the canal from a point not exceeding 35 yards on the Stoke side of the bridge carrying the main road over the canal at Trent Vale, through to its termination in Newcastle. It also gave powers for Stoke-on-Trent Corporation to take ownership of the site of the canal including the Trent Vale Bridge, up to 35 yards on either side of the bridge, for the purposes of widening the road to a width of 50 feet. The NSR was required to contribute £2,700 towards these works. This was a nasty sting in the tail for the NSR, doubtless deemed by Parliament a deserved penalty for all its prevaricating about railways and canals hereabouts! However, the railway company was empowered to sell or otherwise dispose of the other land released, including the canal bed, free of any rent charge to the canal company.

The land was indeed sold over the next few years, in somewhat piecemeal fashion. For example, in April 1927 two rods and 23 perches (706.75 sq. yards) alongside London Road was sold by the London Midland & Scottish Railway

The Timothy Trow Monument in London Road Stoke on 15 July 1976. The inscription reads: *Erected By Public Subscription In Grateful Memory of Timothy Trow, Tram Conductor, Aged 21 Years. Who Lost His Life By Drowning Near This Spot, In An Attempt To Save That Of A Child, April 13th 1894.*

(LMS), as successors to the NSR, to G H Ainsworth, at £200, to erect a garage. The 1921 Act also gave the railway company powers to retain any land acquired in connection with both the 1899 railway scheme and the 1905, 1906 and 1914 railways authorised under the Light Railways Acts. In November 1940 agreement was reached with Stoke-on-Trent Corporation to donate the land where the canal had passed under Clayton Lane, to enable the Corporation to dismantle the bridge and improve the road layout. A further agreement of November 1942 transferred ownership of over an acre at Newcastle to one L Bridgett, for £350. As late as June 1946,

a portion of land at Newcastle was sold to Messrs N C Joseph, three rods and 38 perches (1,166 sq. yards) for £250, the purchaser to be indemnified against any of the perpetual rents payable to the canal company under the NSR Canal Lease Act of 1864, be it noted! Much of the remainder was sold by the LMS, again piecemeal and over several years, to Newcastle-under-Lyme Borough Council. It is worth a mention here that water remains in a small portion of this canal, opposite the main entrance to the City General Hospital – The Avenue – and on the opposite side of London Road to the hospital. Interestingly, at a meeting of the NSR Traffic & Finance

Committee on 9 September 1919, agreement was reached to dredge the canal as far as Trent Vale, at a cost of £3,000. This was a tidy sum in those days and would suggest that little traffic had been using even that section, for some time.

As early as 1 November 1914 the NSR had entered into an agreement with Stoke-on-Trent Corporation regarding road improvements as well as covering over portions of the canal at Campbell Place in Stoke, along with abandonment of a short branch to the Gordon Flint Mill which was adjacent to Campbell Place. The plan here was to cover over the canal forming in effect a tunnel over

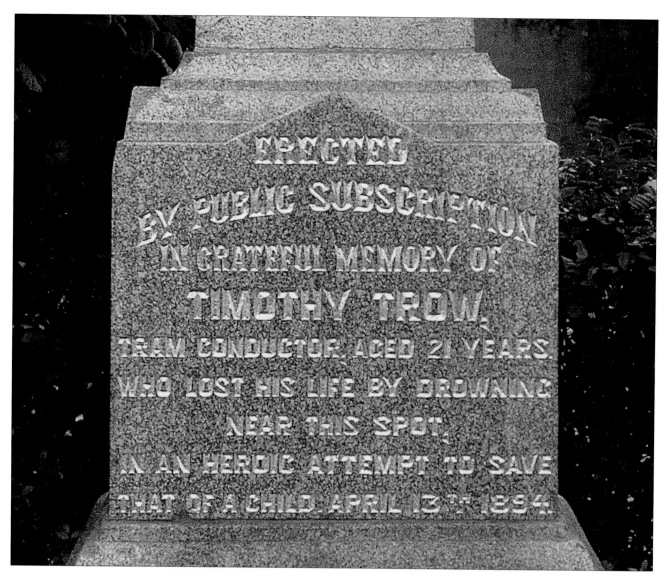

the still navigable section. The flint mill had by this date closed and having been purchased by the Corporation was in the process of being demolished. As with the projected light railway from Trentham to Newcastle, the intervention of the First World War seems to have prevented anything being done, and it was not until 21 February 1934 that the LMS Works Committee discussed a request from the Corporation to resurrect this agreement. Even as late as this the committee decided to ensure in any resurrected agreement that there was a clause to protect the navigation rights of the canal, but in the event the proposed agreement was overtaken by one of much greater significance.

Before continuing the story it is worth mentioning that in 1927 the French Michelin Tyre Company was building a large factory in Stoke, alongside the Lower Canal at Boothen. Rail connection was provided by a branch from the main line at Sideway, south of Stoke, but the company applied to the LMS for permission to take up to 7,000,000 gallons of water every 24 hours from the Trent & Mersey Canal, which ran parallel to the main line where the branch line connected. The application also involved returning 1,000,000 gallons

into the Lower Canal, and agreement was reached at a cost of £50 per annum plus a penalty £50 for every 500,000 gallons average daily quantity taken from the Trent & Mersey but not returned to the Lower Canal. Yet another agreement between the LMS and Stoke-on-Trent Corporation, dated 26 July 1928, covered the extraction of water for condensing purposes for a 1,000kW steam-turbine generator at Stoke Electricity Works, which was also situated alongside the Lower Canal at Boothen. The Corporation was empowered to take up to 125,000 gallons per hour for an average of eight hours per day, returning it all less an allowance of 3% to cover evaporation, and at a temperature 'not exceeding 14° Fahrenheit over that at which it was extracted'. The price was 1/- (5p) per 1,000kW generated. The agreement referred to earlier ones with the NSR of 1908 and 1922, and for similar purposes. The works closed in 1938, presumably when a new and much bigger power station was commissioned in Hanley, the agreement being cancelled in June that year. Perhaps worthy of note is the fact that the agreement was replaced by another one, to take water from the Caldon Canal,

which ran alongside the new power station.

In 1935 the LMS came to an agreement with Stoke-on-Trent Corporation to seek powers to abandon all but a short section at Stoke of the remaining part of the Lower Canal, transferring ownership of the land to the Corporation. The agreement was dated 21 February 1935 and a Bill was submitted to Parliament on this basis for the 1934-1935 session. The plans of the Corporation involved seven separate schemes in connection with road improvements and the construction of sewers, estimated to cost £49,820; the agreement covered the land being handed over free of any charge and at no liability or cost to the LMS, with the Corporation paying all costs associated with the Act. There was, however, one liability that remained with the LMS involving the annual payments to the canal company shareholders, an obligation contained in a clause of the 1864 Canal Lease Act which had still not been repealed.

One might have expected this Bill to go forward unopposed, but this was not the case and the Trent Vale Brick & Tile Company Limited lodged an objection under its common seal. This company owned and operated a brick and tile works at Trent Vale situated south-east of, and adjacent to, the canal, almost at its then termination and just short of the bridge where it had passed under the London Road. The basis of the petition was use of the canal by the company to transport its finished products. The firm pointed out that when it had purchased the existing brick and tile works in 1919, it had been influenced by its site adjacent to the canal, and while at that time the canal was not navigable due to wartime lack of maintenance, it had been assured (presumably by the NSR, although this was not stated) that the canal would be made navigable. This, it is presumed, was the reason for the 1919 dredging mentioned earlier. Nevertheless, the petition claimed that neither the NSR nor the LMS had completed the dredging such that the company had not been able to use the canal. As a consequence its goods had to be taken to Stoke by road for transhipment to either canal or railway – in actual fact exclusively to the railway. This petition cut no ice in Parliament, if for no other reason than that, for the period from 1919, when the company acquired the works, through to 1935 it had in fact not used the canal. Thus the Stoke-on-Trent Corporation Act 1935 (25-6 Geo V ch cxi) duly received the Royal Assent on 2 August 1935. A short stub of the canal was now left, at its junction with the Trent & Mersey in Stoke, for use as a basin and wharf; it ran to a point east of Church Street and in effect consisted of about 330 yards of canal. In 1938 the LMS obtained powers to abandon part of even this small length (1-2 Geo V1 ch xxvii, Royal Assent 2 June 1938) leaving only some 100 yards as a small basin terminating at Aqueduct Street. This was eventually used as a mooring by locally owned pleasure boats. During the recent (2005-6) road improvements to the A500 as it passes through Stoke, even this small section has disappeared, including the original bridge carrying the Trent & Mersey Canal towpath over the entrance to the canal, as well as the bridge taking the canal under Copeland Street. What if any statutory powers were taken to legalise this is however, unknown to the authors.

Rather surprisingly, it has not been possible to find out if and when the Newcastle-under-Lyme Canal Company was finally dissolved, and when the obligation of the LMS to pay the annual rental ceased. The North Staffordshire Railway Act 1904 (4 Ed V11 ch xliv, Royal Assent 24 June 1904) contained powers for the NSR to cease paying the rent with the agreement of the canal company. However, it appears that agreement was not forthcoming as the LMS continued to pay. While the LMS obtained various statutory powers to abandon the canal, powers to wind up the canal company do not appear to have been obtained. As a statutory body, primary legislation would have been required to achieve this. That said, and as mentioned above, it is also doubtful if any statutory powers have ever been obtained for the abandonment of the canal basin in Stoke, as none of the powers that were obtained allowed for the closure of this (admittedly tiny) section. So, despite all the research for this history, a few matters remain unsolved.

In Memoriam

Little remains of the Lower Canal today. Of the section that closed first between Trent Vale and Newcastle the only discernable fragment is the short length still holding water adjacent to the City General Hospital mentioned earlier. Between Stoke city centre and Trent Vale the eagle-eyed will, however, spot the odd bit of evidence here and there betraying its former route, including the iron railings of the bridge that took Corporation Street over the canal. The short tunnel under Campbell Place in Stoke was used during the last war as an air raid shelter and parts of it doubtless remain under the present road layout; the noticeable hump in Church Street also betrays where the canal formerly passed under the road, in the tunnel.

Perhaps the most noticeable and without doubt the best known feature is a small granite monument alongside the London Road at Boothen, opposite James Street, adjacent to what are now the Coronation Gardens. These are in fact on the site of the canal. On Friday 13 April 1894, a young 21 year old tram conductor by the name of Timothy Trow was, along with his driver John Hulme, engaged in running the steam tram engine around its car for the return journey to Stoke from the West End terminus of the line. At around a quarter past four with the manoeuvre complete and ready for the return journey, the two men heard a splash of water from the canal which ran alongside the road at that point. On investigation they saw that a child had fallen in and was in obvious distress. Trow immediately jumped into the canal to undertake a rescue but seems to have been overcome, shouting to his driver 'Oh Jack I have got cramp'. Another passer-by, John Forrester, then jumped in and while he was able to save the child, Trow drowned; an earlier attempt by Henry Lloyd, another passer-by, had also resulted in cramp, but he managed to save himself. Forrester by the way, after recovering the child went into the water again in an attempt to save Trow, but he had to abandon the attempt. The child was Jane Ridgway who lived nearby and was three years old at the time.

Trow's valiant attempt made headlines in the local press and generated a lot of local sympathy; it was to his memory that the monument was erected by public subscription, along with a donation from his employers. At the inquest held at the North Staffordshire Infirmary at Hartshill on the morning following the accident, it was stated that Trow's body was recovered at ten minutes to five, and that the water at the place where he drowned was no less than nine feet deep, which seems rather excessive for a canal. The neat and well made monument was formally unveiled on 22 October 1894 and takes the form of an obelisk eight feet high fashioned from grey granite; it is worthy of more than a second glance when passing. At its unveiling by the then Deputy Mayor of Stoke-on-Trent, Alderman E Baddeley, certificates were presented to Lloyd and Forrester, as well as one to Trow's father. More recently, through the auspices of the Rev. Alan Newman, Minister of Stoke Baptist Church at the time, this delightful monument has been spruced up and a re-dedication service was held on the evening of 14 April 1994. At the service, which was attended by around 150 local residents, were three of Jane Ridgway's seven children, Len Juggins, Mary Mellor and Elizabeth Reeves. Len, who was 82 years old on the day before the ceremony, was born on the anniversary of Timothy Trow's drowning. The renovation of the monument was undertaken by local stone mason Wilf Burt, and the work included re-gilding the inscription. Wilf is a member of the family firm of stone masons, R&W Burt, and it was his great grandfather Robert, along with his brother William, who founded the firm which made the monument all those years ago. This was a very nice touch, and Wilf offered not to charge for the renovation work, an offer gratefully accepted. One is left wondering nevertheless, out of the hundreds of passers-by each day, and of those who stop and study, what they might make of the inscription of Trow 'drowning near this spot', when there is no water to be seen for some considerable distance around!

In concluding this chapter it is worth pointing out that despite the promotion of two railway schemes and one street tramway scheme to cover the ground between Trent Vale and Newcastle, all in effect paralleling or running along the London Road and the site of the canal, none of them came to fruition. The Newcastle-under-Lyme Canal shareholders nevertheless, continued to receive financial remuneration long after their undertaking ceased to have any commercial value!

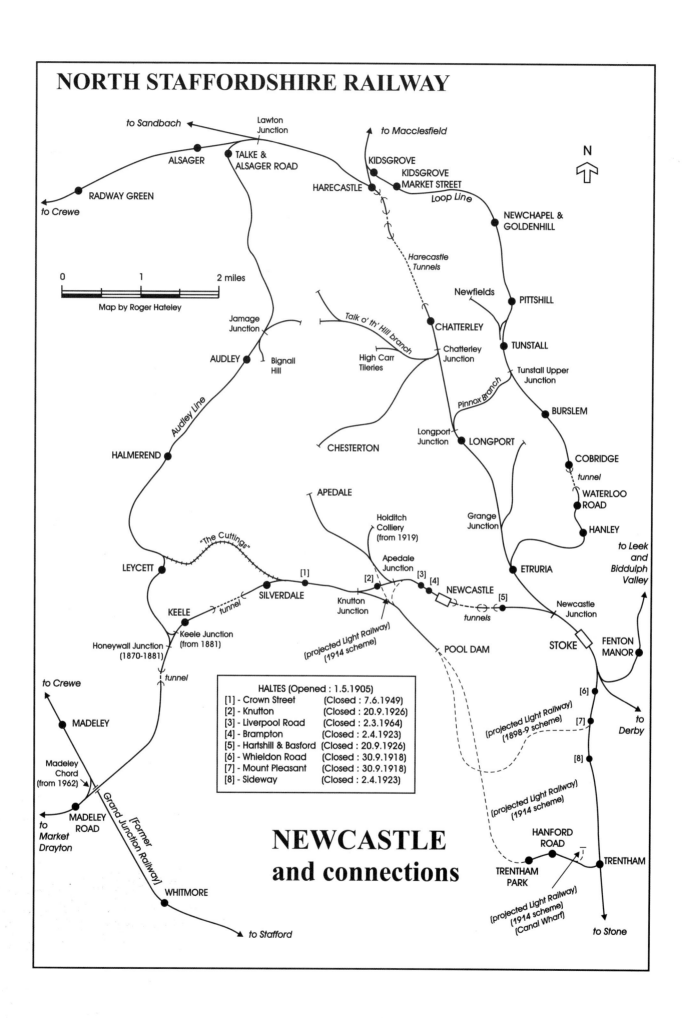

NORTH STAFFORDSHIRE RAILWAY

to Sandbach
Lawton Junction
to Macclesfield
ALSAGER
TALKE & ALSAGER ROAD
KIDSGROVE
KIDSGROVE MARKET STREET
RADWAY GREEN
HARECASTLE
Loop Line
NEWCHAPEL & GOLDENHILL
to Crewe

0   1   2 miles
Map by Roger Hateley

Harecastle Tunnels

Newfields
PITTSHILL
Jamage Junction
Talk o' th' Hill branch
CHATTERLEY
TUNSTALL
AUDLEY
Bignall Hill
High Carr Tileries
Chatterley Junction
Tunstall Upper Junction
Audley Line
Pinnox Branch
BURSLEM
CHESTERTON
Longport Junction
LONGPORT
COBRIDGE
HALMEREND
tunnel
WATERLOO ROAD
APEDALE
Holditch Colliery (from 1919)
Grange Junction
HANLEY
"The Cuttings"
[1]
[2]
Apedale Junction
[3] [4]
NEWCASTLE
[5]
ETRURIA
to Leek and Biddulph Valley
LEYCETT
SILVERDALE
Knutton Junction
tunnels
Newcastle Junction
KEELE
tunnel
Keele Junction (from 1881)
(projected Light Railway) (1914 scheme)
POOL DAM
STOKE
FENTON MANOR
Honeywall Junction (1870-1881)
tunnel
to Crewe

MADELEY

HALTES (Opened : 1.5.1905)
[1] - Crown Street   (Closed : 7.6.1949)
[2] - Knutton   (Closed : 20.9.1926)
[3] - Liverpool Road   (Closed : 2.3.1964)
[4] - Brampton   (Closed : 2.4.1923)
[5] - Hartshill & Basford   (Closed : 20.9.1926)
[6] - Whieldon Road   (Closed : 30.9.1918)
[7] - Mount Pleasant   (Closed : 30.9.1918)
[8] - Sideway   (Closed : 2.4.1923)

[6]
(projected Light Railway) (1898-9 scheme)
[7]
to Derby

Madeley Chord (from 1962)

[8]

to Market Drayton
MADELEY ROAD
[Former Grand Junction Railway]

(projected Light Railway) (1914 scheme)

NEWCASTLE and connections

HANFORD ROAD
TRENTHAM PARK
TRENTHAM
WHITMORE
(projected Light Railway) (1914 scheme) (Canal Wharf)
to Stafford
to Stone

CHAPTER TWO
HOW THE RAILWAY CAME TO NEWCASTLE AND SILVERDALE

Setting the Scene

While recounting the history of the Newcastle canals we have already had to make some mention of railways. These have mostly fallen within the category of abortive schemes from, for example, the early proposed primitive 'railedway' to Partridge Nest to the much later proposal to extend the Trentham Park branch to Pool Dam as a means of combating electric tramway competition. These abortive schemes have been highlighted in order to describe the impact they might have had on the canals and also to demonstrate the attitude of canal shareholders and customers towards railways. The Newcastle-under-Lyme Canal Extension Railway was, of course, an exception to all of this as it became a reality and was actually built by the canal company. It is now time to describe the other railways of Newcastle that became connected to the main line railway system in this country. The key player in this was the North Staffordshire Railway (NSR) but, as we shall see, it was not the first to serve the town.

The North Staffordshire Railway

As was the case with most other main line railways in this country, the NSR was a statutory body by Act of Parliament. In its case there were three separate Acts of Parliament in connection with its formation. One of these, the NSR (Pottery Line) Act 1846 (9-10 Vic ch lxxxv) received the Royal Assent on 26 June 1846. As well as embracing what became the main line of the new undertaking, running from Macclesfield in the north and over the Cheshire border to Colwich and Norton Bridge in the south, also gave powers to build a branch line from Stoke to Newcastle and Silverdale. Between the three Acts the company was also empowered to build what became the Churnet Valley line from south of Macclesfield to Uttoxeter and lines from Stoke to Burton-on-Trent and from Harecastle to Crewe and Sandbach. In addition the Acts gave the company powers to absorb the Trent & Mersey Canal Company, another statutory body, giving the NSR ownership of not only this canal, but others it owned, as well as several tramways that connected the waterways with various industrial,

quarrying and mining operations. The following year the railway company promoted a further Act, the NSR (Alterations & Branches) Act 1847 (10-11 Vic ch cviii, Royal Assent 2 July 1847) which largely consolidated the powers from the three previous Acts, thereby repealing most of their provisions, with the exception of the powers to absorb the undertaking of the Trent & Mersey Canal, the formation of the company itself, and a few other minor matters. As we shall soon see, it also gave powers for the promotion of a second railway to serve the Newcastle area.

Opposition

When the Bills for the original lines of the NSR were progressing through Parliament, Richard Edensor Heathcote (1780-1850) objected and presented a Petition to Parliament. He owned land over which would pass both the main Pottery Line, mentioned above and the branch to Newcastle and Silverdale. The basis of his objection was that the Silverdale branch as projected would have 'shut, or crossed – as best judged by the railway company' the Gresley Canal, which ran chiefly over his land and was used by him, and thereby

Ralph Sneyd (1793-1870) of Keele Hall; Sneyd was a prominent player in the tale of how Newcastle and Silverdale got their railways. The portrait is dated 1842, a stipple engraving by Fredrick Christian Lewis after George Richmond. (Copyright National Portrait Gallery).

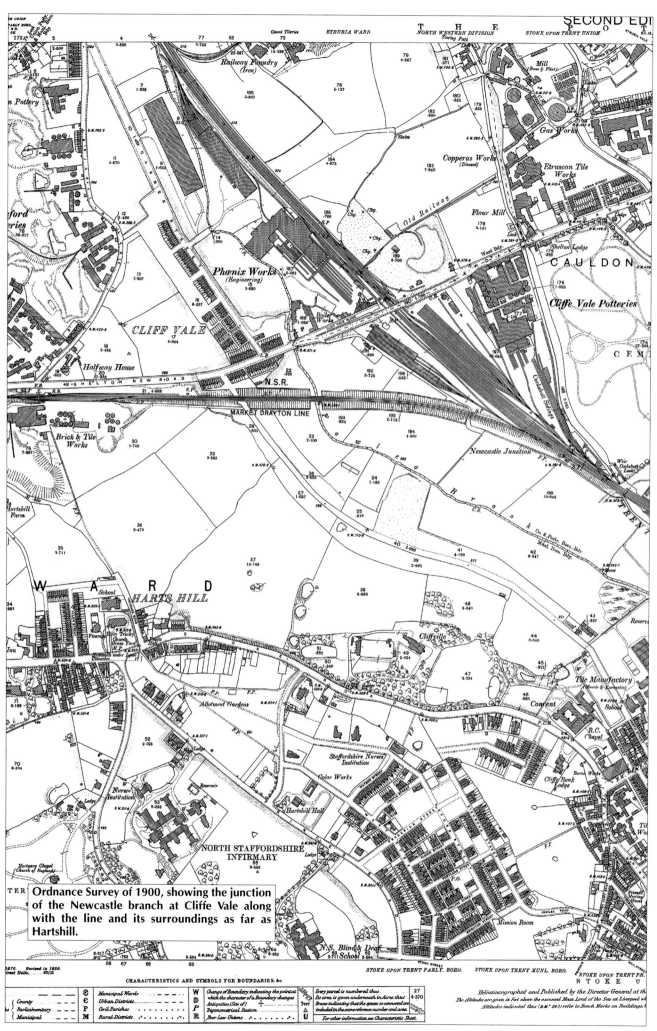

Ordnance Survey of 1900, showing the junction of the Newcastle branch at Cliffe Vale along with the line and its surroundings as far as Hartshill.

means would have to be provided for moving his goods to distant parts over the authorised Silverdale Branch. Heathcote tried to gain further advantage by having a branch line constructed to Apedale, where he owned extensive mines and an iron works and this resulted in the NSR entering into an agreement with him on 30 March 1846, to apply for a Bill in the next session of Parliament to build such a branch. It had clauses to protect his interests, such that if the canal was obstructed during the progress of the works, the NSR would provide means of carrying his traffic at its own expense until the railway was open. In return Heathcote agreed to place the canal at the disposal of the NSR, in order to convert all or part of it into a railway. If however, as events unfolded there was no need to convert the canal, 'that part of it from the east side of the works at Apedale to the wharf at Newcastle shall be given to the NSR without charge within one week of the opening of the railway'. The reason for this was to prevent the canal being used in competition with the new railway.

There was another strong objector to the original NSR schemes, the 1st Earl Granville (1773-1846). The Earl owned and operated ironworks and mines at Etruria and near Hanley and he too, wanted railway access. Therefore, the 1847 Act also provided for a branch from the main Pottery line at Etruria to his works. This branch later became part of the line to serve Hanley, and later still the Potteries Loop Line. In the event the Apedale branch as built did not impinge on the Gresley Canal, such that no provision was made in the NSR Act of 1847 to protect Heathcote's interests.

Ralph Sneyd, owner of the mineral estate at Silverdale, was also involved in the negotiations for the original lines of the NSR. He too, was a substantial land owner in North Staffordshire. It would appear that, knowing of the potential mineral wealth of the Silverdale area, the railway promoters attempted to get Sneyd to agree to the insertion of a clause in the legislation, so that no other railway could pass through his land in and around Silverdale. The principal promoters, who became the first Directors, were conscious of the Grand Junction Railway (GJR) which was not all that far to the west, as well as a private mineral line from the GJR at Madeley to coal mines at Leycett. In return powers would be sought to extend the projected railway beyond Newcastle to Silverdale, but Sneyd was far from happy with this and declined to enter into any such agreement. Newcastle Borough Council somehow got wind of these behind the scenes discussions, sensing that as a result the NSR might delay, or not seek powers to build the line to Newcastle. It used its influence to good effect, a clause being inserted in the 1846 Act, which was carried over into the

Alterations & Branches Act of the following year. It meant that unless the branch as far as Newcastle was built and opened to public traffic, within 12 months of the opening of the main line from Macclesfield to Colwich, it would not be lawful for the railway company to pay any dividends on its stock. As we shall see there were delays in building the line to Newcastle and Silverdale, such that Sneyd, together with his then partner and later lessee Francis Stanier (1808-1856), built their own railway to Newcastle. Despite the clause in the Act of Parliament, the NSR went ahead and paid dividends anyway!

As a result of the agreement with Heathcote of 30 March 1846 (the deed embodying the terms was not actually completed until 10 October) he withdrew his opposition and the three original NSR Acts received the Royal Assent on 26 June 1846. Following this and in accordance with the agreement, the NSR promoted a further Bill in the following session resulting in the Alterations & Branches Act of 1847, as outlined above. Among much else, it gave the NSR powers to build a branch from a junction with the line between Newcastle and Silverdale to Apedale. Notwithstanding the powers the NSR now had, construction of the branch to Newcastle and onwards to Silverdale was delayed. There were a number of reasons for this; to some extent it was due to the depressed state in the money markets at the time, but by May 1849 the NSR decided to get on with the works. Notice was therefore served on the various land owners, including Heathcote, in his case on 1 June, to 'Treat' under the terms of the Lands Clauses Consolidation Act 1845, for the compulsory purchase of the necessary land. The powers of this Act by the way, were incorporated in Acts concerning railways where compulsory powers to acquire land were necessary. If it was not so, any Bill presented would not be in compliance with Parliamentary Standing Orders, and therefore would be unlikely to proceed any further.

Delays

Heathcote took exception to the notice to Treat and on 3 July 1849 filed a Bill in Chancery, on the premise that the NSR powers for the compulsory purchase of land had expired. Indeed they had, the Alterations & Branches Act giving a period of three years from the date of Royal Assent of the earlier Pottery Line Act of 1846, for the land purchase powers for the line to Newcastle and Silverdale. This did not, it should be noted, include the line to Apedale. These powers had therefore lapsed on 26 June 1849, a few days before his injunction; however, for the Apedale branch the period was three years from the date of the later Act, which meant these powers did not lapse until 2 July 1850. While it might seem strange at first that Heathcote should want to stop what he

had earlier been advocating, it was the exclusion of the Apedale branch from the current plans of the NSR that annoyed him, understandably so, his point being that the railway company should honour its agreement with him dated 10 October 1846, and build the line to Apedale.

In his injunction Heathcote pointed out his agreement to make the bed of the Gresley Canal, in whole or part, along with towing paths available for the railway company to assist in building the Apedale branch. His view was that compulsory purchase powers were not necessary in the light of the agreement of 10 October 1846, and that he would do everything in his power to assist. The counter view of the NSR was that while the agreement might well allow the construction of the Apedale branch, it would not allow building of the line from Stoke to Newcastle and Silverdale. The compulsory purchase powers for the land, as Heathcote had pointed out, had expired. The Apedale branch would of course, be of little use without the line onwards from Newcastle to Silverdale, as it was planned to be a branch from it.

Resulting from this stand-off between the two parties, the NSR 'determined' to apply to Parliament (Board Minute of 6 November 1849) for an Act to abandon its powers to build the lines to Newcastle, Silverdale and Apedale. If this should fail, it asked for an extension of time for their construction. On 22 January 1850 Heathcote amended his Bill in Chancery to restrain the NSR from powers to abandon building the railways, and was granted an Injunction against the NSR by the Vice Chancellor of England, preventing the railway company under a penalty of £5,000, from getting powers to abandon the lines, or in fact doing anything inconsistent with the agreement of 10 October 1846. As might be expected the NSR appealed against this ruling and the case was reviewed by the Lord Chancellor on 7 and 8 February 1850. The judgement went in favour of the NSR, the crux of the matter being that while the NSR had powers to build the various lines, the Act did not otherwise require it actually do so. It was also pointed out that Heathcote was in fact, not the 'absolute owner' of the Gresley Canal and therefore, not in a position legally to dispose of it to the NSR, or anybody else, as by the Act authorising its construction, it 'must always be kept open'. To add insult to injury, the railway company was awarded costs. This course of events turned into a test case; in circumstances where a petition by a landowner against a railway company, building a line, was settled by an agreement resulting in the company obtaining powers to build a line for the benefit of the petitioner, but where, subsequently, the railway company sought to abandon its powers and renege on the agreement. It is thus

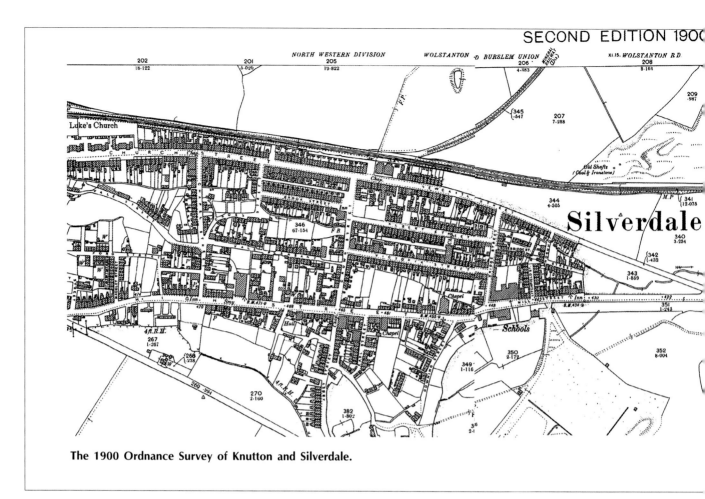

The 1900 Ordnance Survey of Knutton and Silverdale.

quoted in Hodges *Law of Railways* 1888.

The matter, inevitably, did not end there. The House of Commons appointed a Select Committee to consider the NSR Bills, one of which proposed abandonment of the powers to build the lines, and the other an extension of time. The committee sat on 23 and 24 April 1850 and along with considering several other matters embraced by the Bills, as well as further objections to the NSR being granted powers to either abandon the lines, or for an increase in the time allowed for the purchase of land etc., heard evidence. The NSR Resident Engineer, J C Forsyth attended in person, and cross-examination revealed that, following enactment of the 1846 Act, all the landowners involved in the line from Stoke to Newcastle and Silverdale were in fact given the statutory 'Notice to Treat'. In many cases agreements had been reached between them and the railway company on the price, and where claims had subsequently been made, the NSR had lodged the money with the Accountant General under the terms of the Land Clauses Consolidation Act 1845. In other cases, while monies were not paid, agreements had been reached on the relevant figures. He went on to say that work on the construction had commenced in June 1849, when the contractor (this was Thomas Brassey) started work, but soon stopped following an injunction, in this case from Thomas Kinnersly on behalf of himself and two other landowners,

William Taylor Copeland and John Ridgway, the former a prominent pottery manufacturer and the latter a brewer. This case was, like Heathcote's, heard in a Court of Chancery when Thomas Fenton, Kinnersly's solicitor, told the court that two of the Newcastle-under-Lyme Justices of the Peace had in June 1849, appointed Robert Chapman, the Assistant Surveyor to the Borough, to value the land independently under the terms of the Land Clauses Consolidation Act 1845. An agreement had been reached not to take any land for the railway from the Newcastle-under-Lyme Junction (Upper) Canal. This is interesting because, as we saw in Chapter One, and will see shall again later, part of the bed of the canal was in the event used for the formation of the railway.

Once again, as was the case with Heathcote and Kinnersly, the concern was that the powers for the purchase of the land under the Act had expired, although as Forsyth pointed out, agreements were in place with all the landowners, and in some cases, as noted above, the railway company had made payments. He also told the committee that if the contractor had been allowed to continue with the construction of the line, it would by this time have been completed, although in the light of later events regarding the strata through which the Newcastle tunnel passed, this may not have been the case. The committee was able to establish the real concern in questioning Forsyth; this was

a feeling amongst some of the landowners that the value of the land had increased between 1846 when the agreements were reached, and 1850! The recommendation of the Select Committee to Parliament was that the Preamble of the Bill for the extension of time was 'proved', while the one to abandon the powers was not, and that the former should go forward on the basis of giving the NSR an extension of time to complete the works for both the line to Newcastle and Silverdale, and the branch to Apedale.

In the Chancery case papers, incidentally, Heathcote is shown as residing at Harve de Grace in France, and later in Paris. He cannot, presumably, have been personally involved very much in his Apedale estate at this period and his solicitor, Thomas Fenton would thus have been acting very much *in absentia*. Heathcote was, in fact, ill and died in Geneva on 29 May 1850. Fenton was also a shareholder in the Upper Canal, and in addition acted for Thomas Kinnersly, at least in matters concerning the NSR and canals. Another of Kinnersly's concerns was the Upper Canal, of which he was a shareholder. This canal was almost completely dependent on the Gresley Canal for its water supply. If the latter was closed and drained so that it could be used to form all or part of the Apedale branch railway, the Upper Canal would very soon have been devoid of water.

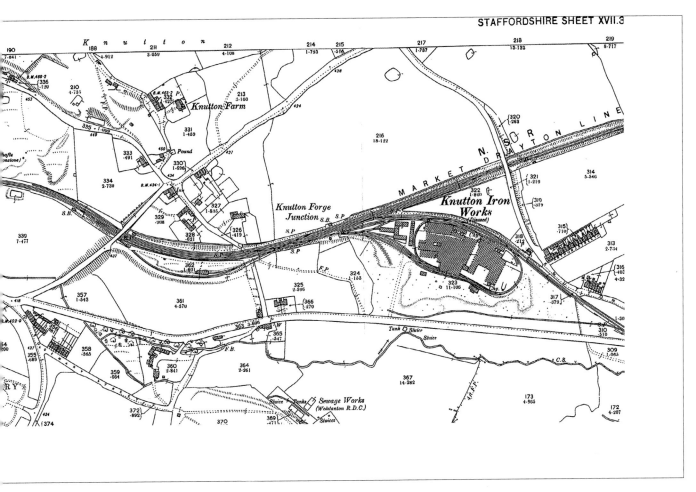

Construction Problems

The original plans and sections for the branch from Newcastle to Silverdale placed the railway east of its eventual route and therefore, east of the Newcastle-under-Lyme Junction Canal (the Upper Canal) over which it was to cross by a swing bridge. The railway line would have then turned west, missing the Gresley Canal by passing immediately to the west of its terminal basin. The route of the Upper Canal between the later site of Newcastle station and where it turned east at the Brampton, and the last five chains of the Gresley Canal at its terminal basin, were within the Parliamentary limits of deviation for the railway line in the Act of Parliament. But it is worth reminding readers again at this point, that neither at this time nor subsequently, were legal powers acquired by anybody for the abandonment of all or any part of the Gresley or Newcastle-under-Lyme Junction (Upper) Canals. Such powers were a legal requirement, as both canals had been built under statutory powers, and while both were indeed eventually abandoned, the owners of the Upper Canal had no powers to do so and were therefore, technically in breach of the law. Nevertheless, nobody seemed to bother!

The problems alluded to above, once construction started, were in connection with the strata of the ground through which the main Newcastle tunnel was driven following deficient surveys. The NSR (Newcastle Branch Extension of

Time) Act 1850 (13-4 Vic ch lv) which received the Royal Assent 15 July 1850, gave powers to extend the time allowed for the compulsory purchase of the land, and for construction of the railway. To speed up the work on the tunnel the Board had agreed, at its meeting on 5 July 1851, to an additional expenditure of £1,000 to sink a further access shaft. This followed a visit to the works by the Chairman, General Manager and Engineer (John Lewis Ricardo, George Parker Bidder and J C Forsyth respectively) and an estimate by the three of them that the branch would bring in an income of £3,000 per annum. The original contracted cost of the construction of the branch from the junction with the main line at Stoke, to a junction with the Silverdale & Newcastle-under-Lyme Railway (SNuLR - to be described later) at Knutton, was £27,000, minus the cost of lining the Newcastle tunnels. The latter was to be paid for by schedule at 23/- per yard (£1 15p), and 5/- (25p) for mining the clay for the bricks, plus 2/- (10p) for contingencies. It was estimated that if the complete tunnels needed lining the cost would be £12,000, but Forsyth reckoned that approximately half the distance would need lining and the cost would, therefore, be in the region of £6,000. The NSR minutes are silent on the eventual outcome. The contract for the construction of the branch to Silverdale had been part of Thomas Brassey's contract awarded in 1846, for the main line from Macclesfield to

Colwich and Norton Bridge. However, in view of the lapse in time before work commenced on the branch, Bidder had reached agreement in November 1850, on behalf of the NSR Board, with Brassey's agent, a fellow called Jones, on the price quoted above including the issue of tunnel lining. In pushing the work forward the company and its contractor then got into hot water in August 1851, for carrying out work on Sundays!

The NSR Reaches Newcastle, Knutton Junction and Apedale

The NSR Traffic Committee noted at its meeting on 24 August 1852 that the Newcastle branch was sufficiently complete to allow opening to passenger traffic, and the date of Monday 6 September was agreed. In the meantime notice was given to the Board of Trade, which appointed Captain Douglas Galton, formerly of the Royal Engineers, to undertake the inspection. His report is dated 3 September 1852, and the only concern he raised was that some of the track in the tunnel was off-centre. This Forsyth, who accompanied him, agreed to rectify. On the understanding that this was done and that passenger trains would be worked by tank engines (as there was no turntable at Newcastle) he gave his authority to open. The report mentions that while the signalling was complete at the junction with the main line near Stoke, at Newcastle it was 'about to be erected', but this does not seem to have prevented him agreeing

Ordnance Survey of 1900 showing the town of Newcastle with its railways.

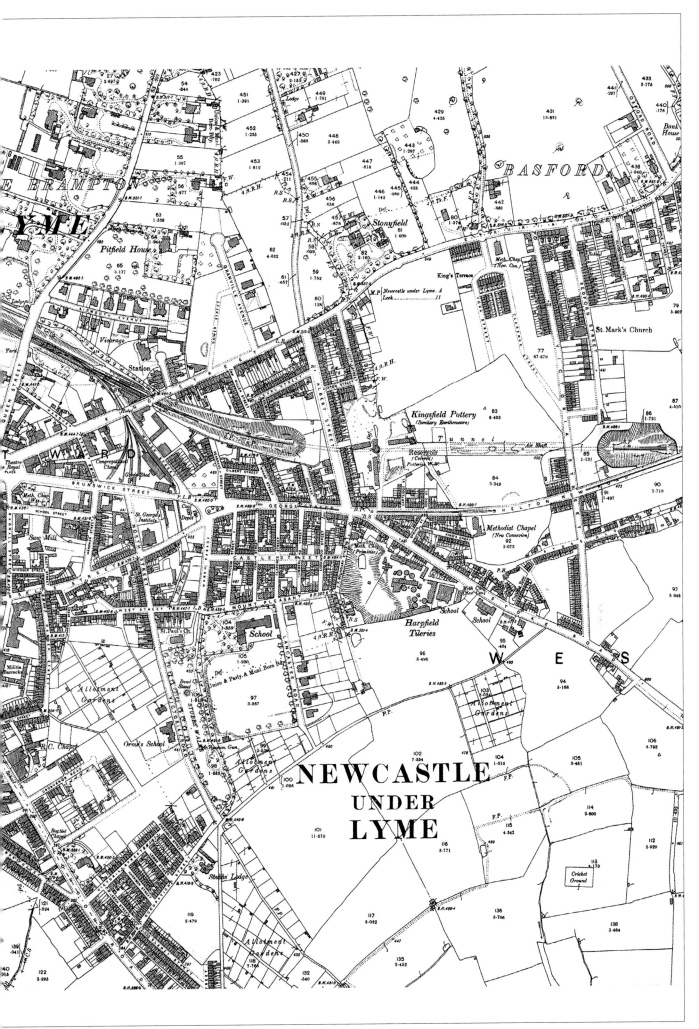

Kent's Lane Colliery at Silverdale survived until May 1996, generating the last remaining traffic on the line between Silverdale and Madeley. The Shelton Iron, Steel & Coal Company and Florence Coal & Iron Company private owner railway wagons in the foreground would date the photograph as post-1918, for it was in that year that the Shelton Company acquired the colliery. The wagons are standing on the Silverdale & Newcastle-under-Lyme Railway, as extended to serve the colliery and iron works.

for the line to be opened for passenger traffic. The line from Stoke to Knutton was, therefore, officially opened on 6 September 1852, but only the section to Newcastle was passed for passenger traffic following the Board of Trade inspection. However, an NSR board minute of 3 July 1852 records that the 'Chairman and Engineer had been over the line throughout with a locomotive, and that it would immediately be practicable to open for goods and mineral traffic'. It is therefore more than possible that goods and mineral traffic had commenced earlier than the official date. The line was single throughout with a passing loop at Newcastle, and made an end-on junction with the SNuLR at what became known as Knutton Junction, later called Knutton Forge Junction.

The Apedale branch was constructed by a contractor called Jones, and his tender of £9,000 including the land and track materials was accepted by the Board on 5 July 1851. Payment was in 4% Bonds in the NSR. Interestingly, there does not appear to have been any tendering process in the letting of this contract, and one is tempted to conclude that Jones was in fact the one and the same gentleman mentioned earlier, the agent of Thomas Brassey. The Board had been well pleased with Brassey's work

on his other contracts, including the arrangement mentioned above for the line to Newcastle and Silverdale. As he was on site, it would be logical to come to an arrangement for the Apedale branch to be included with his other works in the locality. This might also explain the agreement to accept payment in Bonds in the company, a type of arrangement the larger contractors often agreed to. In fact Brassey had recently made a similar deal with the company for building the Ashbourne branch.

It should also be noted that at this time the entire NSR system was operated by a contractor, Joseph Wright & Son of Saltley, albeit using engines and rolling stock owned by the NSR. Wright in turn paid for their use and maintained them at his own cost. As the railway expanded concerns arose over Wright's costs, and the numbers of locomotives and rolling stock needed. In the case of the lines to Newcastle, Silverdale and Apedale, this gave rise to some debate in 1853, as Wright's estimate of the numbers of locomotives and rolling stock required for these lines was more than the members of the Traffic Committee felt to be appropriate.

The construction of the section from what became Apedale Junction to Knutton Junction followed an agreement

between the NSR and Francis Stanier dated 10 May 1852. This followed a Board minute of 5 July 1851, when a request was tabled from Ralph Sneyd, to guarantee the same amount of interest on the cost of construction of the line, as would be paid by the company making it. The agreement was between the NSR and Stanier rather than Sneyd, as by this time it was Stanier who had the lease of the mines and minerals along with other operations at Silverdale. The agreement refers to the section of railway as the 'Newcastle & Silverdale Junction Railway', and it was constructed following a number of undertakings by the parties of the agreement. For example the NSR was committed to complete the line within three months from the date of the agreement at its own cost (we saw earlier that it was probably ready for goods and mineral traffic in July) and to provide passage over the line 'free of tolls' for traffic worked by Stanier himself with his own locomotives and rolling stock. In return Stanier was obliged to pay a sum equal to four pounds per cent per annum of the gross outlay incurred by the NSR in constructing the branch. Stanier was also committed to pay for the maintenance of the line, and for any use made of NSR locomotives and rolling

Silverdale ironworks, looking east in the general direction of Newcastle about 1880. The railway in the foreground is almost the extreme western end of the Silverdale & Newcastle-under-Lyme Railway, extended to serve the works at what was known as the Furnace Bank. Three open-top blast furnaces to the extreme left and the tall building alongside housing the steam beam blowing engine; the chimney on the right served the forges. The row of cottages to the left was for the men employed at the furnaces, along with their families; the foreman enjoyed the larger residence in front.

Later, circa 1900 view of the blast furnaces at Silverdale Iron Works. Notice that compared with the previous view by the time this photograph was taken there were only two furnaces, although they had been converted to hot-blast. That is the hot-blast stove to the rear with the charging hoist between the furnaces and the blowing engine house to the right. The hot-blast piping protruding to the left suggests that it may have been the intention to install a further furnace replacing one of those demolished - originally there were four. The wagons in the foreground which were used internally round the works are of an interesting design.

41

Ketleys Siding signal box, a standard NSR McKenzie & Holland design, on 9 August 1966, looking towards Silverdale. The left-hand set of rails form part of the original Silverdale & Newcastle-under-Lyme Railway; the right-hand rails were originally laid by the NSR in 1862 when the line to Silverdale was opened to passenger traffic. The signal box had earlier been named Gordons Siding and by this time controlled the junction with the Pool Dam branch. The junction had originally been controlled by Knutton Forge Junction signal box, which was further towards Newcastle, prior to simplification of the arrangements after closure of the Knutton Forge.

stock to work his traffic, as opposed to his own locomotives and rolling stock. While the NSR had exclusive rights to operate the line, it was obliged under the terms of the agreement to allow traffic not exceeding 250 tons of goods and minerals per day, belonging to, or in connection with, the business of Francis Stanier, to pass over the line. The traffic covered by this clause included that worked by either the NSR or Stanier's engines and rolling stock. Stanier's concern was that other traffic on the railway company's behalf would restrict his use of the line; it should be noted that at this time Stanier only had the lease of the Silverdale operations and not, as was later the case, those at Apedale too. The agreement was for 21 years from the date of completion of the line, and included sidings exclusively for Stanier's use in what became Newcastle goods yard, along with half an acre of land there for a wharf.

The branch to Apedale or at least part of it, from what became Apedale Junction, opened on or about 11 July 1853 – at least this is the earliest date for which a record exists of any traffic passing over it. However, in this case the traffic was ironstone from Whitebarn Junction, where the Whitebarn Iron Company had a siding, and it was not until 7 November that the remaining half mile or so to the terminus at

Apedale was opened. At the very most, only the last five chains or so of the Gresley Canal at the Newcastle end may have been used for the railway, but this section would have included part of its Newcastle Wharf. In the case of the Upper Canal, a Board minute of 17 April 1851, following a representation by the Engineer, authorised the Stoke Lands Committee of the railway company to negotiate for the purchase of the land and canal bed at Newcastle, provided the price did not exceed what had already been agreed as a fair price for what was referred to as the 'Jubilee Walks land'. This was the land originally intended for the railway, between the later site of Newcastle station and the Brampton. The Engineer had subsequently submitted a plan to use part of the Upper Canal between these two points and alter the proposed site for the station, in substitution for the 'Jubilee Walks land'. As this effectively rendered the canal just about useless, a further section of its bed onwards towards its southern terminus at Stubbs Gate was used to form Newcastle goods yard.

There were three further agreements with Heathcote following the Deed dated 10 October 1846 between Richard Edensor Heathcote and the NSR, outlined above. This Deed, as we have seen, committed the NSR to apply for

powers to build the Apedale branch, and for Heathcote to give up such parts of the bed of the Gresley Canal as were necessary for the construction of the branch – the canal was by this time in his ownership. The railway was to be constructed and opened as expeditiously as possible after the passing of the Act, and the NSR was to maintain the railway for the exclusive use of Heathcote. Following this indenture various 'disputes and differences' arose between the parties, resulting in litigation, so to 'avoid further litigation', the first of the three agreements mentioned above was entered into with John Edensor Heathcote (son of Richard who had died 29 May 1850) on 5 June 1851. In this agreement the Apedale branch was to be constructed within six months of the signing of the agreement and Heathcote was to pay an annual sum equal to 4% of the cost of construction, not exceeding £9,000, along with the costs of the NSR maintaining the branch.

Heathcote was also committed to pay for the use of any engines and rolling stock belonging to the NSR working his traffic over the branch. The quarterly payments were to commence three months after the Board of Trade Inspector 'passed' the branch though in fact this was never necessary as the branch was not used for passenger traffic. The NSR had exclusive rights to

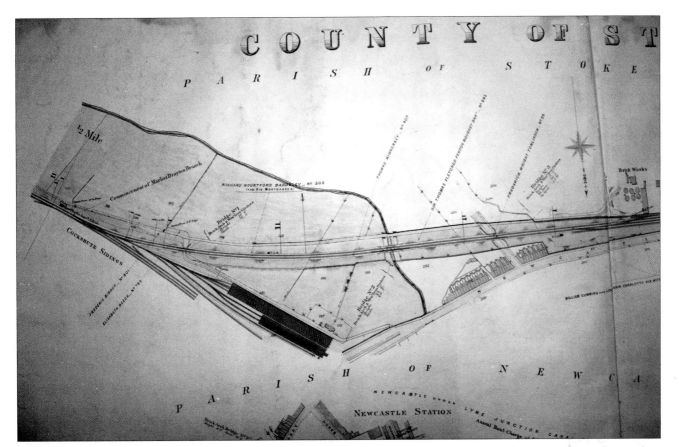

Series of NSR plans, on this and the following pages, from a survey (of about 1900) of the line between Newcastle Junction, where the Newcastle branch joined the NSR main line at Cliffe Vale, to Silverdale including the Pool Dam branch.

a different one in this case, Liddle Elliott, but he was far from happy with the proposals and concluded that there would be 'a continuing danger in the public using them'. Approval unforthcoming, the second Act concerned itself with the diversion of the roads, construction of a new road, two bridges, and a much better layout for both the railway and road traffic. A new road was therefore constructed on the east side of the railway, from Pool Dam to the edge of the village of Silverdale, the present Silverdale and Newcastle Roads, passing under the line by a rail over-bridge just south of Knutton Junction. The present Church Lane, from Knutton village to what became the new Newcastle Road, was diverted to the west and taken over the railway by a bridge which replaced the level crossing. The present Cherry Hill Lane crossed the line by level crossing and was, in the words of the Act, 'stopped up'. However, in later years this road was 'opened up' again, by the construction of an under-bridge taking it under the railway. It was estimated that the works would cost £1,500, to be paid by Sneyd, but the Act conveyed ownership of the new roads, and thus their future maintenance, once complete, to the local authorities; that is, Newcastle Borough and Wolstanton Urban District Councils, as appropriate.

In late 1859 and 1860 the NSR entered into discussions with Ralph Sneyd and his lessees, by this time Stanier & Heath (see below) to lease the

SNuLR. By this time the line was a public one, so statutory powers were necessary. These were obtained under the conditions of the North Staffordshire Railway Act 1860 (23-4 Vic ch xlii) which received the Royal Assent on 15 May 1860; it covered a number of other matters relevant to the NSR but not Sneyd. Although the Act gave the necessary powers to lease the line, they could not be exercised until agreement on the exact terms had been made between Ralph Sneyd and the NSR. The latter had to obtain shareholder approval and the Board of Trade was required to give its approval to the lease conditions. Approval was given at the half-yearly shareholders meeting held on 29 August 1860 and on 31 August 1860 'heads of terms' were agreed with Sneyd, the lease being signed and sealed on 29 November 1860. The lease agreement was for 999 years at a cost of £1,250 per annum, payable twice yearly on 1 January and 1 July with Stanier, or whoever held the Silverdale lease at the time, paying £500 per year for the right to use the line with its own engines and wagons etc, in lieu of any other tolls. Some civil engineering works were considered necessary by the NSR and a contractor by the name of J Wilkinson was appointed to carry them out. It should be noted that the Canal Extension Railway was excluded from the powers of this Act and it remained in the ownership of the canal company, although the NSR acquired the powers Sneyd already had, to use the line.

Complete control of the Canal Extension Railway did not pass to the NSR until it acquired a lease of the Newcastle-under-Lyme Canal, on 1 July 1863.

It is easy to forget of course that all this was really the story of the actions, careers and lives of diverse individuals. Prior to the lease with the NSR, the SNuLR, although in Sneyd's ownership, was leased to Mary Stanier, Robert Heath and Moses and John Mottram Cartwright; these latter two having the siding connection at Knutton. Mary Stanier and Robert Heath were in a partnership dating from 21 May 1857, 'Stanier & Heath'; Mary and her son, Francis Stanier Broade, had replaced Mary's husband when he died in October 1856. The partnership leased from Sneyd the Silverdale & Knutton mining and iron making operations. Later the partnership variously traded as Stanier & Son and the Silverdale Company. From 13 September 1851 an earlier partnership of Ralph Sneyd and Francis Stanier had entered into a 31 year lease, from Ralph Sneyd, of the Silverdale mineral estate and ironworks. This included the SNuLR. Sneyd however, maintained powers 'for the owners of Keele Hall to carry by horse or steam power, bricks, tiles and quarries or any other articles upon the railway from Silverdale to Newcastle-under-Lyme and to deposit same on the wharf at the termination of the railway without charge for carriage or wharfage'. The Stanier & Heath partnership assumed this lease.

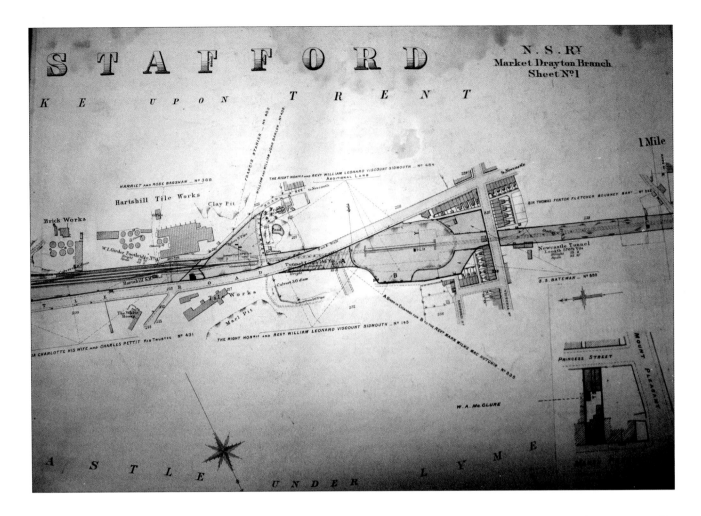

The desire of the NSR to either own the SNuLR, or as events turned out, take a long term lease, should be seen against the background of a number of schemes to gain access to North Staffordshire from the west. Several railways were projected in attempts to share in the rich mineral wealth of North Staffordshire, in which there was enormous interest at the time. The topography of the district and the location of the lines the NSR had already built meant that penetrating the otherwise NSR stronghold from its western flank was seen as the easiest option. There was also a strong desire by traders in the Pottery towns for their products to leave and raw materials to enter North Staffordshire independent of the NSR and Trent & Mersey Canal; the latter, remember, was owned by the railway company. This is an extremely complicated issue, that has already been explored in considerable depth in an earlier publication by one of the authors, *The Potteries Loop Line* (Allan C Baker, Trent Valley Publications 1986). One scheme is, however, worth a more detailed mention at this juncture, as Ralph Sneyd was one of its promoters. Along with the Potteries Chamber of Commerce, which was also keen to suppress the monopoly exploited by the NSR, Sneyd joined forces with the London & North Western Railway (LNWR). A scheme was developed to build a railway from a junction with the SNuLR at Silverdale,

to Madeley, where connection would be made with the LNWR main line from Stafford to Crewe. A Bill was introduced into Parliament, for the Newcastle-under-Lyme, Silverdale & Madeley Junction Railway, in the session 1858-1859. The LNWR was committed to contribute towards the estimated cost of £50,000 for this railway, a little over three miles long with connecting spurs at Madeley in both directions. It would have followed almost the exact course that was eventually taken by the NSR line between Silverdale and Madeley. While this Bill was wending its way through Parliament – it had its first reading on 9 June 1859 – the respective directors of the LNWR and the NSR had been settling another long-standing difference over sharing the Manchester-London traffic, such that some of it would pass over the NSR between Macclesfield and Colwich, rather than entirely over the LNWR via Crewe. When the Marquis of Chandos, Chairman of the LNWR, was called to give evidence to a Select Committee meeting of the House of Lords, in cross-examination he had to admit that had this agreement been in place earlier, the LNWR would not have supported the Madeley railway scheme. The Bill was therefore, there and then, 'thrown-out' of Parliament, as the press used to refer to such matters. Following this Ralph Sneyd appears to have changed his allegiance and abandoned what sympathy he might have had for the

Potteries Chamber of Commerce. He switched instead to the North Staffordshire Railway.

So far as the other schemes to bring railways into North Staffordshire from the west were concerned, suffice it to say that a lease of the SNuLR and ally Ralph Sneyd owning the land were important items in the railway's arsenal. The agreement with Sneyd included clauses to the effect that he would not promote, or assist in promoting, railways through his property without the consent of the NSR. The railway was likewise constrained and the two parties agreed to join in opposing any lines either of them disagreed with. The culmination of a lengthy period of negotiation and Parliamentary debate resulted in the granting of powers to the NSR, to extend the line from Silverdale to Market Drayton, build several branches to serve the Audley coalfield, along with a few other mineral lines deeper in its territory. In granting the NSR powers to build these lines rather than its rivals, Parliament insisted that the company should build three other lines that had been authorised and for which it was seeking powers to abandon. The three lines were what became known as the Potteries Loop Line (from Hanley to Kidsgrove) and the Pinnox and Newfields branches (at or near Tunstall).

Improvements and Railways to Audley and Market Drayton

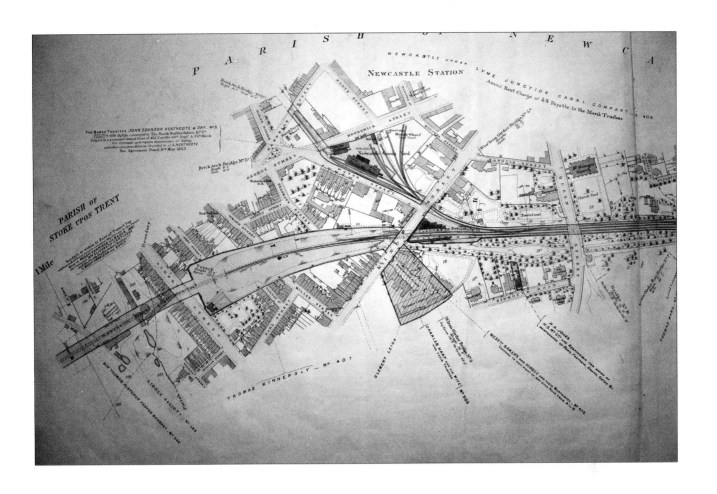

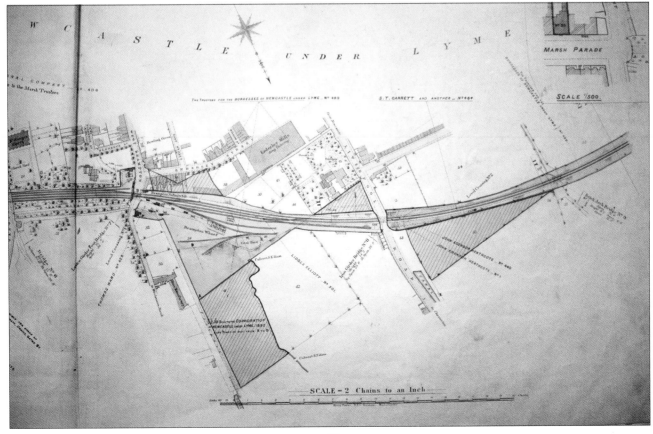

53

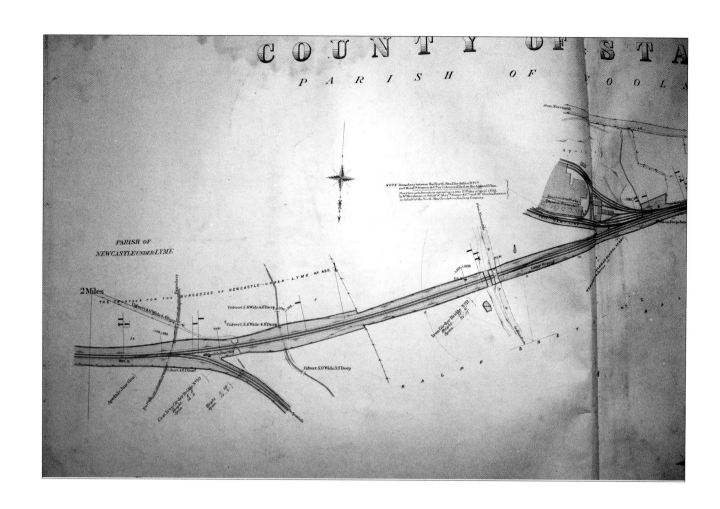

COUNTY OF STA

PARISH OF WOOLS

PARISH OF
NEWCASTLE-UNDER-LYME

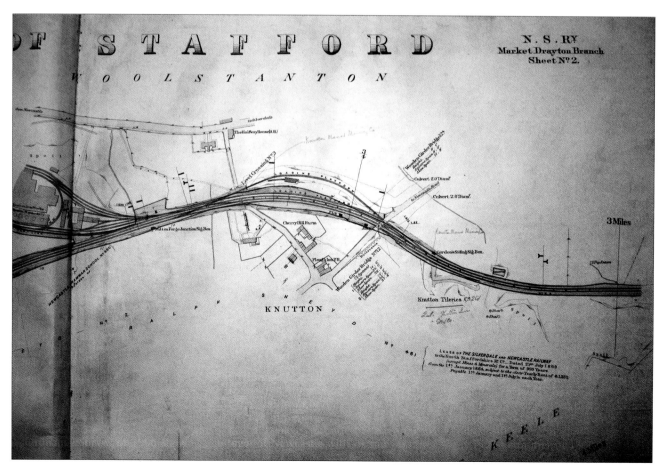

OF STAFFORD

WOOLSTANTON

N.S.RY
Market Drayton Branch
Sheet No 2.

KNUTTON

KEELE

54

On 7 April 1862 the NSR commenced a passenger service between Newcastle and Silverdale. Before it started various works had to be undertaken, including the laying of a second line of rails alongside and to the north of, the existing line of the SNuLR from Knutton Junction to a new passenger station at Silverdale. This station was situated east of what became the permanent station to serve the village, constructed when the line was extended to Market Drayton. The Board of Trade inspection of these arrangements was undertaken by Captain Rich and his report is dated 1 April 1862. While generally satisfied with the arrangements, he was concerned about a level crossing (on the present Albermarle Road) at one mile and 46 chains. It had been regarded as an occupation road rather than a public thoroughfare, so a level crossing had been provided instead. The company gave an undertaking that, should it be unable to prove to the satisfaction of the Board of Trade that it was indeed an occupation road, it would within twelve months erect a bridge. The papers are however, silent on the outcome, although in later years a bridge eventually appeared. Agreement was given to open the line, subject to an undertaking regarding the method of working; only one engine in steam or two coupled together could be used and, as there was no turntable at Silverdale, passenger trains had to be hauled by tank engines. Thereafter, the two lines between Knutton Junction and Silverdale were operated as separate single lines, with the passenger trains only being authorised to use the new line. It is interesting to note that, to gain access to the station (which was adjacent to the Parish Church of St Luke's) the new NSR passenger line had to cross the earlier Sneyd line on the level. A relatively minor, but nevertheless interesting fact is that on the first day, while 1,333 passengers travelled from Silverdale, only 704 are recorded as having returned, leaving one to speculate on what happened to all the others! The takings amounted to a princely £29 11/11½d (£29 60p).

In 1864 the NSR obtained powers under the North Staffordshire Railway Branches Act 1864 (27-8 Vic ch cccix, Royal Assent 29 July 1865) to build a railway from Silverdale to Market Drayton. At the same time it also obtained powers under the North Staffordshire Railway (New Works) Act 1864 (27-8 Vic ch cccviii, Royal Assent 29 July 1864) to build a line from Silverdale to Audley and Alsager. Construction of both was delayed for a number of reasons, and in the event special arrangements had to be made with the Board of Trade to extend the powers, and dispensation was agreed between the parties such that a further Act of Parliament was not necessary. However, as a prelude to the new lines being opened, the NSR undertook

works to turn the two single lines from Knutton Junction to Silverdale into a double track railway. In these works the NSR line became the up and the SNuLR the down line, thus conforming to the usual arrangement of left-hand running. There was a new station at Silverdale, as alluded to above, suitable for through traffic to Market Drayton. At this stage the line to Audley and Alsager was for goods and mineral traffic only; the junction with the SNuLR was at the east (that is, the Newcastle) side of the new station so that trains using it would not pass through the station.

The Board of Trade inspection of the new arrangements was undertaken by Colonel W Yolland, who reported on 29 January 1870. In view of the number of sidings and junctions on the former SNuLR, several recommendations were made, so that authority was not given to open the line for passenger traffic 'until additional works had been undertaken'. In the Colonel's own words: *Between Knutton Junction and Silverdale the sidings are so numerous that it is more like a station yard than anything else. The Company are making the necessary arrangements for a good system of signalling, with points and signals properly interlocked, but cannot complete anything until the authority of the Board of Trade is given for using the present mineral-line as a second passenger line.* He made a number of recommendations involving the sidings at Knutton Forge, where they all connected with the main line, as well as at Gordon's Junction, Grove Branch Junction and Silverdale. The works recommended were in due course undertaken by the NSR and a second, more successful, inspection took place the following month. Later there was a problem with Stanier, as his siding accommodation at Knutton had been reduced to allow for the new works, and the NSR had to purchase additional land and lay new sidings to compensate.

The line from Silverdale to Market Drayton, where connection was made with the Great Western Railway (GWR) line from Nantwich to Wellington, as well as the double track section from Knutton Junction to Silverdale, was opened for all traffic as a double line of railway on 1 February 1870; before, as events turned out, all the alterations had been completed. However, the line from Silverdale to Audley and Alsager, which passed through deep cuttings east of the collieries and iron works at Silverdale on its way to Leycett, although completed, may not have been brought into use, or if it was, very soon fell out of use. There were reasons for this, and the oft-quoted one that the section of line was difficult to maintain, due to mining substance and slippage of the cutting sides, may not be the complete picture. There was in fact little need for it, as almost all the mineral traffic on the Audley line was directed to the opposite end at Alsager, rather than Silverdale and onwards to Newcastle

and Stoke. The only source of mineral traffic at the southern end of the Audley line was the colliery at Leycett, and while most of its output went via the private colliery owned mineral line to the LNWR at Madeley (referred to briefly in Chapter One) such traffic that did flow via the NSR, was directed to the west via Market Drayton, where the colliery company markets were. This was one of the reasons why the connection to the line from Silverdale to Market Drayton near Keele faced west, rather than towards Silverdale; the other was to placate the promoters of the earlier schemes to bring railway access to the Potteries from the west, by means other than the NSR. The operating practice was for trains headed towards Market Drayton to pause at the junction at Honeywall, while the engine tripped to and from the colliery at Leycett to exchange traffic – although the connection to the colliery was not made until the middle of 1872, two years after the line opened. The track at Honeywall was laid out for these movements and any traffic that was destined for the Stoke direction would be left at Honeywall, and collected later by trains headed in that direction. The working timetables for the period all show such movements. It was later decided to open the Audley line to passenger traffic, and it was desirable that trains should call at both Silverdale and Keele. The best place for a station at Leycett was on the wrong side of the junction there with the earlier line to Silverdale, so trains had, perforce, to run via the junction at Honeywall. As we have seen, the junction there faced the wrong way for a direct movement, so while the Board of Trade allowed passenger trains to start running, it was on the strict understanding that a new connecting spur was built facing in the opposite direction, so that trains could run without reversal. By this time the traffic flows from the colliery at Leycett tended to run eastwards, so when the new spur opened the earlier one closed. Passenger services commenced on the Audley line on 28 June 1880, and the new connecting spur opened on 1 October the following year.

In December 1870 the NSR decided to obtain estimates to lay a second set of rails between Newcastle and Knutton Junction, such that the complete line from Newcastle to Market Drayton would then be double track. Forsyth's estimate of £5,967 was approved on capital account by the NSR Traffic & Finance Committee on 17 January. The work was not undertaken with any degree of urgency, and although not inspected by Colonel Frederick Henry Rich of the Board of Trade until March 1872 (his report is dated 12 March) the line had been brought into use for all traffic the previous month. This was under an arrangement between the railway companies and the Board of Trade, whereby the former could bring

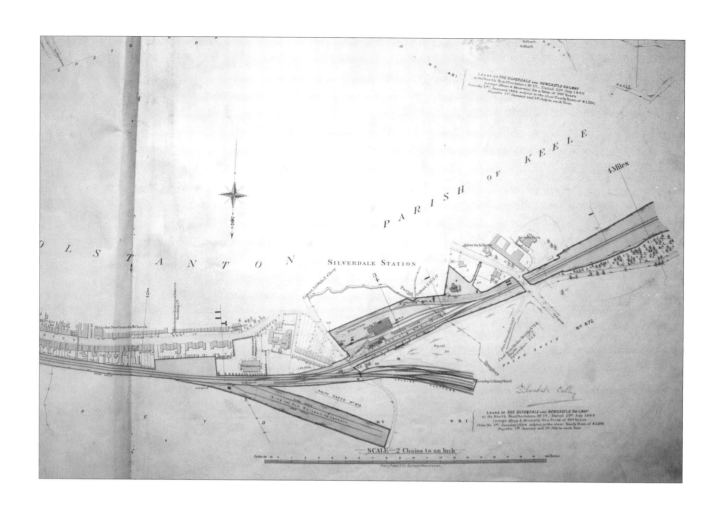

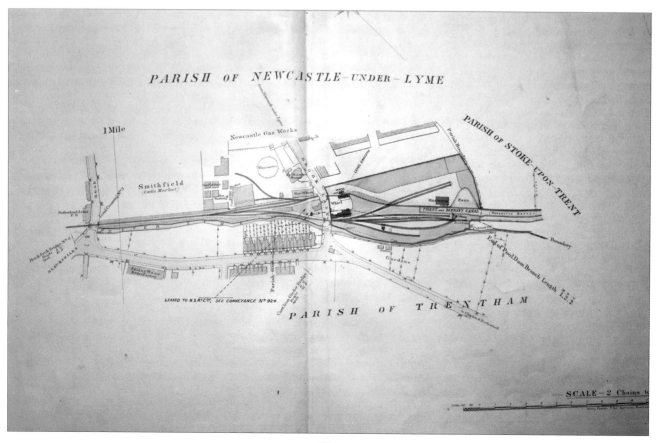

into use certain types of new works provided they complied with a range of 'standing conditions'; this was to avoid delays while inspections were arranged. However, as with many other railway companies the NSR was on several occasions berated for applying a too liberal interpretation of this 'rule'! There is no evidence however, that this was the case here.

It is interesting to relate that, despite these rather piecemeal works in doubling the line from Newcastle to Silverdale, as well as the later doubling of the section from Newcastle Junction at Stoke to Hartshill, the NSR also obtained statutory powers for improving the line between Hartshill and Newcastle. These powers included either expanding the existing tunnels, building additional ones, or opening out the area to form a cutting. As events turned out, this section was destined to remain as single track. Powers were, however, contained in the North Staffordshire Railway Act 1867 (30-31 Vic ch cxlii, Royal Assent 15 July 1867). This granted miscellaneous other powers, for a short new railway in Burton-on-Trent and extensive mutual running powers over the LNWR. The prospect of either

widening the tunnels or opening out into a cutting was discussed again in August 1887 but the cost was, not surprisingly perhaps, felt to be too great and there the matter rested.

A third set of rails was laid between Newcastle and Brampton Sidings as part of an extensive scheme for rationalisation of Newcastle station, which included new platforms, new buildings, a new signal box and other works. The scheme also included new sidings at Brampton, widening of over-bridges, and a number of other improvements. In view of the extent and cost, the work was planned as several separate schemes and NSR Board approval was required following meetings held on 9 July 1873 and 30 December 1874, as well as at later dates. In fact this third set of rails was originally in two separate sections, in effect two down loops, one each side of Queen Street bridge carrying the main road from Newcastle to Burslem and Tunstall. An enormous amount of work was therefore undertaken over the next few years, some of which required further Board approval, and it appears that the complete third set of rails from Newcastle to Brampton were not

brought into use until some time in 1875. One of the reasons for this third set of rails was to provide what was in effect a long shunting neck for Newcastle goods yard, so that shunting operations need not impinge on operation of the main line. Worth a note is that it was not necessary to widen the cutting by any significant amount between Newcastle and the Brampton to accommodate the third set of rails. Remember this was the route of the Upper Canal, and the works were already wide enough. The canal builders had done their work well.

The section of single line between Stoke Newcastle Junction, where the Newcastle line joined the main NSR line from Stoke to the north, and Hartshill, was converted to double track by the laying of a second set of rails, to the north of the existing one. The new arrangements were brought into use on 9 April 1884, following a Board of Trade inspection by Major Francis Arthur Marindin. His report is dated the same day the line opened, and includes comments regarding the increase in width of the embankment, widening the bridge over North Street, and signalling alterations at Hartshill. Thereafter the only section that was single track, from Stoke Newcastle Junction to Market Drayton Silverdale Junction, on the GWR line from Nantwich to Wellington, was in the two tunnels between Hartshill and Newcastle. The tunnels, as we've seen, made the cost of improving this section prohibitive. Many years later, as will be related in Chapter Five, the section beyond Silverdale to Market Drayton, along with the Audley line, was converted to single line. At the same time the junction arrangements at Keele Junction, west of Keele station, were removed and henceforth, between that point and Silverdale, the Market Drayton and Audley lines ran alongside each other as completely separate single line railways, thus emulating the much earlier arrangement between Silverdale and Knutton already described.

Francis Stanier (1838-1900) who, together with his father, was so instrumental in the railways and industry in and around Newcastle.

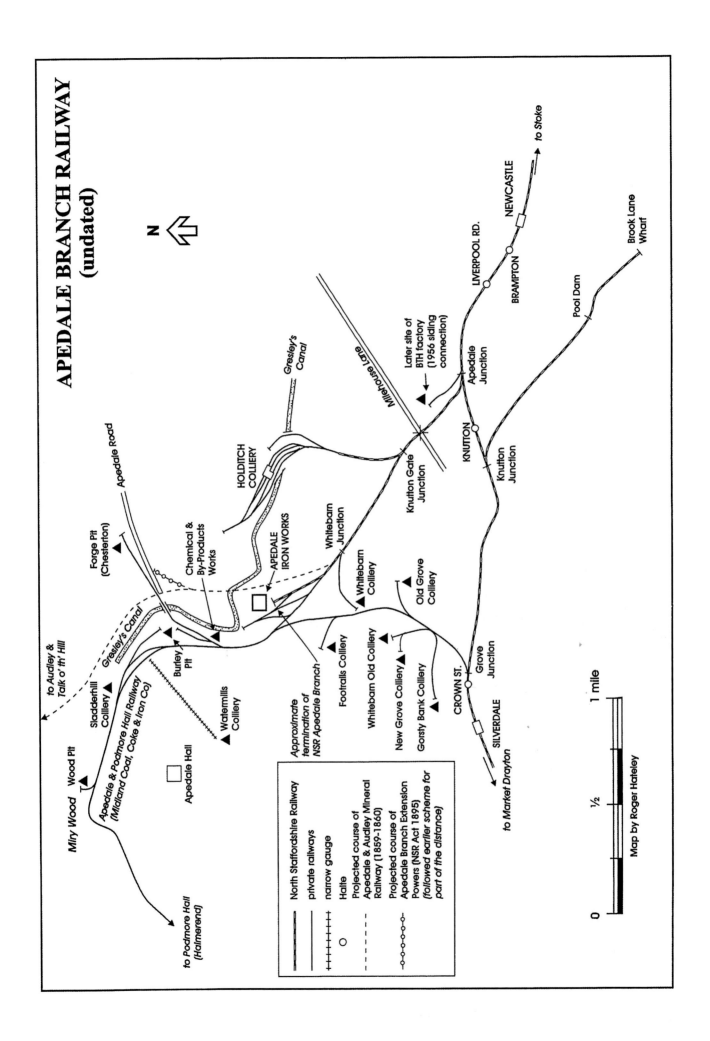

APEDALE BRANCH RAILWAY (undated)

N

Map by Roger Hateley

North Staffordshire Railway
private railways
narrow gauge
Halte
Projected course of Apedale & Audley Mineral Railway (1859-1860)
Projected course of Apedale Branch Extension Powers (NSR Act 1895) (followed earlier scheme for part of the distance)

to Audley & Talk o' th' Hill

to Podmore Hall (Halmerend)

Miry Wood   Wood Pit

Sladderhill Colliery

Apedale & Podmore Hall Railway (Midland Coal, Coke & Iron Co)

Gresley's Canal

Watermills Colliery

Apedale Hall

Burley Pit

Forge Pit (Chesterton)

Apedale Road

Chemical & By-Products Works

Gresley's Canal

HOLDITCH COLLIERY

APEDALE IRON WORKS

Approximate termination of NSR Apedale Branch

Whitebarn Junction

Footrails Colliery

Whitebarn Colliery

Whitebarn Old Colliery

New Grove Colliery

Old Grove Colliery

Garsty Bank Colliery

CROWN ST.

Grove Junction

SILVERDALE

to Market Drayton

Millhouse Lane

Knutton Gate Junction

Later site of BTH factory (1956 siding connection)

Apedale Junction

KNUTTON

Knutton Junction

LIVERPOOL RD.

NEWCASTLE

BRAMPTON

Pool Dam

Brook Lane Wharf

to Stoke

0   ½   1 mile

58

CHAPTER THREE
THE APEDALE BRANCH

Origins

This branch has already been referred to, in Chapter Two, as its development was inextricably linked with other Newcastle railways. Here we study it in greater detail. It was always recorded in official documents as one mile and 46 chains long, from its junction with the line from Newcastle to Silverdale at what became known as Apedale Junction, to its termination at Apedale, where it made an end-on connection with the lines of the ironworks and collieries. The plans and sections however, as submitted in the Bill for powers to build the line, quoted its length as one mile four furlongs, one chain and 60 links, which equates to one mile 50 chains and 40 inches. Therefore, the line as built was slightly shorter, roughly four chains, and while it was originally intended to almost abut the Gresley Canal, right in the midst of the iron works, it instead terminated at the eastern extremity of the works site.

It was opened in two stages, as far as Whitebarn Junction, exactly one mile, on 11 July 1853, where the mining operations of the Whitebarn Iron Company (Lawton Luke & Company) were served, and onwards to Apedale itself on 7 November the same year. The Whitebarn Company by the way, had originally applied for rail connection as far back as 18 November 1851. Worth a note is that in the official NSR schedule of opening dates, June 1856 is erroneously quoted as the period when the complete branch opened. The junction with the main line was made into a double one when the main line itself was converted to double track in 1872, along with the first 250 yards of the branch. The line descended from the junction at 1 in 101 and then 1 in 300 for roughly half its distance; there was a short level section, before it climbed again at 1 in 190 for the remainder. There was a level crossing over what later became Milehouse Lane, a busy thoroughfare between the main turnpike road from Newcastle to Talk at Milehouse, and the village of Knutton – this level crossing was roughly at the bottom of the dip in the railway line.

The Gresley Canal avoided this natural low point, by following the course of the main and later turnpiked road from Newcastle to Talk as far as the southern extremity of the village of Chesterton, before turning east towards Apedale. It then followed roughly the line of what is now Holditch Road. By this route it maintained a level course and obviated the need for any locks.

Raison d'être

Before proceeding any further with the history of the branch, it is perhaps worth exploring the reason for its construction, and an earlier scheme that would also have served the area. Mining operations at Apedale go back to a very early date and as we saw in Chapter One they were the reason why Gresley, as the land owner of the estate, financed construction of a canal to Newcastle. As iron ore was extracted from the mines as well as coal, furnaces were erected on the site by Abraham Parker as early as 1783, and by 1854 there were four modern furnaces here. By 1825 at least, Thomas Firmstone had the lease of the mines and ironworks, which he operated until 1839, when his lease terminated and the landowner, John Edensor Heathcote, elected to take over

This view taken on 17 April 1964 shows the extreme end of the what was then left of the Apedale branch, with the remaining earth works of the iron works and collieries clearly discerned beyond. The branch had been retained this far after closure of the iron works and collieries in 1930, to provide run round facilities to assist in shunting trains at Holditch colliery, the method by which this was undertaken being fully described in the text. (Martin R Connop-Price - Authors Collection)

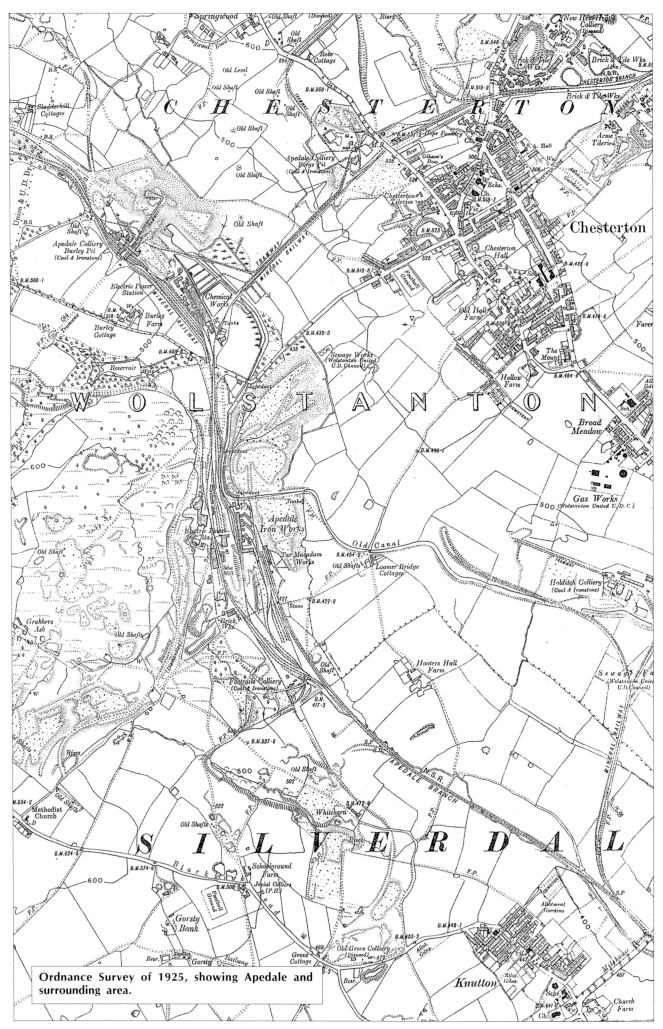

Ordnance Survey of 1925, showing Apedale and surrounding area.

The Apedale branch where it joined the main line, 9 August 1966. The line to the extreme left, protected by the signal with the small arm, served the British Thomson Houston Company factory.

the operations himself. Firmstone, as already related, then concentrated his activities at nearby Leycett and Madeley Heath. On 13 October 1866, Francis Stanier Broade, Mary Stanier and James Undall, trading as Stanier & Son, took on the lease of the Apedale mineral estate and ironworks from John Edensor Heathcote. When he died in 1869 his nephew, Justinian Heathcote Edwards-Heathcote (1843-1928) became owner of the Apedale estate. Edwards-Heathcote, son of the Rev. EJ Edwards, vicar of Trentham, had married John Edensor Heathcote's sister. He adopted the additional surname of Heathcote when his uncle died. A Captain in the Staffordshire Yeomanry 1875-1881, DL, JP, he was Conservative MP for North-West Staffordshire 1886-1892. The Apedale lease was for 35 years with powers to 'determine' – that is, terminate – on 1 April 1890, which as events turned out is what happened. Francis Stanier had taken on the additional surname of Broade in 1856, when he inherited the estate of his cousin, Philip Barnes Broade (1803-1852) of Fenton Vivian. His name actually became Francis Stanier Philip Broade, as this was a condition of the will; in 1876 he resumed his original surname.

The Apedale & Audley Railway
In 1859 the Apedale & Audley Railway was projected from Apedale heading due

north three miles, two furlongs and seven and half chains to a place called Parrots Drumble, a little short of the village of Talke Pits; this was deemed 'railway number one'. There was a branch heading south, 'railway number two' which left 'number one' where it crossed the main road from Bignall Hill to Audley, roughly halfway between the two places. It was projected as two miles, five furlongs seven and three quarter chains long, terminating a little short of Leycett, at a place called Red Hall, which was adjacent to Hayes Wood; that is, the wood itself, and not the place that later went by the same name. Between its proposed termination, via Halmerend and a little way further north, the route was roughly the same as that later adopted by the NSR Audley line. The junction between the two lines faced north, so that trains from Apedale to Hayes Wood would have had to reverse. Although the NSR was supportive of this scheme, for which the plans, sections and books of reference were deposited with Parliament on 30 November 1859, the Bill proposed incorporation of a new company. The powers included provision for the NSR to make, use and work the railway as well as subscribing towards its capital and holding shares. The line was surveyed by the NSR engineer J C Forsyth, whose estimate of cost was £65,000. It would have been a difficult

line to work. Railway number one would have been either level, or at gradients in the range 1 in 51 to 1 in 55 for its entire distance. Railway number two was also steeply graded, with sections as steep as 1 in 51. In fact, apart from the initial five furlongs or so from the junction with railway number one, there were no level sections at all.

While it is by no means clear who all the promoters behind this scheme were, clearly it was intended to tap the mineral resources at Talk o' th' Hill, Leycett, and in the Audley area, along with anything else of value along the way. There was however, plenty of opposition, including from Heathcote, who made clear to the NSR Traffic & Finance Committee on 3 January 1860, his 'determination to give every opposition in his power to a Bill of which he had received a notice for making a railway from Audley (sic) to the NSR at Apedale'. This was at a time when he was arguing long and hard for reductions in the rates charged by the NSR for the movement of his traffic. Other objections came from landowners over whose land the line would run, including Sir Thomas Fletcher Fenton Boughey Bt (1809-1880), Ralph Sneyd, and the Surveyors of Highways for Halmerend, Bignall End and Audley. One of Heathcote's complaints was that the line would obstruct the view from his seat at Apedale Hall. This was, of course, before the NSR and Sneyd

61

Apedale Junction on 28 December 1964 with 3F 0-6-0T 47596 passing on the main line with the Pool Dam branch trip working. (Martin R Connop-Price - Authors Collection).

patched up their differences and began a more fruitful relationship. As a result of the NSR pact with Sneyd, the Bill was withdrawn by its promoters, who realised they stood little chance of financing the scheme without the support of the NSR, as a result of which it never even reached an initial reading in Parliament. John Lewis Ricardo, the Chairman of the NSR, was able to give the news to those shareholders attending the 28th half-yearly meeting of the company, held at the London Tavern at Bishopsgate in London, on 16 February 1860. He declared that, following the agreement recently reached with Ralph Sneyd to lease the SNuLR, as well as the Bill for the independent line supported by Sneyd and the LNWR from Silverdale to Madeley having been 'thrown out' of Parliament, the line promoted with NSR support from Apedale to Audley had been withdrawn.

Before leaving this scheme for a railway from Apedale to Audley, it is worth mentioning that one of the supporters we are aware of was the newly formed North Staffordshire Coal & Iron Company Limited, which had only recently erected furnaces and taken over mining operations at Talk o' th' Hill. This company, which would have been served by erstwhile 'railway number one', was one of the earliest to avail itself of limited liability under the original Companies Act of 1856 – it was

registered on 12 May 1857. Largely to placate this company after the Apedale & Audley Railway proposals had been dropped, Ralph Sneyd promoted an Act of Parliament, Mr Sneyd's Railway Act 1861 (24-5 Vic ch lxxi) which received the Royal Assent on 28 June 1861. Its purpose was to extend a short branch that passed over his land at Chatterley to the workings at Talk o' th' Hill and Jamage. This line left the NSR main Pottery Line at Chatterley, the junction facing north, and originally terminated at High Carr, where there was a small colliery – it was a little over five and a half furlongs long. The Act gave powers to extend the line, again over land owned by Sneyd, to serve both the operations at Talk o' th' Hill, which were on land leased by the new company from another local landowner, Sir Smith Child, as well as land at Jamage in the ownership of the representatives of the late John Wedgwood. This second plot of land was served by a short spur off the line to Talk, almost at its termination. An Act of Parliament was necessary as the new railways had to cross public roads in five places. One of these was the Turnpike Road from Newcastle to Talk. Sneyd and his associates had already had their fingers burnt, so to speak, over the SNuLR for, as we have already seen, when first built it crossed public roads without the statutory authority required by law.

Arrangements with the NSR

Mention has been made in Chapter Two that Francis Stanier had the lease of the Silverdale mines and ironworks from Ralph Sneyd, having earlier had some sort of working arrangement with him; the formal partnership is dated 13 September 1851. Stanier later entered into a further partnership, in this case with Robert Heath who had previously been his manager at Silverdale, and who is perhaps better known for his later activities at Kidsgrove and in the Biddulph Valley. This partnership had leased a further tract of land from Ralph Sneyd at Knutton and in 1855 had built a sizable forge and mill there, consisting of 60 puddling furnaces and five rolling mills, using both coal and iron from Silverdale. In view of the agreements with Ralph Sneyd regarding the SNuLR, traffic between Silverdale and Knutton was free of any tolls. On Stanier's death on 13 October 1856 the partnership with Heath was dissolved, although operations seem to have continued much as before. Stanier left his entire estate to his wife Mary (1816-1880) and she entered into a similar partnership with Robert Heath; the partnership deeds were signed on 21 May 1857. This partnership was in turn dissolved, in this case on 31 October 1860, and by mutual consent, Heath by this date being heavily involved in operations in the Biddulph Valley. The valuation of the plant and machinery at Knutton

Class 4 2-6-4 tank engine 42226 about to leave the Apedale branch with a loaded coal train from Holditch Colliery on 11 September 1963. Notice the signalman waiting to collect the single line token from the fireman. It was unusual for this class to be used on these trains. (Martin R Connop-Price - Authors Collection)

Knutton Gate level crossing on the Apedale branch, looking towards Apedale Junction, on 26 September 1954. In late 1966 and early 1967 the NSR crossing keepers house was demolished and the signals removed; thereafter the crossing gates were worked by the train crews with the keys attached to the single line token.

Knutton Gate level crossing, where the Apedale branch crossed the Milehouse Lane; view towards Apedale Junction in late 1966. This was after the crossing keepers house and signals had been removed.

Knutton Gate Junction, where the Apedale and Holditch Colliery branches diverged, in late 1966. View looks towards Apedale Junction. The Holditch branch is on the left, the line to Apedale on the right; Knutton Gate level crossing gates can just be discerned in the distance.

Empty train for Holditch Colliery drawing forward towards Knutton Gate level crossing on 14 April 1960; 4F 0-6-0 44484 has run round its train at Apedale, prior to propelling back into the colliery yard. Notice the old crossing gates in the foreground and the relatively new houses to the right. (Martin R Connop-Price - Authors Collection)

amounted to £20,712 13/ 5d (£20,712 67p), along with a stock of pig and manufactured iron valued at £7,050 13/ - (£7,050 65p); this was split between the partners, and on 1 March 1861 Robert Heath sold his share to Mary Stanier. A new partnership was then formed consisting of Mary Stanier, her son Francis Stanier Philip Broade (1837-1900), who had 'come of age' in 1858, which event seems to have precipitated termination of the agreement with Robert Heath, and James Udall, of Knight & Udall, Newcastle solicitors. James's brother Thomas, who we met earlier, was also involved in this legal partnership. The new partnership traded variously as the Silverdale Company, Stanier & Son and, after taking on the Apedale lease as related above, The Apedale Company or, on occasions, The Apedale Iron Company.

Over a period of years a number of coal and ironstone winnings were developed in the area between Apedale and Silverdale. The Whitebarn undertaking (mentioned earlier) occupied this tract of ground, along with a completely separate pit known as Whitebarn Old, along with the Old and

New Grove pits and the Gorsty Bank Colliery. To serve these outlying workings a standard gauge line was built from Apedale, to join the SNuLR at what became known as Grove Junction, a mile and a half or so from Newcastle and roughly halfway between Knutton Junction and Silverdale. The junction faced Silverdale, where the bulk of the traffic was destined. It has not been possible to ascertain exactly when Grove Junction was brought into use, but it was not mentioned in Captain Rich's report when he inspected the line from Newcastle to Silverdale on 27 March 1862, preparatory to passenger traffic being introduced on that section. However, it is shown on the plans the NSR submitted to the Board of Trade in January 1870, as part of its application for permission to use the SNuLR between Knutton and Silverdale as a second line of rails, making the section Knutton-Silverdale in effect a double line for all traffic. Hitherto, it will be recalled, the SNuLR and the NSR operated separate single lines between these two places. The plans show a double line junction, with the Grove branch becoming single almost immediately.

Colonel W Yolland mentions in his report that the points and signals at Grove Junction were not interlocked, recommending that this situation be regularised by interlocking. He made a number of other recommendations that have already been outlined, all of which the NSR complied with. We are thus left to assume that Grove Junction was constructed some time between 1862 and 1870. As it was a junction with a passenger line, it should have been submitted to the Board of Trade for approval, though no record seems to have survived. It would be unusual if authority had not been given at an earlier date for Colonel Yolland not to have raised the point in his report. On the other hand, an earlier inspection would certainly have made recommendations in respect of the interlocking of points and signals, which the railway company would have been required to address.

After the Stanier partnership acquired the Apedale lease, by using the private mineral line from Apedale to Grove Junction, traffic could be moved between Apedale, Silverdale and Knutton free of tolls, rather than via

Left. Francis Stanier of Peplow Hall, one time Francis Stanier Broade, when Mayor of Newcastle-under-Lyme in the period 1896-1899.

Below. Aerial view of the Knutton Forge in about 1900. The main line from Newcastle to Silverdale runs across the top centre behind the chimneys, with the Pool Dam branch curving away to the bottom right. To the centre left is Knutton Forge Junction signal box and to the bottom left is the main road from Newcastle to Silverdale. This was one of the new roads built by Ralph Sneyd under powers of the Silverdale & Newcastle-under-Lyme Railway Act of 1860, so that level crossings, regarded as dangerous, could be dispensed with; details are explored in the text.

The Knutton Forge, from the Pool Dam branch (in the foreground). The house on the extreme right can also be seen in the preceding photograph, in that case also on the extreme right.

the Apedale branch which would have incurred NSR rates and charges. This emulated the practice with Stanier's traffic between Silverdale and Knutton. However, traffic from Apedale to Knutton would have had to go to Silverdale first, to enable the engine to run round its train as the junction at Grove faced in that direction. As an aside, in May 1873 and again in January 1878, it came to the notice of the Traffic & Finance Committee that Stanier & Co were using wagons that were not fit for use on the Company's lines, and the General Manager, who considered some of them dangerous, was instructed to sort the matter out!

Industry at Apedale

Before continuing with the history of the Apedale branch it is worth saying something of the operations at Apedale. By the time the Stanier lease of the site was surrendered, in January 1890, there were three collieries tapping the lower and middle seams, known as the Burley, Watermills and Sladderhill, working between them nine different coal seams. Of these the Burley was the thickest but the coal was hard-won. The shafts were sunk to a depth of 475 yards and in their day were said to have been the deepest in the country. Burley was equipped to draw 1,000 tons in an eight hour shift, a remarkable achievement in those times. At Watermills one of the shafts was 350 yards deep, with machinery capable of lifting 400 tons in an eight hour day. This pit could have drawn far greater tonnages, for while a new winding engine of greater capacity

had been installed, the consequent alterations to the shafts had not been undertaken; as a result the new engine had never been used. At Sladderhill the shafts were 200 yards deep, where the water from all the pits collected, so the pumping engines were also placed there. At the time the daily output from the three pits amounted to 1,000 tons. At that rate, it was estimated, there was a working life for the pits of 26 years. In addition there were two other pits drawing coal (from the upper seams) as well as extracting ironstone. The New Recovery Pits reached a depth of 175 yards, and the Lilly Pits the same depth; there was a fault between the underground workings of the two, throwing them off by 200 yards. They were not profitable in their own right although the coal and ironstone, when mixed with stuff of better quality, was quite suitable for the blast furnaces that were on site. Supporting all the pits were the usual washing and screening plant and machinery for loading the coal in wagons, and moving the waste to the adjacent tips. There were also facilities for 'calcining' the iron ore. This was a process whereby the ore was concentrated by burning, often in the open air, to drive off moisture, carbon dioxide, etc, oxidising it to ferric oxide ready for smelting in a blast furnace.

The blast furnaces were regarded as the most modern in North Staffordshire and indeed they were capable of producing pig iron as economically as any in the district. There were six, three 65 and three 55 feet high, working on the hot blast system. They were

supported by 11 hot blast stoves which also supplied steam, supplementing that from the boilers, to the beam blast engines. The charging equipment was hydraulically operated and each furnace was capable of producing 280 tons of pig iron per week. Coke for the furnaces came from a twin battery of 200 beehive coke ovens, 100 ovens in each, between them capable of producing 300 tons of coke per day. It was a complex industrial site, with a brick making plant capable of making 40,000 bricks a day from the marl extracted from the pits, as well as all the necessary workshops, power station, railway sidings, locomotives and so on. However, there was no plant for the further manufacture of the iron, and this was one of the reasons Stanier and Heath built the forge and mill at Knutton. Presumably, as this was before any of the Stanier Partnerships became involved in Apedale, this was the reason for selecting the Knutton site, rather than one at Apedale. Silverdale did have its own forge and mill, although it did on occasions send pig iron to Knutton for processing. Before leaving this description of the plant at Apedale, it is worth explaining something of the topography of the site and how the plant was laid out from the point where the NSR Apedale branch terminated, and the works lines commenced.

The whole of the complex was situated in the Apedale valley, with the ground rising steeply on both sides. The Gresley Canal avoided this high ground, by cleverly gaining entry to the valley on its eastern flank, just prior to where the ground began to rise. The Apedale

The Knutton Forge locomotive KNUTTON, new from Scottish builder Andrew Barclay Sons & Company, in 1900. In 1915 it was sold to the Cowpen Coal Company at Cambois in Northumberland; thereafter shunting at Knutton was undertaken by an engine from Apedale, which travelled daily over the NSR to and from the forge.

branch terminated in a large fan of sidings were traffic was exchanged, many of the sidings being equipped with loading platforms, where the pig iron was transferred from the small wagons used internally, into main line railway wagons. From here onwards along the valley the various operations were strung out in a long line of almost one and a half miles. First of all came the coke ovens, followed by the blast furnaces, to the west of which were the workshops and later a power station. There followed a gap of about 500 yards before the later site of a replacement battery of coke ovens, 82 Simon Carves by-product recovery ovens dating from 1905 (42) and 1913 (40), along with a substantial chemical works. Immediately beyond the ovens was the Burley pit and associated screens, Watermills colliery being some distance to the west, on slightly higher ground, and connected to the Burley Pit screens by a narrow gauge rope-hauled tramway. A further 500 yards along the valley the Sladderhill colliery was situated. There were also over the years a number of other pits, for example Footrails colliery. This was adjacent to the exchange sidings, a comparatively small drift mine, or 'foot rail' in local parlance, mining ironstone, as well as the Forge Pits at Chesterton. These pits were adjacent to the Chesterton to Bignall End road (Audley Road), and were served by a rope-hauled tramway which climbed out of the valley. The coal and ironstone was transported on this tramway for processing at the Burley Pit screens, as there were no such facilities at the Forge Pits.

The Midland Coal, Coke & Iron Company Limited

After the Stanier lease was terminated the whole of the Apedale operation was taken over by a newly formed limited company. The Midland Coal, Coke & Iron Company Limited (MCCI) was registered on 3 January 1890 with a capital of £375,000, to acquire not only the lease of the Apedale estate along with ownership of all the surface equipment, but also the lease of the Podmore Hall and Halmerend mineral estate. The pits on this estate had been worked by a partnership, Copper & Craig and included the ill-fated Minnie Pit which in January 1918 was the scene of the worst ever colliery disaster in the North Staffordshire coalfield. As was the case at Apedale, mining in this part of the coalfield dates from a similar period, the mineral estate being yet another part of the Heathcote empire. As at Apedale, at one period the Heathcotes worked the minerals themselves with direct labour. By 1866 Cooper & Company had the lease and by 1888 William Young Craig had become a partner; subsequently they traded as Cooper & Craig. W Y Craig (1827-1924) hailed from Northumberland and became a prominent mining engineer in North Staffordshire. Earlier on, he had been responsible for important coal mining operations in Durham, Shropshire and Denbighshire, and maintained an interest in Shropshire after his move to North Staffordshire. From 1880 to 1885, he served as Liberal Member of Parliament for North Staffordshire. Craig and Justinian Heathcote Edwards-Heathcote were among the principal shareholders in the MCCI, Edwards-Heathcote the Chairman, and Craig the first Managing Director.

The Knutton Forge was not included in the MCCI assets and remained in the ownership of the Stanier Partnership (sometimes trading as the Knutton Iron Company) until 1893. At this time the MCCI, having been over-capitalised on formation as a result of an action taken out in the Court of Chancery by the debenture holders, was forced into liquidation on 25 May 1893, under supervision of the Court. As a result a new company was registered on 1 December 1893, with the same name but with a reduced capital of £187,000, later reduced to £135,333. Edwards-Heathcote remained as Chairman, as well as being the principal shareholder, and like all the other shareholders in the original company, was a lot worse off financially for it. The Knutton Forge closed in February 1893 (Stanier & Co had written to the NSR to say it was closing on 22 February) as a direct result of the problems at Apedale. Operations there, under the management of the Receiver, continued on a limited scale though without the coke ovens, chemical plant and blast furnaces. The latter, in contemporary phraseology, had 'blown-out', so with no iron production at Apedale there was no requirement for the forge at Knutton. On 20 February 1900 a new company was registered to operate the Knutton Forge; titled the Knutton Iron & Steel Company Limited, in July 1901 it became a subsidiary of the MCCI with Justinian Heathcote Edwards-Heathcote as Chairman, and Fredrick John Jones as Managing Director.

One of the first developments of the new company was the building of a private mineral railway from Apedale to Halmerend, to serve the Podmore Hall and associated collieries. However,

Apedale Hall, seat of the Gresleys and the Heathcotes in 1930, long after the family had moved on. Latterly it was the residence of William Hill, the Managing Director of the Apedale works who was also the General Manager of both the Apedale complex and the Knutton Forge. The hall was demolished soon after closure of the operations at Apedale; indeed not long after this photograph was taken.

The Apedale blast furnaces, looking west towards Halmerend in about 1900. About this time the hand charged open-top furnaces had been converted to mechanically charged, enclosed, hot blast. Notice the hot blast stoves behind the furnaces and the mechanical charging hoist in the centre. In the foreground are the railway sidings serving the furnaces, for removal of the pig iron and slag. At this time only two of the furnaces were in blast; from the right they are Nos.1 and 3, with the pig beds, where the pig iron was run into the moulds, in front of No.2.

APEDALE FURNACES

The Burley Pit about 1893, shortly after formation of the Midland Coal Coke & Iron Company Limited; notice the newly painted lettering on the wagon in the left foreground. This view looks east towards Chesterton; observe the new headgear being erected in front of the right-hand pit shaft, part of a plan for increased production, and the ventilating fan cowling to the extreme left. The coal is being loaded direct into railway wagons as there was neither screening nor washing plant at this time.

these pits were connected to the NSR and had been since July 1870, when the Audley line opened from Silverdale and Keele to Alsager. The Apedale & Podmore Hall Railway, almost two and a half miles long from the Burley Pit to a head-shunt at Podmore Hall, while primarily intended to move coal from the Halmerend pits to Apedale for coking and use in the blast furnaces, was also intended to circumvent the NSR rates and charges. Apedale coal destined for northern or western markets and routed via Crewe or Market Drayton, would be taken to Halmerend for transfer there to the NSR, and onwards by the Audley line. Similarly, coal from the Halmerend pits heading south, would go via Apedale and the NSR Apedale branch. The line opened some time in the period 1898-99, the exact date having gone unrecorded; it is reported to have cost around £9,000 and was certainly very well engineered. Its course exists today as a footpath.

Operation of Private Trains
In addition to the lessees of Silverdale being able to work their own traffic between Silverdale and Pool Dam, as well over the Canal Extension Railway to the Brook Lane wharf in Newcastle, once the Stanier Partnerships held the Apedale lease, they could also operate to and from the Knutton Forge without paying the NSR tolls. Although the SNuLR and the Canal Extension Railways were leased to the NSR,

agreements had been made when the lease was signed to cover the operation of private trains. Nevertheless, at the Traffic & Finance Committee meeting held on 7 March 1882, an application was discussed from Messrs Stanier & Company, for terms to use the NSR line, with its own engines and trains, between Apedale and Knutton, via Apedale Junction. The traffic per week was estimated at 2,400 tons of coal, coke and pig iron. It was agreed to offer a fixed sum of £2,400 per annum rather than a road toll of 4½d (2p) per ton. This, although the minutes are silent, appears to have been agreed, for on 3 May expenditure of £488 was agreed for alterations at Apedale Junction to accommodate 'Messrs Stanier working between Apedale & Knutton'. Likewise we have no information as to exactly what these alterations were, although £251 was authorised for signalling alterations by McKenzie & Holland, the NSR's favoured signalling contractor. This work presumably included a cross-over road, as the junction faced Newcastle and not Knutton. Why there was a need to route the traffic this way rather than via Grove Junction is another mystery, as it was not until 1897 that the junction arrangement there was taken out of use. Maybe some of the traffic was getting too heavy for what was quite a lightly laid mineral line with minimal engineering works. However, on 2 February 1886, the Traffic & Finance Committee was considering a request

by Stanier & Co for a reduction in tolls for traffic hauled by its own engines to Knutton via Grove Junction. This was deferred for 'consideration and inspection' and at the meeting held on 30 March it was agreed to leave the tolls at the level they were. This was after the agreement of 10 May 1852, between Stanier and the NSR for the use of the SNuLR free of tolls, had expired. The agreement was for 21 years from the opening on the NSR line from Newcastle to Knutton, which had taken place in September 1852, so the agreement expired in 1873; in June in fact. However, Sneyd, and/or his lessees operating at Silverdale retained a right to use the SNuLR and Canal Extension Railways, free of tolls in perpetuity, but subject to an annual rental to cover the operation and maintenance aspects.

Presumably the Apedale-Knutton trains started to operate as soon as the alterations were complete at Apedale Junction, but the earliest timetable we have is dated July 1883. There were three return paths, one of which went through to Silverdale, calling at Knutton Forge on its return journey. The first train left Apedale at 8.15am to arrive at Knutton at 8.27am; return was at 9.0am, due back at Apedale at 9.12am. The second train left Apedale at 10.30am to arrive at Knutton at 10.42am, returning at 11.20am, to arrive Apedale at 11.33am. It was the afternoon train that went through to Silverdale, leaving Apedale at 3.50pm to arrive at Silverdale at

CHAPTER FOUR
RAILWAY FACILITIES AND OPERATIONS

The Railway at Newcastle

In this Chapter we describe the railway facilities and operations at Newcastle. There were five focal points:
Pool Dam and Brook Lane Wharf.
Newcastle Goods Yard, including Marsh Wharf.
Newcastle Station.
Brampton Sidings.
Knutton.

Pool Dam and Brook Lane Wharf

As the SNuLR was the first on the scene, it is appropriate to start here. This railway, as described in Chapter Two, was built to serve the ironmaking and coal and iron ore mining at Silverdale. Coal and iron was taken to Pool Dam and, later, to the Brook Lane canal basin, when the Newcastle-under-Lyme Canal Company extended the branch by building the Canal Extension Railway. The trains returned with raw materials, principally limestone and iron ore, brought by canal. Much of the limestone would come from the NSR's own Cauldon Low quarries. Prior to the opening of the Canal Extension Railway, transhipment between Pool Dam and the canal was by horse and cart. There were never any passenger facilities on the branch although, as described in Chapter One, there had been schemes for a passenger service on this line.

Once the NSR line from Stoke via Newcastle made a junction with the earlier line at Knutton in 1852, the line to Pool Dam became known as the Pool Dam Branch. Although the Canal Extension Railway was built without statutory powers, there would appear to have been some sort of agreement with the local authority not to use locomotives, doubtless as it crossed three public roads. When this was regularised in a later Act of Parliament, the stipulation prohibiting the use of locomotives was embodied within it. This prohibition was not repealed until 1881. When the Newcastle-under-Lyme Gas Company, along with Ridgway's Brewery in Lower Street, applied in August 1874 to have access to the railway, the company declined to provide any facilities, as it would not have been able to use locomotives for the traffic. Probably as a result of this, the Gas Company was the last to use the Lower Canal, although some of its traffic did later move to rail, a siding being provided in December 1897. This was an awkward arrangement requiring a second level crossing over Brook Lane to provide the necessary headshunt, with a trailing connection into the gas works yard.

The single line Pool Dam Branch served the Knutton Iron & Steel Company's siding although this

Post-Second World War aerial view of Newcastle-under-Lyme, looking north-west. At the extreme bottom right is the Brook Lane Wharf, at the termination of the Canal Extension Railway, which can be seen passing in front of the gas works running towards Pool Dam and Knutton. The line from Newcastle to Silverdale passes along the top but as it was largely in a cutting, cannot be seen.

81

Class 3F 0-6-0T 47587 shunting at Brook Lane Wharf on 27 August 1964. (Martin R Connop-Price - Authors Collection)

Bridge carrying the Pool Dam branch over the Silverdale Road on 24 April 1967, looking towards Knutton. The building on the left is the SPD warehouse, on the site of the former Knutton Forge, which was rail connected at the time; the signal is the fixed distant for Ketleys Siding. The tall house on the right with the very pointed gable end, partly obscured by the bridge fencing, can also be seen on the picture of the Knutton Forge in Chapter Three.

Shunting operations during lifting of the track in the gas works siding at Newcastle on 19 April 1965. The view is towards Pool Dam with the Canal Extension Railway on the extreme left; the level crossing over Brook Lane is directly behind the photographer. The engine is BR Standard Class 4 2-6-0 76023, Stoke shed having several of this class on its allocation at the time. Notice the remains of part of the gas works behind, which had ceased production by this time. (Martin R Connop-Price - Authors Collection)

company also had connections to the main line at Knutton Forge Junction. There were at various times other private sidings on the branch. Silvester & Company's Castle Hill Foundry, situated roughly midway between Knutton and Pool Dam, would appear to have been the first. There were sidings on both sides of the line, and this is particularly interesting in that they were accessed by a turntable on the branch itself. The agreement with Silvester was dated March 1864, making this one of the earliest private sidings served by the NSR; the foundry seems to have closed around the turn of the century. Ridgway's Brewery eventually got a siding, a short spur to the north between Pool Dam and Blackfriars, though there is no record of when this was laid. There was also the Gas Works connection, mentioned previously. The NSR Traffic & Finance Committee minutes mention two other private sidings connected to the line, but nothing else is known about them. In October 1884 a sum of £265 was agreed for a siding at Pool Dam to serve Bostock's Works, followed by £104 in June 1895, for a further siding at Pool Dam, in this case for a Mr Ashwell. Local trade directories have not helped to identify exactly what these individuals were about, no more has it been possible to locate exactly where the respective

sidings might have been situated. In May 1883 revised junction arrangements were introduced at Knutton Forge, including a new signal box, and in June 1899 Dick Kerr & Company Limited, who were contractors at the time undertaking extensions to the Gas Works, had a siding agreement with the NSR. The Bostock agreement incidentally, specifically mentions coal traffic and there were sidings at Pool Dam and coal landsale wharfs, so it may have been located there.

In June 1882, the Stanier interests rented a portion of the wharf exclusively for their own traffic, which at that period would have included coal from both Silverdale and Apedale; the lease cost £50 per annum. In September the same year the NSR agreed to spend £500 extending the sidings at Pool Dam and in August 1898 provided additional accommodation for the Butterley Company, by this time lessees of the Silverdale works. In January 1903 the NSR purchased almost 7,000 square yards of land at Pool Dam as part of its scheme to build a new railway from Stoke to make connection with the branch at Brook Lane Wharf. Mention has been made of this in Chapter One and it is assumed the land would have been used for a passenger station, as it was intended to introduce passenger traffic. In August 1904 yet more siding

accommodation was provided for goods and mineral traffic at the canal wharf, at a cost of £1,000. The last significant addition in NSR days would appear to have come early in 1905, following an agreement with the Florence Coal & Iron Company of Longton to provide siding accommodation at Pool Dam for the landsale of coal. These were quite extensive works and cost £1,207, the initial lease being seven years.

The branch was distinguished by the three level crossings, at Pool Dam, Blackfriars Road and Brook Lane, all of which were ungated and had to be protected by a flag man. The crossings caused considerable annoyance to later day motorists, especially at Brook Lane where it was the practice to fly shunt wagons into the sidings. The Corporation was frequently complaining about the crossings and in August 1882 the NSR did agree to make some improvements. In the previous June train staff working had been introduced on the branch and as there were no tickets, the line was worked under the 'one engine in steam or two coupled together' arrangements, and this remained the case until the line closed. Exactly how the branch was worked prior to 1882 appears to have gone unrecorded. The bridge carrying the line over the Silverdale Road, though built to comply with Board of Trade

A train on the Canal Extension Railway on 7 January 1965 heading towards Pool Dam, having just crossed Blackfriars Road. The shunter is running ahead of 3F 0-6-0T 47596 with his flag ready to stop the road traffic at Pool Dam. Unless special instructions were issued, trains were only allowed to use the branch between sunrise and sunset as the three level crossings were not protected by gates.

Pool Dam level crossing on 17 October 1964. The 4F 0-6-0 44571 and its train are just leaving the Canal Extension Railway at its junction with the Silverdale & Newcastle-under-Lyme Railway, and about to enter the goods yard at Pool Dam. (Martin R Connop-Price - Authors Collection)

The Pool Dam local trip working crossing the Silverdale Road in September 1962, hauled by 4F 0-6-0 44499. Notice the brake van is at the front of the train. The engine would have run round its train at Ketleys Siding prior to entering the branch and, as the gradient was largely descending to Pool Dam, special instructions were in force for this method of operation. (Martin R Connop-Price - Authors Collection)

recommendations as embodied in the 1860 Act, always seems to have caused problems; the line crossed the road at an angle and clearances were restricted. In July 1899 the British Electric Traction Company entered into discussions with the NSR to improve the headroom under this bridge by one foot, as it had authority to extend the electric street tramways of the Potteries Electric Traction Company (PET) which it owned, from Newcastle to Silverdale. Negotiations dragged on for some time, inevitably over who should pay. Agreement finally came in May 1900, the tramway company paying £200 of the £300 involved. The trams started to run soon after this, so the work must have been put in hand quickly.

Newcastle Goods Yard
Newcastle goods yard was built partly on the site of the former Junction Canal and partly on land formerly owned by the Marsh Trustees. The link to the goods yard left the down main line by a trailing connection just west of Newcastle Station. The yard could also be reached from a third line which ran parallel to the main lines on the south side between Newcastle and the Brampton. This had originally been a headshunt for the goods yard, terminating by the bridge carrying Queen Street over the railway, while on the other side of the bridge

there was a loop between that point and the level crossing at Brampton Sidings. As a part of the 1867 doubling of the line from Newcastle to Knutton this bridge, along with the cutting, was widened. The cutting, of course, had originally been part of the route of the Upper Canal, and there were now three lines between Newcastle and Brampton Sidings, up and down running lines and a down loop. The goods yard connection passed under King Street, utilising the original canal bridge with its very limited clearance of 11 feet 8 inches – the normal NSR loading gauge was 13 feet 5 inches. The goods yard was split into two. The western part was known as Marsh Wharf, as it partly occupied land reclaimed by the Marsh Trustees; eventually it comprised four sidings, devoted to the private trains from Apedale. This was subject to the various machinations and later agreements between the NSR and the Heathcotes outlined earlier. The eastern part of the goods yard was devoted to NSR general merchandise traffic, excepting a short extension which continued under Brunswick Street to a coal merchant's depot which existed until at least 1922. Sometime thereafter, the former canal bridge brick arch under Brunswick Street was sealed up.

As early as November 1852 £4,000 was approved for the erection of a

goods warehouse (initially termed simply a goods shed) although in the event in April the following year, Thomas Brassey's tender for £3,000 was accepted for the work. It will be recalled that Brassey was building the line from Stoke to Newcastle and onwards to Knutton, so he would have had men and equipment available. The warehouse was a substantial building alongside Water Street, intended for perishable traffic. It was an elegant structure with walls of Staffordshire blue brick with a plinth having a low pitched slate roof with ornamental eaves cornice, including projecting stone lintels and a stone label course. The elevation to Water Street was particularly fine having 11 double-brick radius arched windows, each having keystones to the outer arch and stone cills to the semi-circular headed metal windows. The two outer windows were blind with additional narrow single arched blind openings at each end of this elevation. Certainly in later years a single line of rails passed through the building and there were two tracks in the open in the cutting between the warehouse and Water Street. These tracks and the line through the warehouse were connected by a wagon turntable located immediately prior to the bridge under Brunswick Street. There were two further sidings for NSR traffic to the west of the warehouse. A

Newcastle-under-Lyme gas works in the 1930s with Brook Lane Wharf in the middle distance. Notice the two level crossings; the one to the left is on the headshunt for the gas works traffic. The building with the white roof to the right is the Priory Garage, with Clayton Road to the extreme top right.

grain shed was added at a cost of £644 in December 1875, followed in June 1876 by an agreement to erect a goods office, Kirk & Parry's tender against a schedule of prices being accepted. The following year, in August, alterations were made to the main line signalling so far as it affected shunting of the goods yard. The cost amounted to £920, so the works must have been quite extensive. Alterations and extensions were made to the layout in August 1883 following the NSR purchase of 500 square yards of land from the Stanier interests, after which the arrangements seem to have been satisfactory until the new century. In January 1900 the warehouse was extended. The goods yard facilities catered for all types of goods, mineral and live stock traffic; a crane was provided in July 1906 with a lifting capacity of three tons, although latterly there was one with an increased capacity of 10 tons.

The early operation of Newcastle goods yard is something of a mystery. The NSR Working Timetable for July and August 1905 has a 'Newcastle Shunting Engine' leaving Stoke shed at 5.40am

and Stoke at 6.0am on weekdays for Newcastle goods yard shunting 'as required'. This included Brampton sidings and a trip to Hartshill, until 4.20pm when it returned to Stoke shed via the LNWR yard at Stoke. By 1913 the locomotive also worked a trip to Pool Dam at a convenient time except on Saturdays, when it returned from Newcastle at 3.25pm. There is no mention of a 'Newcastle Shunting Engine' in the working timetable from July 1915; doubtless, as a war time economy, the shunting at Hartshill, Newcastle and Brampton sidings was undertaken instead by train engines, the workings having suitably lengthened timings to allow for it. This arrangement seems to have continued, and was still in force in 1921. In 1905 only the 0-6-0 saddle tanks 58A and 59A were permitted to enter the goods yard, while by 1920 the Kerr, Stuart 'Argentina' class 0-6-0 side tanks 74 and 75 were listed as permitted to pass under Newcastle goods yard bridge. The official NSR locomotive diagram book gives a maximum height above rail level for the Kerr, Stuart engines of 11 feet

5½ inches; 74 and 75 would therefore have had a clearance of 2½ inches, not terribly generous! The saddle tanks would not have passed under the bridge in their original form but after rebuilding at Stoke to a more squat arrangement whereby the maximum height was 11 feet 3 inches from rail level to chimney top they were able to pass with a clearance of 5in.

By 1914 Newcastle goods yard was worked by four electrically operated capstans and steel wire ropes which were connected by the shunting staff to the wagons for movements within the yard. Electrical power was supplied by Newcastle-under-Lyme Corporation whose diesel generating plant was in Goose Street, next to the gasworks. One of the diesel engines installed there shortly after the end of the First World War began its life in the German submarine UB67 which was interned on 24 November 1918 under the terms of the Armistice and later surrendered to Great Britain; it was broken up at Swansea in 1922. What a way to power a capstan in Newcastle goods yard!

We suspect that all shunting by NSR locomotives in Newcastle Goods Yard had ceased by 1914 and that the saddle tanks 58A and 59A only operated there between 1905 and 1914. The A suffix to the NSR locomotive numbers by the way, indicates that the locomotives in question had been placed in what was referred to as duplicate stock, being replaced in capital stock by new locomotives. This practice, often followed by the pre-grouping railways, was to satisfy the accountants, as it enabled the overall locomotive fleet to be increased, while the number of locomotives allocated against authorised capital remained the same. Of course, Newcastle goods yard was still accessed by the Manning Wardle and Yorkshire Engine Company saddle tanks operated by the MCCI and its predecessors as they would readily pass under King Street Bridge into the Marsh Wharf section of the goods yard.

Newcastle Station

The Newcastle station which opened to traffic on 6 September 1852 was temporary, for the NSR had determined to 'await the requirements of the public' before erecting a permanent structure on the same site. Various improvements came about in piecemeal fashion over a number of years. The first enlargement, at a cost of £500, was planned as early as June 1854 and an additional platform on the up side was built in January 1870, preparatory to opening of the line onwards from Silverdale to Market Drayton that year. In July 1873 further improvements were agreed and undertaken over the next few years at a cost of £5,000, which resulted in the up side awning being moved to Bucknall, and the waiting shed to Rudyard. Kirk & Parry undertook much of this work at a schedule of costs rather

Train for Pool Dam on the Canal Extension Railway on 7 November 1964 with the gas works, or what was left of it, to the left. The engine is one of the BR Standard Class 2 2-6-0 tender engines, 78056. (Martin R Connop-Price - Authors Collection)

The goods yard at Newcastle, a view taken from the bridge taking King Street over the railway on 4 May 1956. The former Newcastle-under-Lyme Junction Canal ran alongside the retaining wall to the left, and that is Water Street running parallel, presumably taking its name from the canal. The truncated siding to the extreme right originally served that part of the yard exclusively used for Apedale traffic. The electric capstan to the bottom left was used for hauling railway wagons and vans, as by this date there were no locomotives small enough to pass under the former canal bridge which gave access to the yard.

'Jinty' 47280 at the entrance to Newcastle goods yard on a wet July day in 1962; loaded coal train on the up line to the right. (Martin R Connop-Price - Authors Collection)

Newcastle (so far as the NSR, LMS and BR were concerned it was always plain Newcastle!) station looking towards Stoke on 25 April 1964. The booking office was at street level; the back of it can be seen above the platform canopy, with the Borough Arms Hotel beyond on the opposite side of King Street. Notice the paint date, 10/56, painted on the end of the canopy on the up platform to the left.

Empty coal train approaching Liverpool Road Halt on 29 July 1964 hauled by tender first Class 5 4-6-0 45146. (Martin R Connop-Price - Authors Collection)

The Trains

The vast majority of the passenger and goods trains at Newcastle were operated by the NSR but there were interesting variations which added much colour to the scene. The Great Western Railway (GWR) exercised a right to run over the whole of the Market Drayton Branch with a daily goods train from Shrewsbury to Stoke and back. These were not statutory running powers under any Act of Parliament but rather a mutual agreement between the two, sealed on 10 August 1896. The arrangements had actually come into force with the NSR working timetable for the previous month, the GWR having a morning return working between Shrewsbury and Stoke and the NSR an overnight train to and from Wellington. The arrangement also allowed for the NSR to work, on behalf of the GWR, a passenger train from Market Drayton to Hodnet and back, along with a cattle train, on alternate Tuesdays to coincide with Hodnet cattle market. It will be recalled that the lessees of the operations at Silverdale and at Apedale had arrangements with the NSR to work some of their own traffic. The Silverdale trains worked to and from Knutton Forge, Pool Dam and the Brook Lane canal wharf, a legacy from Ralph Sneyd's original ownership of the line. From Apedale the operations consisted of trains to and

from Marsh Wharf in Newcastle goods yard, Knutton Forge, Pool Dam and Brook Lane wharf. There were variations over the years with trains not running to all the destinations at the same time. Later, as described in Chapter Three, the MCCI ran passenger trains for its own workmen from Apedale, initially to and from Newcastle Station but latterly only as far as Apedale Junction. The running of private trains over its metals, while not perhaps encouraged by the NSR, was tolerated where costs could be saved and advantageous terms agreed. In most cases the trains were included in the working timetables, but there were frequent changes that only found their way into the weekly operating notices. In the case of the Silverdale trains, the powers were statutory and embodied in the agreements, themselves outlined in the Act of Parliament for the NSR to lease the SNuLR. These trains, perhaps obviously, did not run on Sundays, neither did any other goods or mineral trains operate on the Market Drayton,

Audley lines and branches. The Sabbath was strictly observed in those distant times.

Passenger Services

Passenger services commenced running between Stoke and Newcastle on 6 September 1852. The inaugural service on weekdays provided for no less than fourteen trains in each direction, six minutes being allowed for the journey. There was a reduction to nine trains each way on Sundays. By December 1852, the service had been modified to provide 11 trains from Stoke to Newcastle on weekdays and 12 return trains. On Sundays there were six trains each way.

By 1865, 12 trains were being operated between Stoke and Newcastle, four of which ran through to Silverdale. In the opposite direction 11 trains left Newcastle for Stoke, four of which originated at Silverdale. This was reduced to four trains in each direction on Sundays, three of which ran through to Silverdale. Some of these early trains ran beyond Stoke to Longton on

	1862		1863	
	Pass.	Revenue	Pass.	Revenue
From Newcastle	13948	£14	15862	£185
To Newcastle	16168	£196	17945	£219
From Silverdale	1419	£26	1921	£34
To Silverdale	1067	£20	1394	£27

Photograph taken from Church Lane, which runs between Silverdale and Knutton, looking towards Newcastle on 4 May 1956. The train, hauled by an unidentified Class 4F 0-6-0 running tender first, is destined either for the Pool Dam branch, or has just left the branch. Engines had to run round in the sidings here before trains proceeded on or off the branch. The area on the right betrays evidence of the former mine loading stages and sidings, where coal and ironstone arrived from a number of outlying pits, either by horse and cart or primitive tramways, to be loaded to rail. The site of the Knutton Forge is behind the centre of the train.

Down loaded coal train passing the site of Knutton Forge Junction in September 1962, hauled by 4F 0-6-0 44499; view looks towards Newcastle. The lines in the foreground include the run round loop for the Pool Dam branch. By this time all the traffic for the branch came from the Newcastle direction; for reasons of history the junction faced the opposite way towards Silverdale, so run-round arrangements had to be made. The Pool Dam branch can just be discerned curving away in the middle distance to the right of the end of the train. The area to the extreme right is the site of the Knutton Forge, by this time (perhaps surprisingly in view of its former use) partly occupied by allotments. It is now a housing estate. (Martin R Connop-Price - Authors Collection)

Two views taken on 14 January 1966 showing the Pool Dam branch train at Knutton with BR Standard Class 2 2-6-0 78056 in charge. In the first picture the train is arriving from Newcastle on the main line, while in the second it has been propelled back from Ketleys Siding, where the junction with the main line was situated; the engine is about to run round the train prior to proceeding along the branch. The signal in the second view is the Ketleys Siding down home. (Martin R Connop-Price - Authors Collection)

Empties for Brampton Sidings approaching Ketleys Siding on 9 August 1966 behind Class 4 2-6-0 43024. By this date the line between Stoke Newcastle Junction and Newcastle had been severed, and this train would have come from Crewe via Madeley Chord. The wagons were for a scrap metal merchant at Brampton still using rail. Notice the remains of the former tileries and brick works to the right. On this occasion the authors were exploring the layout hereabouts along with the remains of former mineral workings, never expecting to see a train, and had to hastily collect their wits to get this shot. Later they followed the train to Brampton Sidings for more photographs.

weekdays with corresponding return workings. Some interesting statistics have survived for passenger traffic on the branch for the three months ending 31 August 1863, compared with the corresponding period the previous year and these are tabulated *(on page 93)*.

It will be seen that more passengers travelled to Newcastle than those departing, the reverse being the case at Silverdale, which leaves us wondering why this should be so?

The character of Newcastle station changed on 1 February 1870 when the branch was extended to Market Drayton to join the GWR. The purely local nature of the station was no more; not only was it possible now to travel east to Stoke but also west beyond Silverdale to Keele, Madeley Road, Pipe Gate, Norton-in-Hales and Market Drayton. Moreover, a change could be made there for the GWR service to Wellington, where connections could be had for Wolverhampton and Birmingham, as well as Shrewsbury and beyond into Wales. It has to be added, however, that the GWR connections were sometimes poor or non-existent! A sobering example of this is recorded in *The Railway Magazine* for October 1907: *The most*

peculiar working of the North Staffordshire Railway's passenger trains to 'foreign' lines is that of the one on Tuesday only, over the Great Western Railway to Hodnet, a distance of 5¾ miles. This train starts from Market Drayton at 11.55am, arrives at Hodnet at 12.4pm and returns empty at 12.10pm arriving at 12.19pm. Tuesday is Hodnet market day, and the running of this through train [it left Stoke at 11.5am and Newcastle at 11.11am] *by the North Staffordshire Railway is an instance of the arrangements made by that enterprising railway to provide convenience for the public. If the train were not run through, passengers for Hodnet market, from the North Staffordshire Railway would have to wait at Market Drayton from 11.55am* [the train actually arrived at 11.50am] *until the 1.46pm Great Western Railway train. The Railway Magazine* did not get this quite right. As previously mentioned the NSR train only ran on alternate Tuesdays. The train was actually run by the NSR on behalf of the GWR for which the former company was paid 7/6d (37.5p) per trip. Presumably this arrangement came into being because the GWR had neither engines nor rolling stock available at Market Drayton. At this period other NSR trains ran through

to Hodnet on Thursdays and Saturdays, leaving Market Drayton at 2.56pm and arriving at 3.5pm. They also returned empty.

Poor GWR connections or not, Newcastle had assumed a new importance. At the outset there were four trains from Stoke to Market Drayton on weekdays with corresponding return trains. The service was reduced to two trains each way on Sundays. Newcastle's status was enhanced still further on 28 June 1880 when passenger trains began running over the Audley Line. Passengers from Newcastle could now travel directly to Leycett, Halmerend, Audley, Talk & Alsager Road (opened 1 July 1889) and Harecastle (later Kidsgrove Central and now Kidsgrove). Initially, the Audley Line trains had to reverse at Honeywall Junction, just west of Keele, but a new east-curve was opened on 1 October 1881 and the original west facing curve at Honeywall abandoned. This eliminated the need to reverse. The NSR Public Timetable for July-September 1889 shows that six trains ran to Market Drayton on weekdays with six return trains, excepting Wednesdays when an additional return train ran to

Silverdale station and goods yard about 1910, looking towards Newcastle with St Luke's church prominent. The original NSR station before the line was extended to Market Drayton was just to the left of the church. The rake of six-wheel NSR coaches in the goods yard are doubtless stabled there between trains to suit the shifts of the workmen at the adjacent colliery. The chimneys just visible to the left of the station masters house, on the right, mark the site of the Knutton Forge.

The Silverdale Station Master John Peake, his wife Sarah Ann and their family. The couple had no fewer than ten children, all of whom are gathered here. Three of the boys in 1911 were railway clerks, having joined their father in the service of the NSR. We have no date for this photograph, but it doubtless stems from some time during the First World War, when one of the sons enlisted in the Army. John was born at Keele in 1860 and had been in the service of the NSR all his working life, prior to Silverdale at Keele. His wife was three years younger and at the time of the 1911 Census they had been married 27 years.

NCASTLE STATION (N. S. R.)   BAGGULEY, Stationer,

This photograph, again not a particularly good one, is one of only two known to the authors showing an engine or train at Newcastle in NSR days. The down train is headed for Silverdale hauled by a Class A 2-4-0 tank engine, in this case No.35 built at Stoke in 1881. Notice the driver handing the single line token to the signalman and the rather nice covered walkway from street level and booking office to the up platform.

accommodate market day traffic. Three trains ran to Harecastle via the Audley Line with an extra train on Mondays and Saturdays with a further additional one on Saturdays only. There were corresponding return workings. On Sundays there were two Market Drayton trains with corresponding return workings with three Audley line trains to Harecastle but only two returns. In addition to these through services, several trains ran locally between Stoke and Newcastle. Newcastle station and its passenger traffic was set fair to prosper, which indeed it did until 17 March 1900, when the first electric tram ran in the town centre.

Enter Street Tramway Competition
At the turn of the 19th century the NSR was in its prime. Its network of lines was nearly complete and it had succeeded in virtually monopolising passenger traffic in the northern half of the county. In 1899 the railway conveyed 8,314,719 passengers, exclusive of season ticket holders, a record. However, in that same year a serious competitor arrived on its doorstep in the form of the Potteries Electric Traction Company (PET) which had been incorporated the previous year. Between 1899 and 1905 the PET opened 31 miles 58 chains of electric tramways in the very heart of NSR territory. This

included the conversion of the seven miles and 39 chains of steam tramway formerly operated by the North Staffordshire Tramways Company Limited (1879-1899) which had never been a serious threat to the NSR. The steam tramways were dirty and slow but this new-fangled electric traction was altogether different; it was convenient, clean and cheap!

The new tramway system paralleled the NSR Loop Line from Goldenhill to Hanley, ran on to Stoke and then proceeded to Fenton, Longton and Meir. Moreover, the PET attacked the most profitable part of the Market Drayton Branch traffic by building tramways to Newcastle and Silverdale, the two most important intermediate stations. The tramways ran past peoples' homes whereas many of the NSR stations were inconveniently situated away from the town centres, Newcastle being a prime example. Direct tramway connections from Newcastle led to Hanley, Stoke, Longton, Burslem, Tunstall, Silverdale and Chesterton, all opened by 1901.

The NSR General Manager, the renowned W D Phillipps (1839-1932) played the situation down in public but behind the scenes was dismayed and angry. At an enquiry held at Stoke in 1901, convened by the Light Railway Commissioners to consider further tramway extensions, the NSR complained that 800,000 passengers had

been lost in a single year through the new competition. The tramway company did not deny that the electric trams attracted short-distance passengers from the NSR, but claimed that the new tramway innovation was also creating traffic in its own right.

By 1905 passengers conveyed on the NSR had dropped by nearly 1.8 million per annum, to 6,528,906. Gross receipts had fallen from £220,207 in 1899 to £209,431 in 1905, in spite of increased ticket prices. This decline is dramatically illustrated by figures extracted from the annual returns to the Board of Trade shown in Appendix I. The NSR had had enough. It was time to fight back and the main battle ground was centred upon services to and from Newcastle, which had been particularly badly affected.

Steam Rail Motors
W D Phillipps went on the offensive and convinced the NSR Board of Directors at their meeting on 9 August 1904 to introduce a steam rail motor service. *The Railway Magazine*, in its issue for June 1905, gave a very full report which is worth quoting at length: *Readers of the RAILWAY MAGAZINE have always recognised that Mr. W.D. Phillipps, the experienced General Manager of the North Staffordshire Railway is ever in the van with regard to improvements in railway working and services.*

Another train typical of those that would pass through Newcastle in NSR days, in this case a much earlier one of around 1895. The engine is fitted with the vacuum brake as required under the Regulation of the Railways Act 1889. The scene is Pipe Gate and the train is en-route from Market Drayton to Stoke, with Class A tank No.35, a long term resident of Market Drayton shed it would seem. The train consists of early four-wheel coaches with a couple of vans at the rear. The driver is clearly proud of his engine but perhaps surprisingly the station staff on the right have not taken the opportunity to be included, as was quite usual in the relatively early days of photography; likewise where is the fireman?

Although this photograph was taken on the Audley line with an up train passing Rookery Colliery near Audley, it is nevertheless an NSR train typical of those used on the line through Newcastle. The engine is one of the B Class 2-4-0 tank engines No.2, built at Stoke in 1890, and the train will be one from Harecastle via Audley and Newcastle to Stoke. The period would be about 1910.

16

NEWCASTLE AND MARKET DRAYTON, AND AUDLEY BRANCHES.
(WITH THROUGH SERVICE TO GREAT WESTERN STATIONS.)

STATIONS.	WEEK-DAYS.	SUNDAYS.
L&NW London, Euston *d.*		
Birmingham, N.S.		
Wol'hampton, H.L.		
Stafford		
L & NW BUXTON ¶ *d.*		
Macclesfi'ld, Hibel Rd.		
" Central		
STOKE dep.		
NEWCASTLE		
SILVERDALE		
KEELE		
LEYCETT		
HALMEREND		
AUDLEY		
TALK & ALSAG'R RD		
✻ HARECASTLE		
MADELEY ROAD		
PIPE GATE, for Woore		
NORTON-IN-HALES		
MARKET DRAYTON *a.*		
Market Drayton dep.		
Hodnet arr.		
Wellington		
Shrewsbury		
Birmingham, S. H.		
Stourbridge Junc.		
Kidderminster		
Worcester		
Malvern		
Leamington		
Oxford		
Reading		

✻ (*Kidsgrove*) § Foregate Street. ¶—*Via* Middlewood. A—*Via* Stockport, L. & N. W. B—On *Saturdays* Passengers travel *via* Stockport.
C—*Saturdays excepted*, Newcastle to Market Drayton. D—*Saturdays only*, Newcastle to Market Drayton. E—Calls on *Wednesdays* by Signal to pick up Passengers only. The Trains on this Line do not run in connection with the other Trains.

On Sundays, a Train leaves Stoke for Newcastle at 4 40 p.m.

BURTON BRANCH—BURTON TO TUTBURY.

Miles from Burton	STATIONS.	WEEK-DAYS.												SUNDAYS.		
		mrn	mrn	mrn	aft	aft	aft	aft	aft					mrn	aft	
	BURTON, Station Street dep.	8 0	8 55	11 5	2 0	2A35	4 20	7 0	8A35	...	...	...	...	9 0	6 20	...
	" Horninglow	8 4	8 59	11 9	2 4	2 39	4 24	7 4	8 39	...	...	...	...	9 4	6 24	...
5¼	TUTBURY arr.	8 12	9 8	11 20	2 13	2 48	4 35	7 13	8 48	...	...	...	...	9 13	6 33	...

A—*Saturdays only.*

Part of the NSR Public Timetable for July, August and September 1889, regarding services on the line from Stoke to Market Drayton including the Audley line and connecting services.

NEWCASTLE AND MARKET DRAYTON, AND AUDLEY BRANCHES.
WITH THROUGH SERVICE FROM GREAT WESTERN STATIONS.)

STATIONS.	WEEK-DAYS.	SUNDAYS.
G.W. Ry. Reading		
Oxford		
Leamington		
Malvern		
Worcester		
Kidderminster		
Stourbridge Jun.		
Birmingham, S. H.		
Shrewsbury		
Wellington		
Hodnet		
Market Drayton arr.		
MARKET DRAYT'N dep.		
NORTON-IN-HALES		
PIPE GATE, for Woore		
MADELEY ROAD		
✻ HARECASTLE		
TALK & ALSAGER RD		
AUDLEY		
HALMEREND		
LEYCETT		
KEELE mrn		
SILVERDALE		
NEWCASTLE		
STOKE arr.		
Macclesfield, Central arr.		
" Hibel Road		
L & NW BUXTON ¶ arr.		
Stafford arr.		
Wolverhampton, H.L.		
Birmingham, New St.		
London, Euston 1145		

✻ (*Kidsgrove*) ¶ *Via* Middlewood. † *Mondays* only from Malvern. § Foregate Street. B—*Via* Stockport, L.&N.W. C—*Via* Stockport, L. & N. W. On *Saturdays*, Passengers reach Buxton at 1 45 p.m. D *Via* Stockport, L. & N. W. *Tuesdays, Thursdays, Fridays and Saturdays only.*
The Trains on this Line do not run in connection with the other Trains.

On Sundays, a Train leaves Newcastle for Stoke at 8 55 p.m.

BURTON BRANCH—TUTBURY TO BURTON.

Miles from Tutbury	STATIONS.	WEEK-DAYS.												SUNDAYS.		
		mrn	mrn	aft	aft	aft	aft	aft	aft					mrn	aft	
	TUTBURY dep.	8 17	9 20	12 38	2A17	3 5	5 46	8 8	9A0	...	...	...	...	11 0	7 24	...
	BURTON, Horninglow arr.	8 26	9 30	12 49	2 27	3 16	5 56	8 18	9 10	...	...	...	...	11 10	7 35	...
5¼	" Station Street "	8 30	9 33	12 53	2 30	3 20	5 59	8 21	9 13	...	...	...	...	11 13	7 39	...

A—*Saturdays only.*

17

Mr. Phillipps, with a keen eye to the economical working of the traffic on certain portions of the North Staffordshire Railway, and in view of the competition to which the railway is subjected by the municipal rate-supported electric trams, some time since suggested to the directors the advisability of utilising steam rail motor cars for serving certain portions of the system.

The directors accepted the views of the General Manager, and orders were given for the designing and construction of suitable rail motor cars.

The first of the cars has just been delivered, and in June the service will be in active operation between Silverdale and Trentham, serving the following places:-
Silverdale, Station
Silverdale, Crown Street
Knutton
Newcastle, Liverpool Road
Newcastle, Brampton
Newcastle, Station
Hartshill and Basford
Stoke
Whieldon Road
Mount Pleasant
Sideway
Trentham

It will be observed that the motor cars stop at several halts in addition to the railway stations.

The service caters especially for workmen, the first car leaving Stoke as early as 4.35am., and weekly tickets available for one journey in each direction are issued at extremely cheap fares, some as low as 6d for the 12 journeys. These tickets are nipped each day, and given up on the Saturday.

The motors are designed to haul 40 passengers in the main coach (with their complement of luggage), together with one loaded trailer of equal passenger capacity up gradients of 1 in 60, at a speed of about 20 miles an hour, and are capable of reaching and maintaining a speed of 30 miles an hour or more on the level, with a high rate of acceleration from rest. Provision is made for readily detaching the carriage from the motor if required at any time.

The 'halte' (in the somewhat prosaic NSR parlance) at Whieldon Road was located directly opposite the rail entrance to the Kerr, Stuart locomotive works and served the up side only; the Inspecting Officer (see below) specifically mentioned that only up trains were to stop!

The rail motors were purchased from Beyer Peacock & Company Limited of Manchester, a firm which had not produced a rail motor before but managed to secure orders for eight in 1905; it was its only foray into the rail motor market. The three that went to the NSR were delivered in June (Works Nos.4643-4) and December 1905 (Works No.4793). Beyer, Peacock's remaining rail motors went to the London, Brighton & South Coast Railway (Works Nos.4721-2) and to Cuba, for use on the British-owned United Railways of Havana (Works Nos.4659-4661). The first two cost £1,850 each, the Beyer Peacock

Outside Cylinders	8½in x 14in
Driving wheel diameter	3ft 8in
Wheelbase	9ft 6in
Heating surface – tubes	327.4sq ft
Heating surface – firebox	41.6sq ft
Grate area	7sq ft
Boiler pressure	180psi
Water capacity of tank under coach	380 gallons
Water capacity of tank in bunker	40 gallons
Coal capacity	15cwt
Weight in working order	32tons 9cwt 1qtr
Overall height above rail level	13ft 2in
Height from rail level to centre line of boiler	6ft 6in
Overall unit – length over buffers	50ft 6in

The cylinders were later bored out to 9in diameter.

tender being accepted on 4 October 1904; the third one was more expensive at £2,050; the tender for this unit was accepted on 8 August the following year. The rail motor expenditure was allocated to a 'suspense account' and not to capital stock, which presumably explains the separate numbering system. On 3 October 1905 it was decided to include steam heating of the carriage portion at an extra cost of £42. This was fitted to the first two only after delivery, it would seem. The 2-2-0 tank engine units all had conventional boilers with outside horizontal cylinders and Walschaerts valve gear. This valve gear and the Belpaire firebox boilers were innovations on the NSR. Full technical details of the NSR examples taken from the Beyer Peacock general arrangement drawing are given above. The coach portions of the units were built by the Electric Railway & Tramway Carriage Company of Preston, whose main production (in a touch of irony) at that time was electric tramcars. The coaches were exactly 35ft in length, the rear end being supported by a conventional carriage bogie with wheels of 3ft 7½in diameter with a wheelbase of 8ft. The main portion of the coach consisted of an open saloon seating 40 third class passengers; additionally there was a smoking compartment with six seats. Folding steps were provided externally interlocked with the vacuum brake to prevent the rail motors starting with the steps extended as some of the new 'haltes' had lower level platforms; Whieldon Road was one example, costing a grand total of £14! When running backwards the driver rode in the guards compartment and while he only had complete control of the brake, he could close the regulator remotely; the remainder of the controls were handled by the fireman under the driver's instructions through a system of bell communication using a cable carried inside the carriage roof. The carriages were lit by electricity. Rather grandly, a brass Staffordshire Knot was fixed to the centre of the cab side panels with the letters NSR in the three interspaces with the engine running number, also in brass, immediately

below. They bore NSR Nos.1, 2 and 3 in order of construction. Had the NSR aspirations to operate certain of its branch lines as light railways and if the Trentham Park Branch extension to Pool Dam had come about, no doubt further rail motors would have been purchased but, as explained later, this was not to be.

Before the rail motor service could be introduced the NSR had to seek authority from the Board of Trade Railway Department, not for the use of rail motors, but for the 'haltes' it proposed to build, as the facilities provided would fall far short of those found at normal stations. Following the construction of the 'haltes' at Silverdale Crown Street, Knutton, Liverpool Road, Brampton, Hartshill, Whieldon Road and Mount Pleasant, Colonel E Druitt duly reported.

Board of Trade Railway Department
1 June 1905
I have inspected the following motor 'haltes' for passenger traffic on the North Staffordshire Railway. The cars are at present to run between Silverdale, Newcastle, Stoke and Trentham Stations and in addition the following platforms have been built viz:
Silverdale Crown Street - level crossing with two ground platforms at rail level.
Knutton - two platforms three feet high 40 feet in length.
Liverpool Road, Newcastle - two platforms 40 feet long three feet high.
Brampton - level crossing two ground platforms at rail level.
Harts Hill (sic) - a single platform 40 feet long and three feet high.
Whieldon Road Stoke - an up ground platform at rail level to be used by up trains only.
Mount Pleasant - two platforms 40 feet long and three feet high.
The raised platforms are all of timber and are approached by steps and paths from the nearby roads with the usual gates to be opened by the guard on arrival. Lamps have been provided in all cases and the arrangements are very complete. The double bogie cars are worked by steam with vacuum and hand brakes, which can be applied from either end of the car. Steam can be cut off

Market Drayton, Audley, and Apedale Branches.

WEEK DAYS. Down.

Miles from Stoke	Station	1 Pas	2 Pas	3 Ord. Goods Stoke to Silverdale	4 Ord. Goods Stoke to Brampton	5	6 Ord. Goods Stoke to Apedale	7 Ord. Goods Stoke to Market Drayton	8 Pas	9 Pas	10 Pas	11	12 Pas	13	14 Pas (WO)	16 Pas	17 Pas	18 Ord. Min'l Stoke to Apedale	19	20	20a	21 Pas	22	23 G.W. Goods Stoke to Coleham
		a.m.	a.m.	a.m.	a.m.		arr dep	a.m.	a.m.	a.m.	a.m.		a.m.		a.m.	a.m.	a.m.	a.m.				a.m.	arr a.m.	dep a.m.
...	STOKE	4 55	5 30	5 35	6 0			6 35	7 0	7 17	7 33	7 53	8 15		8 51	9 3	9 20	9 25				10 20		10 30
...	Newcastle Junction																							
	Hartshill Siding	4 58	5 33					6 40		7 21	7 36	7 50	8 18		8 54	9 6	9 23							10 33
2	Newcastle	5 2	5 35	5 50	6 45				7 23	7 39	7 58		8 20		8 56	9 9	9 26	9 40				10 25		10 38
...	Brampton Siding				6 48																			
...	Apedale ...... arr						6 50											9 47						
...	Pool Dam Wharf																							
...	" Sidings	5 8		5 55																				
	Knutton Forge			6 30																				
4¾	Silverdale	5 17		6 55			Return at 7.25 a.m.	7 29	7 45						9 16	9 33							10 44	
6	Keele	5 22						A		7 49					9 20	9 37						10 50	11 26	
7½	Leycett	5 23								7 53														
9	Halmerend									7 57														
10½	Audley									8 1							See note							
13½	Alsager Road									8 8														
15¼	HARECASTLE									8 13														
8¾	Madeley Road																9 43						11 40	11 50
11½	Pipe Gate														9 34	9 49							11 40	11 50
14	Norton-in-Hales														9 43	9 55							11 56	12 6
17¼	MARKET DRAYTON							7 45								9 50	10 1						12 15	2 50

Column notes (Down, cols 3, 4, 6, 7, 18, 20, 22): Col 3 — Calls at Ketley's Sidings 6.50 a.m.; Return at 7.40 a.m., Arrive Newcastle 8.10 a.m. Col 4 — Return at 8.10 a.m. Col 6 — Return at 7.25 a.m. Col 7 — Mondays only to Silverdale; Return at 9.50 a.m. Col 18 — Return at 10.40 a.m.; See note. Col 22/23 — Coleham arr. 7.0.

No. 16—The Engine and Men of this Train shunt as required at Market Drayton and load Cattle. Return with 4.20 p.m. Train.

No. 17—Engine of this train to shunt as required at Market Drayton.

Section of NSR Working Timetable dated October 1915, on this and the following pages, covering trains on the line from Stoke to Market Drayton including the Audley Line. The private trains operated by the Apedale and Silverdale Companies were covered by separate tables and are therefore not shown here.

Market Drayton, Audley, and Apedale Branches.

WEEK DAYS. Down.

Station	24 Ord. Goods Stoke to Diglake	25 Pas	26 Ord. Goods Stoke to Silverdale (M&S)	27 Rail Motor	28 Pas (SO)	29 Pas (S)	30 Pas (SO)	31 Ord. Goods Stoke to Apedale	32 Pas (S)	33	34 Rail Motor	35	36 Ord. Goods Stoke to Market Drayton	37 Ord. Goods Pratt's Sidings to Leycett (M)	38	39	40 Pas	41 Ord. Goods Newcastle Jct. to Brampton	42 Pas	43 Pas	44 Ord. Min'l Stoke to Apedale	45	46 Pas	47 Pas (S)
	arr dep a.m.	a.m.	arr dep a.m.		p.m.	p.m.	p.m.	p.m.	p.m.		p.m.	p.m.	arr dep p.m.	arr dep p.m.			p.m.	p.m.	p.m.	p.m.	p.m.		p.m.	p.m.
STOKE		11 15	11 35		11 40	11 50	12 10	12 27	12 27	12 35	12 55	1 15	1 30	1 45	1 0 1 55			2 26	3 X0	3 10	3 58	4 20	4 55	5 10
Hartshill Siding			11 37	11 44	11 50	11 53	12 13	12 30	12 58			1 33	1 50		2 1			2 29	3 13		4 23			
Newcastle	11 20	11 41		11 55	12 15	12 32	12 32	12 50	1 1	1 20	1 35	1 53		2 5 2 10			2 32	3 15	4 4		5 1	5 15
Brampton Siding	11 43					12 33			1 22		See note		2 10	2 12 2 20				3 8		4 35			
Apedale ...... arr							1 5															
Pool Dam Wharf ... dep																						
Knutton Forge	11 48		12 0										A&D 2 23	2 35								
" Sidings		12 5	12 20			12 38		1 7	1 37		1 41	2 20 2 45	3 0		2 39		4 11	5 8			
Silverdale	12 10	12 35 11 48 12 25			12 42	12 46	1 7 1 33	1 37	1 41		2 50 2 58	3 4 3 10		2 43		4 15	5 12			
Keele	12 45	1 0 11 52 11 57			12 49		1 11	1 41			3 17		2 47		4 20			
Leycett	1 8	1 15 12 2							T	V		2 51		4 25			
Halmerend		12 7										2 56		4 30			
Audley		12 15										3 4		4 38			
Alsager Road		12 19										3 9		4 43			
HARECASTLE																	
Madeley Road						1 17							5 18	
Pipe Gate						1 23			3 10	3 50	See note	See note		5 25	
Norton-in-Hales						1 29			3 58	4 5			5 32	
MARKET DRAYTON						1 35			4 15		See Note		5 37	

Column notes: Col 24 — Return at 1.35 p.m.; Arrive Diglake 1.26 p.m. Col 26 — Return at 1.46 p.m.; Suspended. Col 31 — Conditional; Return at 2.35 p.m. Col 35 — See note. Col 36 — Return at 8.15 a.m. Col 37 — Return at 3.30 p.m.; See Note. Col 40 — Return empty, Newcastle to Stoke on Wednesdays. Col 41 — Newcastle Jct. Return at 3.20 p.m. Col 44 — Return at 5.35 p.m.

No. 35—Runs to Silverdale on Saturdays only.

No. 36—The Engine of this Train Shunts the Coal Sidings at Market Drayton. Perform all the Yard Shunting at Pipe Gate and Norton-in-Hales, and Marshalls Traffic for No. 49 Up Train Tu. & W. Ex.)

No. 37—An engine and men leaves Pratts Sidings at 12.50 p.m. for Stoke Yard daily to work this train and No. 35 return train, afterwards when required work a special between Stoke and Silverdale. Does not run beyond Silverdale when traffic is very light Stations forward.

No. 40—Saturdays only, Newcastle to Harecastle. On Fridays will work 2.37 p.m., Newcastle to Stoke.

No. 41—Inspector HAND will arrange to work this train.

Down.	WEEK DAYS.		50	51	53	54	55	56	56a	57	58	59	60		61	62	SUNDAYS. 1	2	3	4	5	6	7	8	9	10	11	12
	Rail Motor.	Pas	Rail Motor.	Pas			Pas	Pas			Pas	Pas	Ordinary Goods, Stoke to Wellington		Pas	Pas	Empt	Pas	Pas		Pas		Pas		Pas	Pas		
							M & SO	MS				SO	arr	dep														
	p.m.	p.m.	p.m.	p.m.			p.m.	p.m.			p.m.	p.m.	p.m.	p.m.	p.m.	p.m.	a.m.	a.m.	a.m.		p.m.		p.m.		p.m.	p.m.		
STOKE	5 20	5 40	6 20	6 45	...	...	7 55	7 55	...	...	8 45	9 5	...	9 35	9 50	11 10	8 25	9 2	11 5	...	2 30	...	4 50	...	7 45	8 38	...	...
Hartshill Siding	5 23	5 43	6 23	6 48	...	...	7 58	7 58	...	...	8 48	9 8	...	...	9 53	11 13	8 28	9 5	11 8	...	2 33	...	4 53	...	7 48	8 41	...	...
Newcastle	5 26	5 45	6 25	6 50	...	...	8 1	8 1	...	...	8 51	9 11	...	...	9 55	11 15	8 30	9 8	11 11	...	2 36	...	4 55	...	7 51	8 44	...	...
Brampton Siding	5 27		6 26	...	...	...	...	...	...	...	...	...	...	...				...	...	...	...	...		...	...	...	...	...
Apedale	...	...	...	...	...	...	...	...	...	...	...	...	...	...	...	See Note.	...	...	...	...	...	...	...	...	...	...	...	...
Pool Dam Wharf	From Trentham Park.	...	...	...	...	...	...	...	...	...	...	...	...	...	...		...	...	...	...	...	...	...	...	...	...	...	...
Knutton Forge		...	...	...	...	...	...	...	...	...	...	...	...	...	...		...	...	...	...	...	...	...	...	...	...	...	...
,, Siding		...	6 30	...	...	...	...	8 5	...	...	...	...	...	...	...		...	...	...	...	...	...	...	...	...	...	...	...
Silverdale		...	6 33	...	...	...	8 7	8 13	...	...	8 57	9 18	A	...	...	11 21	...	9 15	11 18	...	2 42	...	...	...	7 58	8 51	...	...
Keele		...	6 37	...	...	...	8 11	8 17	...	...	9 1	9 22	10 0	10 5	...		...	9 19	11 22	...	2 46	...	...	...	8 2	8 55	...	...
Leycett		...		...	...	...	8 15	8 22	...	...	...	9 27	...	...	...	...	...	...	11 27	...	2 50	...	...	...	8 7	...	...	...
Halmerend		...	...	...	...	...	8 19	...	...	...	...	9 32	...	...	...	...	...	...	11 32	...	2 54	...	...	...	8 12	...	...	...
Audley	...	...	From Trentham Park.	...	...	...	8 23	...	...	...	...	9 37	Wellington arrive 12.10 a.m.	Return at 1.0 a.m.	...	...	...	...	11 37	...	2 59	...	...	...	8 17	...	...	...
Alsager Road	...	...		...	...	...	8 29	...	...	...	...	9 45			...	...	...	...	11 44	...	3 5	...	...	...	8 25	...	...	...
HARECASTLE	...	...		...	...	...	8 33	...	...	...	...	9 50			...	...	...	...	11 49	...	3 10	...	...	...	8 30	...	...	...
Madeley Road	...	...		...	...	...		...	...	...	9 7				...	...	...	9 25		...		...	...	...		9 2	...	...
Pipe Gate	...	...		...	...	...	...	...	...	...	9 14	...		10 16	...	...	...	9 32	...	...	...	...	...	...	...	9 9	...	...
Norton-in-Hales	...	...	...	...	...	...	...	...	...	...	9 20	...	...	10 19	...	...	...	9 39	...	...	...	...	...	...	...	9 16	..	...
MARKET DRAYTON arr	...	...	...	...	...	...	...	...	...	...	9 26	...	10 30	10 50	...	...	...	9 45	...	...	...	...	...	...	...	9 22	...	...

No. 61.—Returns with 10.0 p.m. from Newcastle except on Mondays when it will return empty.

No. 62—Saturdays only, Newcastle to Silverdale.

Miles from Market Drayton.	Miles from Harecastle via Audley Line.	WEEK DAYS. Up.	1	2	3	4	5	6	8	8a	9	10	10a		11		12	13	14	15	16	17	18	19		20	22	22a
			Ordinary Goods, Wellington to Market Drayton	Pas	Pas		Pas	Pas	Pas	Ordinary Goods, Brampton to Newcastle Juncton.	Pas	Ordinary Minerl Apedale to Stoke	G. W. Goods, Shrewsbury to Stoke		Ordinary Mineral, Silverdale to Stoke.		Ordinary Minerl Knutton to Pool Dam.	Pas	Pas	Pas		Pas	Ordinary Miner'l Apedale to Norton Bridge	Ordinary Goods, Market Drayton to Stoke			Rail Motor.	
			M												See note.													
			a.m.	a.m.	a.m.		a.m.	a.m.	a.m.	a.m.	a.m.	a.m.	arr a.m.	dep a.m.	arr a.m.	dep a.m.	a.m.	a.m.	a.m.	a.m.		a.m.	a.m.	arr. a.m.	dep. a.m.		noon	
...	...	MARKET DRAYTON dep	Place Traffic in position for unloading, or Empties for loading at Market Drayton. Wellington dep. 1.0 a.m., Market Drayton arrive 1.40 a.m	...	...	...	...		...	...	...	...	6 50	7 45	...	...	...	...	8 30	...	...	...	...	...	9 50	...	...	...
3¼	...	Norton-in-Hales		...	...	..	...	Mondays only from Silverdale	...	...	...	Arrive Newcastle Junction 7.58 a.m.	...	...	...	...	...	...	8 37	See Note	...	...	...	...	...	...	...	...
5½	...	Pipe Gate		...	...	...	...		...	...	...		A	D	Calls at Ketley's Siding, 7.45, 8.30		...	...	8 44		...	...	...	A	...	...	...	...
8½	...	Madeley Road		...	...	...	...		...	...	...		Shrewsbury depart	1.5 a.m. Return at 10.30 a.m.			...	...	8 51	...	...	...	...	...	See note.	...	To Stone.	...
...	...	HARECASTLE		...	...	...	...		...	...	...						...	...	...	9 0	...	...	...	...		...		...
...	1¾	Alsager Road		...	...	...	...		...	...	...						...	...	See Note	9 5	...	...	...	...		...		...
...	4¾	Audley		...	...	...	...		...	...	...						...	...		9 13	...	...	...	...		...		...
...	6¼	Halmerend		...	...	...	...		...	...	...						...	...	...	9 19	...	...	...	...		...		...
...	7¾	Leycett		...	5 50	...	...		...	...	...	Return at 9.25 a.m.			...	...	...	...	...	9 25	...	...	...	...	...	...		...
11¼	9¼	Keele		...	5 54	...	...	...	...	...	...		...	...	...	...	...	...	8 58	9 30	...	...	...	...	...	...	...	...
12½	10½	Silverdale		...	5 58	...	...	7 35	...	...	...		...	D	...	7 40	...	...	9 2	9 35	...	...	...	10 25	10 45	...	...	...
...	...	Knutton Sidings		...	6 2	...	...	...	...	See note.	...		...	See note	8 35	. .	8 20	...	...	...	...	...	...	...	...	...	...	...
...	...	,, Forge		...	...	...	...	...	...		...		...		...	9 56	...	...	...	...	...	...	...	...	...	...	...	...
...	...	Pool Dam Wharf		...	...	...	...	...	...	...	...	...	...		...	...	8 40	...	...	...	...	...	...	...	...	...	...	...
...	...	Apedale		...	...	...	...	...	...	...	...	7 25	...		...	...		...	...	...	...	...	10 40	...	...	...	...	...
...	...	Brampton Siding		...	...	...	...	...	...	8 10	...	7 50	8 30		10 0	...		...	...	...	...	...	10 50	...	...	...	...	...
15¼	13¼	Newcastle		5 40	6 9	...	6 50	7 40	8 10	...	8 30	...	...	8 40	...	10 15	Return at 9.15 a.m.	9 3	9 10	9 42	...	10 30	...	10 55	11 5	...	12 0	...
...	...	Hartshill Siding		5 43	...	. .	6 53	7 43	8 13	...	8 32	...	...	...	...	10 20		9 5	9 13	9 44	...	10 33	...	...	...	...	12 3	...
...	...	Newcastle Junction		...	...	...	...	...	...	8 20	...	8 20	8 45	9 15	10 25	10 40		...	...	...	...	...	11 20	11 10	11 35	...	...	...
17¼	15¼	STOKE	...	5 45	...	...	6 55	7 46	8 15	...	8 35	8 25	9 20	...	10 45	...	...	9 8	9 16	9 48	...	10 35	11 25	11 40	...	...	12 5	...
			Runs on Sunday Mornings.													Return at 11.15 a.m								Works a Special to Chatterley or as required.				

No. 10a—On Mondays calls at Pipe Gate to attach Cattle Traffic.

No. 8a—Thence with 9.30 a.m. Cliff Vale to Crewe.

No. 11—Performs necessary work on Pool Dam Branch.

No. 14—Will not convey H.C., excepting from Market Drayton or beyond for Stoke or beyond.

No. 15.—Worked by Engine and Men of No. 2, page 29. Engine and Men to Longport and Harecastle at 10.0 a.m.

No. 19—Must convey from Market Drayton wagons for G.N. route to connect at Newcastle Junction with the 2.25 p.m. Chaddesden train.

All Up Passenger Trains starting from Silverdale or beyond must arrive at Newcastle 2 minutes before the booked time for departure.

WEEK DAYS. Up.

	23	24	25	26	27	27a	28	29	30	31	32	32a	33	34	35	36	37	39	39a	40	41	42	43
	Pas	Pas	Pas	Pas	Pas		Ordinary Goods, Silverdale to Stoke.	Pas	Pas	Ordinary Goods, Apedale to Stoke.	Rail Motor.	Ordinary Goods, Brampton to Newcastle Junction	Ordinary Mineral, Diglake to Stoke.	Pas	Ordinary Goods, Leycett to Stoke	Rail Motor.	Empty Coaches.	Pas	Pas	Pas	Pas	Rail Motor.	Pas
	S O	S	H C	S O			M & S				S				M			S O	S O	W & S	W O & S O	S	
	p.m.	p.m.	p.m.	p.m.	p.m.		arr p.m.	dep p.m.	p.m.	p.m.	arr p.m.	dep p.m.	p.m.	p.m.	arr p.m.	dep p.m.	p.m.	p.m.	p.m.	arr p.m.	dep p.m.	p.m.	p.m.	p.m.
MARKET DRAYTON dep	...	...	12 25	...	...		...	...	...	...	...	...		3 10					4 20		4 20		...	
Norton-in-Hales	...	...	12 31	...	...		...	...	...	...	See note.	...		3 17					4 27	4 20	4 27		...	
Pipe Gate	...	...	12 37	...	...		...	...	...	...		...		3 24					4 33	4 33	4 34		...	
Madeley Road	...	...	*	...	...	Runs from Silverdale on Saturdays only.	...	...	...	...		...	Diglake depart 1.35 p.m.	3*30					4 39	4 39	4 40		...	
HARECASTLE	...	...	...	...	...		2 0	2 15	...	...	...	...		See note				4 10			...		...	
Alsager Road	...	...	...	...	...		2 5	2 20	...	...	...	...						4 15		...			...	
Audley	...	...	...	...	...		2 12	2 27	...	...	...	...						4 22		...			...	
Halmerend	...	...	...	12 55	...		2 17	2 32	...	...	...	...	1 42	1 50				4 27		...			...	
Leycett	...	...	...	1 0			2 22	2 37	...	...	...	2 50	1 57	2 15		3 30		4 32		...			...	
Keele	...	...	12 49	1 4	1 48		2 26	2 41	...	1 45	...	2 55	2 20	2 30	3 36	3 36	3 45		4 37	4 45	4 46	4 47	...	
Silverdale	...	...	12 53	1 4	1 48		2 30	2 45	...	1 45	...	2 59	2 35	3 25	3 40	3 40	4 0	5 0		4 48	4 49	4 60	4 52	...	
Knutton Sidings	...	...		1 8		1 50	2 10		...	...	3 5					5 5	5 45						...	
„ Forge	...	...	...	...	...		See note	See note	...	...	...	...			Arrive Newcastle 3.46.			Arrive Newcastle 4.48.		See note.			...	
Pool Dam Wharf	...	...	...	...	...				...	...	...	...											...	
Apedale dep	...	...	...	...	...				...	2 35	2 55												5 36	
Brampton Siding	...	...	1 13						2 45	2 55	3 11	3 20		D										
Newcastle	12 32	12 38	1 15	1 55			2 37	2 52		3 13	3 35		3 40	3 50	5 58	6 5	4 15	4 45	4 52	4 56	4 58	5 5	5 20	5 38	5 52
Hartshill Siding	12 34	12 40	1 4	1 18	1 58		2 22	2 33	2 55	3 3	3 30		3 42	3 45		6 12	4 17	4 47	4 53	4 59	5 8	5 22	5 41	5 54
Newcastle Junction							2 36			3 3	3 30		3 42	3 45		6 12	6 35							
STOKE	12 37	12 43	1 6	1 21	2 0		2 42	2 57		3 35			4 5	3 56	6 40		4 20	4 50	4 57	5 1	5 10		5 26	5 44	5 58

No 25—Does not convey Horse Boxes or Private Carriages excepting from Market Drayton or beyond for Stoke or beyond. Stops by Signal to pick up passengers and to set down on notice being given to the Guard at Pipe Gate.

No. 26—Suspended. Returns to Brampton at 3.0 p.m. Inspector Hand will arrange to work train No. 41, page 37.

No. 29—Fridays excepted, Harecastle to Newcastle.

No. 30—Fridays only, Harecastle to Newcastle; and Saturdays excepted, Newcastle to Stoke.

No. 32—Runs 10 minutes later on Fridays only.

No. 39—On Saturdays leaves Silverdale at 2.40 p.m., Knutton Sidings arrive 2.55 p.m., depart 3.30 p.m. Calls at Brough's Siding on Mondays only.

No. 34—Wednesdays only, Market Drayton to Newcastle, returns empty, Newcastle to Stoke on Wednesdays. Calls at Madeley Road to pick up Passengers for Audley Branch Stations.

No. 40—Must be despatched from Market Drayton to time.

All Up Passenger Trains starting from Silverdale or beyond must arrive at Newcastle 2 minutes before the booked time for departure.

	45	46	47	48	49	WEEK DAYS. 50	51	52	53	53a	54	55	57	58	59	60	SUNDAYS. 1	2	3	4	5	6	7	8	9	10
Up.	Ordinary Goods, Apedale to Newcastle Junction	Pas	Pas	Rail Motor.	Ordinary Goods Market Drayton to Stoke.	Pas			Pas		Ordinary Goods Market Drayton to Stoke.	Pas			Pas	Pas	Pas	Pas	Pas	Pas		Pas	Pas			Pas
	arr p.m.	dep p.m.			T V arr p.m.	dep p.m.	p.m.			M S				S O				S O		a.m.	a.m.		p.m.		p.m.	p.m.		p.m.
MARKET DRAYTON dep			...	...		5 30	6 55	...	...	...	8 15	...	...	...	...	...	9 57			...	7 25	...	...	
Norton-in-Hales			...	...	5 42	5 50	7* 4	...	...	...		See note	...	...	...	...	10 5			...	7 33	...	...	
Pipe Gate			...	...	5 58	6 15	7*12	...	...	...			...	...	...	...	10 12			...	7 41	...	...	
Madeley Road	Newcastle arrive 6.35, depart 7.13, Newcastle Junction arrive 7.20, depart 7.40, thence to Ford Green.		...	...		7 19		...	...	...			...	...	...	...	10 19			...	7 49	...	...	
HARECASTLE			5 35	...				...	...	...	9 20		...	10 5					1 40			9 0	
Alsager Road	Pratt's Sidings arrive 7.47 p.m.		5 40	...		See note.		...	...	...	9 25		...	10 10					1 45			9 5	
Audley			5 47	...				...	...	...	9 33		...	10 17	Saturdays only from Silverdale.				1 52			9 12	
Halmerend			5 52	...				...	...	...	9 37		...	10 23					1 57			9 17	
Leycett			5 57	...	6 50		7 26	...	...	8 40	9 43		...	10 27			10 26		2 2			9 21	
Keele			6 1	...	6 55	6 40	7 20	7 31	...	8 45	9 47		...	10 33		10 26	2 6		7 56	9 25	
Silverdale			6 5	...	6 55	6 40	7 20	7 31	...	8 49	9 53		...	10 37	11 30	10 30	2 10		8 1	9 29	
Knutton Sidings			...	...	7 1			...	...				...								
„ Forge			...	...				...	...		L. & N. W. Yard to attach arrive 9.38 depart 10.0		...	See note.							
Pool Dam Wharf			...	...				...	...				...								
Apedale dep		5 35	...	...	7 27			...	...		9 0		...								
Brampton Siding	5 43		...	...				...	...				...								
Newcastle		5 55	6 12	6 55	7 5	7 45	7 38	...	8 56	9 15	10 0	...	10 45	11*20	8 45	10 37	2 17	5 0	8 9	9 36
Hartshill Siding			6 15	6 58	7 8	7 48	7 40	...	8 53		10 2	...	10 47	11 22	8 47	10 39	2 19	5 3	8 12	9 38
Newcastle Junction	6 5	6 30	...	...	7 50	8 0		...	9 30		10 2	...								
STOKE			6 17	7 0	7 10	8 5	7 43	...	9 1	10 3	10 5	...	10 51	11*25	8 51	10 42	2 22	5 7	8 15	9 42

No. 49—On Tuesdays leave shed at 4.0 p.m. to marshal traffic thence to Hodnet at 4.45, arriving there at 4.55, returning at 5.10 p.m. with Cattle, arrive Market Drayton at 5.25 p.m., usual working afterwards. On Wednesdays Engine to leave shed at 3.40 p.m., for Cattle loading.

No. 50—Arrives Norton-in-Hales 7.1 and Pipe Gate 7.9 p.m.

No. 55—Mondays only Harecastle to Newcastle.

No. 60—Runs 20 minutes later on Saturdays from Newcastle.

All Up Passenger Trains starting from Silverdale or beyond must arrive at Newcastle 2 minutes before the booked time for departure.

Celebration to mark the opening of the electric street tramway from Stoke to Newcastle on 17 March 1900. This new tramway provided the NSR with so much competition, along with other routes opened about the same time, that rail motors were introduced in an effort to stem the tide. The location is The Ironmarket in the centre of the town; many of the buildings are still extant.

Manufacturer's photograph of the engine portion of the first of the NSR's three rail motors, all of which were built by Beyer Peacock & Company of Gorton in Manchester in 1905. Rather ironically, the carriage portions were built by the Electric Railway & Tramway Carriage Company of Preston, who also built the tramcar No.46, second in line in the previous illustration!

from the trailing end, but not applied and they have an electrical bell communication between the two ends of the cars.
The steps for the ground platforms are suitable and are worked from a lever in the trailing platform. The cars are seated to hold 40 passengers.
I can recommend the Board of Trade sanction the above mentioned platforms for single motor traffic only, if trailers are used the platforms will need extension.
E Druitt

Although a further 'halte' was established at Carter's Crossing, on the line from Stoke to Derby, the platforms, as sanctioned by the Board of Trade, never were in fact extended; so it appears that trailers were never used with rail motors stopping at them. Only one platform was required at Hartshill as the 'halte, was on the single track section immediately on the Stoke side of the short tunnel taking the line under Shelton New Road. At the Brampton the platforms were immediately on the Silverdale side of the level crossing, the down side platform being directly in front of the signal box. The platforms at Liverpool Road were on the Newcastle side of the bridge taking the road over the railway, with access by individual flights of stairs from road level. Access to the up side platform at Crown Street was from an existing public subway leading to a footpath to Black Bank, while the down side was reached by a roadway leading to an occupation crossing. The platforms were immediately north of the former Grove Junction, and directly opposite Crown Street.

This was by no means the first time the provision of a passenger station at Knutton had been investigated. One had been considered back in March 1875, when alterations were needed to the junction connections for the Knutton Forge, as well as the bridge carrying the Knutton Road over the railway, in part due to mining subsidence. In the event it was not built which was surprising, in view of the close proximity of both the Forge and the village of Knutton. In December 1890 the NSR received a petition for a station from the local residents, but nothing was done. The issue was considered again in both May 1892 and March 1897 to no avail; the Traffic & Finance Committee recorded in its minutes that it was 'not considered desirable to proceed'. The rail motor halte, when finally built, was located on the Silverdale side of the bridge which took Knutton Lane over the railway. Pedestrians reached it by individual flights of steps from the road down to each platform. The halte at Sideway came later, the NSR writing to the Board of Trade on 21 November 1906 requesting permission to bring it into use. Colonel Druitt was again appointed to make the inspection and his report is dated 15 February 1907. He describes the arrangements as

'similar to Brampton', with timber platforms made of sleepers at ground level. He goes on to mention the halte was only for the use of workmen at the adjacent ironworks (the Stafford Coal & Iron Co. Ltd., Great Fenton Collieries and Ironworks) and that the level crossing was a private one, although there was a public footpath. He suggested adjacent shunting operations should be stopped when the platform was being used by passengers and that a name board should be provided, along with lighting. The NSR wrote on 9 March confirming that these recommendations had been accepted and the works completed.

All the new 'haltes', with the exception of Sideway, opened on 1 May 1905. Liverpool Road Halt was directly located on the tramway route to Chesterton at Cross Heath. A special time table was devised for the rail motors which was duly printed in Bradshaw; local time tables emphasised *One Class Only*. By the summer of 1913 the workings had been extended to Stone and also covered the Trentham Park Branch, opened on 1 April 1910. Initially, the rail motors appear to have been a resounding success as from 1906 the passenger carryings certainly began to move in an upward direction, again with a corresponding increase in revenue (see Appendix I). No doubt W D Phillipps made the most of this and considered the rail motors to be a wise investment. Their use was subsequently extended to other parts of the NSR system, including an early morning working from Creswell. Great results were anticipated from an experimental service that operated from Newcastle to Hanley, reversing at Newcastle Junction, at a return fare of 4d, but it did not last. The popularity of the rail motors gradually waned, as the following figures show.

Year	Annual Miles
1905	20,525 (Half year only)
1906	61,597
1907	52,453
1908	56,559
1909	54,342
1910	60,204
1911	60,704
1912	52,709
1913	54,237
1914	42,105
1915	Not available
1916	Not available
1917	Not available
1918	Not available
1919	7,730
1920	7,926
1921	6,102
1922	32,129

The First World War obviously took its toll on rail motor maintenance and availability and they did have their problems. The out of balance forces from

the driving wheels and reciprocating parts were directly transmitted to the passengers in the carriage – much to their discomfort. They could run at much faster speeds than the officially permitted maximum of 30 mph, which probably further increased passenger discomfort, with almost 60 mph being recorded on one occasion! However, they were not really powerful enough to take the anticipated additional loaded trailer; this was self-defeating – or at least self-limiting – when their express purpose, after all, was to bring about an increase in passengers. When they were on rare occasions coupled to a trailing carriage, the rail motor always had to run round it at terminal points, which again nullified one of the advantages over conventional locomotives and trains. After the First World War, a major decline set in but there was a brief revival in 1922 only to be dashed by the Grouping – see Chapter Five.

In December 1904 the NSR considered obtaining powers to operate passenger services using rail motors on several branch lines which were not at that time authorised for passenger traffic. This was at the time of what might be called the 'light railway mania', following the enactment by Parliament of the Light Railways Act of 1896. The purpose of this legislation was to help the development of parts of the country by the construction of railways in situations where lines built under previous legislation would struggle to be competitive. In particular it allowed railways to be built and operated under far less stringent conditions, or for a relaxation of standards on existing lines. There was however a price to be paid, which in the main consisted of a speed restriction of 25 miles per hour. As a result of this legislation a whole plethora of lines were projected, and many built all over the country, in a lot of cases to a narrow gauge. In the case of the NSR, application was made in May 1905 to the Light Railway Commissioners appointed under the Act, to work several mineral lines as light railways for passenger traffic. So far as the lines covered by this book are concerned, these were the Pool Dam and Apedale branches; it is however worth mentioning that powers were also sought for the Chesterton and Talk o' th' Hill branches to be similarly worked. Powers were granted under two Light Railway Orders, the North Staffordshire Railway (Light Railway) Orders 1905 and 1906.

The granting of the powers followed a lengthy inquiry held by the Commissioners at the North Stafford Hotel on 22 July 1905, when all those for and against the proposals had an opportunity to be heard. Not surprisingly the PET was a very strong objector, making the particular point, of its undertaking to the Board of Trade to run minimum services on its

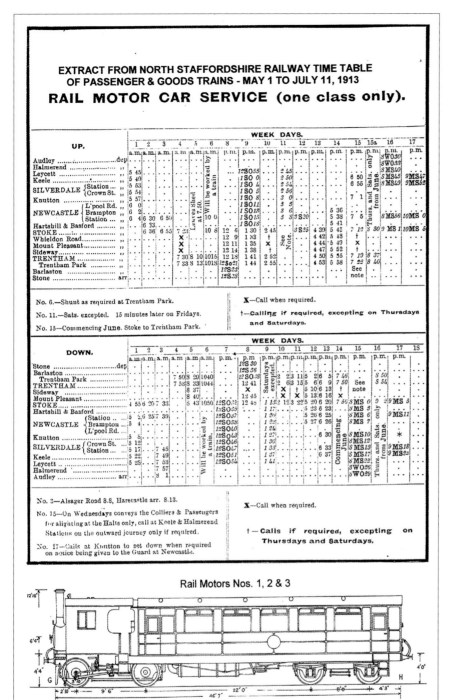

Typical rail motor service working timetable, in this case for the period May to July 1913, along with a drawing by R W Rush – courtesy The Oakwood Press.

operators of the period for engines used on light branch line trains, and stemming from the small engines of that name used on the London, Brighton & South Coast Railway.

Mention has already been made in Chapter One of the light railway for which powers were obtained in 1914, a line to connect the Trentham Park branch to the Pool Dam branch at Brook Lane Wharf. Had this line been built, the rail motors might well have formed the staple motive power. The onset of the First World War ended the project, despite a start being made at the Trentham end by the construction of a substantial bridge. In spite of their problems the rail motors were a brave counter to the trams.

Other Pre-Grouping Locomotives

The first locomotives to enter Newcastle ran on the SNuLR between Silverdale and Pool Dam. Almost nothing is known about them but a painting of 1861 by Henry Lark Pratt, which hangs in Newcastle Museum, shows a locomotive on the railway next to St. Luke's Church in Silverdale. It is in the background and is indistinct but it has a tall chimney. Of course, the painter may have exercised some artistic licence but it could depict a locomotive built by Thornewill & Warham of Burton-on-Trent in about 1859. This bore the firm's works number 162 and was delivered new to the Silverdale Coal & Iron Company. Private locomotives from Silverdale continued to work the Pool Dam Branch until the Second World War and, as previously mentioned, there were also private freight workings from Apedale on to the Pool Dam Branch and also to Newcastle for minerals and workmen. Some of these workings continued until 1930. The owners of the ironworks and collieries at Silverdale and Apedale purchased locomotives from various private locomotive builders and these engines were frequent visitors to Pool Dam and Newcastle. They are listed in Appendix II using information extracted from *Industrial Locomotives of North Staffordshire* (Allan C Baker, Industrial Railway Society, 1997). This work records that some of the locomotives listed were interchanged between these two sites and gives full details of their rather confusing series of names and subsequent history. Also listed in Appendix II are other industrial locomotives that worked within the vicinity of Newcastle. Once again these were often transferred between locations explaining why some locomotives are listed under more than one heading.

A photograph exists of 0-6-0ST SILVERDALE, Manning Wardle works number 169, which was steam tested at Leeds on 7 November 1865 and 'sent away same day to the Silverdale Company, Newcastle, Staffs'. The locomotive is shown in its original livery with elaborate lining typical of Manning

tramways, while under the present proposals the NSR would have no such commitments; except that is, for one 'parliamentary' train each way per day on each line. The railway company was represented by its solicitors along with Messrs W D Phillipps and C J Crosbie Dawson, General Manager and Engineer respectively, and the PET by its solicitors and Traffic Manager Mr F Hatch. The result of the inquiry was a recommendation that the majority of lines be so authorised, but there were exceptions, including the Pool Dam branch. In view of the earlier powers the company had obtained to operate passenger trains on the Pool Dam branch under its 1899 Act outlined in Chapter

One, the Commissioners took the view that having not used these powers, the railway company should not be given them by different means. In the event, despite the powers that were granted, the NSR did not operate passenger trains on any of the lines authorised to be used as light railways, either those mentioned here, or any of the others so authorised. It did consider later on, in 1906, using small engines and converting some coaches for push-pull operation to supplement the rail motors, but this came to nothing. The class of engine intended to be used is not mentioned in the minutes but they were described by the generic term 'terrier' engines, a common name among railway

Wardle practice and has a commodious cab. When the order for this locomotive was placed a request for a 'special canopy and block buffers' was stipulated. At the time of the photograph, the block buffers have clearly been replaced by the spring variety but of main interest is the 'special canopy' which we like to think was specifically requested for the workings to Pool Dam. For some reason the cab was removed after 1882.

In 1915 the MCCI purchased two inside cylinder 0-6-0STs from the Yorkshire Engine Company of Sheffield. They were delivered to Apedale, works numbers 1275 and 1276 and named HALMEREND and APEDALE respectively. A third locomotive of the same type, works number 1356 and named KNUTTON followed in 1917. Amazingly for this period, they were all cabless when delivered and were at once dubbed the 'Big Engines' in contrast to the still cabless Manning Wardles which became known as the 'Small Engines'. The 'Big Engines' took over the workmen's trains and so became regular visitors to Newcastle station. The MCCI management obviously liked their locomotive men to brave the elements on those open footplates, although in 1919 all three Yorkshire Engine Company locomotives were at last provided with cabs. The livery in MCCI days was dark blue, lined out in gold.

Of course, the majority of the locomotives working in and around Newcastle were those owned by the NSR. The rail motors, 0-6-0 saddle tanks 58A and 59A along with the Kerr, Stuart 'Argentina' 0-6-0 side tanks 74 and 75 have already been discussed. We know of only two photographs actually depicting locomotives at Newcastle in NSR days, Class A 2-4-0 tank No.35 running bunker first on a down passenger train and Class D 0-6-0 tank No.152, also on a train in the down platform, but this time running chimney first and with the target letter C on the lamp iron above the front left-hand buffer. Class B 2-4-0T No.48 saw many years service on passenger trains and engines from all three classes were regular performers on the line and therefore frequent visitors to Newcastle.

Insofar as freight traffic was concerned the NSR working time table for November 1879 gives a scale of engine loads for goods and mineral traffic on the Market Drayton Branch, referring to the following locomotives:
0-6-0 Tender Engines – Schedule A
Nos.66 to 68, 74, 75, 82, 83 to 99, 104 to 113 and 118 to 123
0-6-0 Tender Engines – Schedule B
Nos.64, 65, 69, 70, 76 to 81, 100 to 104 and 114 to 117

The above 0-6-0s were of various vintages with some dating back to 1864 but also included more modern examples of Classes E and 69. They were permitted to handle the following loads through Newcastle (table right).

The scale was based on loaded wagons of six tons with a warning that *Where Eight or Ten Tons Loaded Wagons are on a Train discretion must be used and the number of wagons correspondingly reduced*. Three empty wagons counted as two loaded. The working of these cabless saddle tanks with a loaded loose-coupled goods train of 38 wagons, equivalent to 228 tons behind the engine almost beggars belief. The conditions on the footplate through the single bore Hartshill Tunnels must have been horrendous perhaps even more so in the down direction when steam had to be applied on the 1 in 102 gradient. No wonder the permitted load for the tank engines in this direction was reduced to 156 tons!

More powerful freight locomotives were eventually utilised on the branch workings. The 100 Class 0-6-0s introduced in 1896 were used and the 159 Class 0-6-0s built by Nasmyth Wilson in 1900 began to feature, especially the first one, No.159 which was allocated to Market Drayton shed on delivery. Locomotives of this class worked the through goods trains to Wellington under the mutual agreement with the GWR. In contrast during this period the GWR's reciprocal working between Shrewsbury and Stoke would probably be handled by a 'Dean Goods' 0-6-0 tender engine, from Shrewsbury shed.

The 'New L' class of 0-6-2Ts introduced in 1908 became regular performers on passenger and freight trains. Indeed, between October 1921 and March 1922 Nos.18, 25 and 72 participated in a series of trials over the Market Drayton branch to compare the performance of superheated and non-superheated tank engines. Passenger trains were tested too, along with the daily goods train to Wellington. No.25 was the superheated engine while the other two used saturated steam. No doubt many other NSR classes than those mentioned here could be seen at Newcastle from time to time. There is photographic evidence of Class KT 4-4-0 No.38 at Shrewsbury in 1920, which may have travelled by way of Newcastle and so the station could even have witnessed the ultimate in NSR express locomotive power!

One Day in 1915

We have chosen Tuesday 13 July 1915 to paint a portrait of activity at Newcastle station during the First World War using information from the NSR working time table in operation from 12 July to 30 September 1915. All the planned movements are listed in Appendix III. Of course, every train may not have run to time and there may in addition have been local trip workings and specials. Nonetheless, there was a great deal of activity despite the onset of war. In summary, there were 62 passenger trains, 26 goods or mineral trains and six MCCI private trains. The down passenger trains totalled 30 of which 17 terminated at Newcastle. In the opposite direction there were 32 up passenger trains, 19 of them originating from Newcastle and two terminating there. The passenger trains included four to Market Drayton and three to Harecastle via the Audley Line with corresponding return trains. All this made a grand total of 94 trains, full of variety and interest.

Now, to pick out a few highlights. The stillness of the early morning was ended at 4.55am with the noisy arrival of the empty stock for the MCCI Apedale *Paddy* or, to use its politically incorrect but historically accurate title *The Nigger*. Imagine a train of four ancient ex-NSR four-wheeled carriages arriving at Newcastle's up platform behind the spanking new cabless Yorkshire Engine Company six-coupled saddle tank HALMEREND bedecked in dark blue livery with brasses well polished. Imagine also the bustle on the platform crowded with chattering miners and other employees who paid 9d (4p) per week for the privilege of travelling on this train. If your imagination works a little overtime you can readily witness the first train to arrive at Newcastle on that particular Tuesday morning in July 1915 as HALMEREND expeditiously ran around its train.

The next event was the arrival in the down platform of the first NSR train of the day, from Stoke to Leycett. The madder lake livery of the tank engine at its head would contrast with the dark blue of the MCCI locomotive but this time the carriages would be lit! The NSR train left at 5.2am also well loaded with workmen followed very quickly at 5.5am by the *Paddy* which, because of the timing of the NSR train, must have left from the up platform gaining access to the down line via the crossover immediately to the west of the station. The *Paddy*, which was not fitted with continuous brakes ran on beyond Apedale, where

		Schedule A Goods Min		Schedule B Goods Min	
Down direction		30	22	27	19
Up direction		35	28	32	24

0-6-0 saddle tank engines Nos.47 to 50, 56, 57 and 60 to 63 were permitted to take the following loads:

	Goods Min	
Down direction	26	20
Up direction	38	28

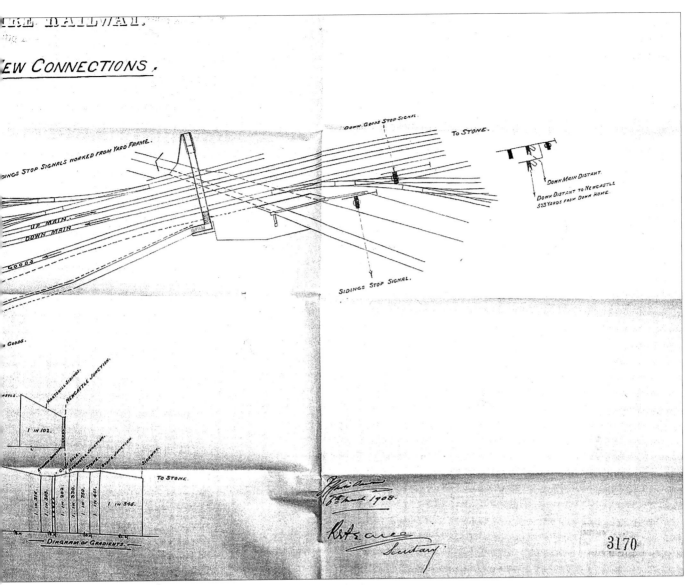

carrying the crimson lake livery including Nos.2305, 2306 and 2315 which were allocated to Stoke. Goods trains were handed over to Fowler class 4F 0-6-0 tender engines and class 3F 'Jinty' 3F 0-6-0Ts. During the early 1930s, it was common practice for an ex-LNWR 'Precedent' (sometimes called 'Large Jumbos') 2-4-0 tender engine to work an evening milk train from the creamery at Pipe Gate. At this time several were allocated to Rugby and were used to pilot the 4pm ex-Euston to Manchester train, the Mancunian, as far as Stoke. The Jumbo would then be detached for servicing at Stoke before proceeding tender-first through Newcastle to Pipe Gate to collect the milk. Engines known to have worked this service were LMS Nos. 5000 PRINCESS BEATRICE, 5001 SNOWDON, 5011 DIRECTOR and 5012 JOHN RAMSBOTTOM, the latter looking rather odd in LMS crimson as its namesake had a lot to do with the design's antecedents!

The Apedale *Paddy* for MCCI ceased to run on 19 July 1926 on the eve of the general strike and was never reinstated but MCCI trains continued to operate to Marsh Wharf in Newcastle until April 1930. Private trains from Silverdale to Pool Dam are still shown as running in

the LMS working time table for 1939 and there is some evidence that industrial locomotives from Silverdale shunted Pool Dam and Brook Street Wharves during the Second World War. The LMS Public Timetable for the winter of 1926/27 shows six passenger trains to Market Drayton on weekdays with five returns. An extra train was run each way on Wednesdays for the market. There were only two trains via the Audley line to Harecastle on weekdays with three return trains. An early morning train ran to and from Halmerend. Extra trains were run on Saturdays but the Sunday service was meagre, with only three trains to and from Market Drayton and only one train each way on the Audley line. Decline had set in although Newcastle was still reasonably well served by additional trains which ran between there and Stoke. By this time the early NSR four-wheeled carriages had given way to six-wheelers which lasted well into LMS days. Some of the NSR side corridor stock also came into use on the Market Drayton trains. Insofar as freight traffic was concerned a major blow occurred in April 1930 with the cessation of all iron and coal production at Apedale following the failure of MCCI. However, the Apedale

Branch continued in use to serve Holditch Colliery which had opened in 1919.

In 1929 there were problems with the main Newcastle tunnel which had never been entirely trouble free even in NSR days. In June the LMS Works Committee authorised a large sum, £18,000, for the reconstruction of 110 yards of the side walls with brick lining. The following month a tender of £4,459 was accepted from the Widnes Foundry Company for cast iron segments for strengthening sections of the tunnel and the works were reported as complete in February 1930. In January 1931 it was agreed to widen the trunk road bridge carrying Liverpool Road over the railway with the Borough Council and Staffordshire Country Council bearing all the costs. During the 1930s a number of under-bridges between Stoke, Newcastle Junction and Silverdale were reconstructed, in some cases to improve the width of the roadways. In April 1943, the bridge carrying King Street over the railway in Newcastle was strengthened with the costs shared between the Council and the LMS, the split being £6,760 and £4,950 respectively. At the same time two bridges between Newcastle Junction and

The southern, Stoke end portal of the longer of the two Newcastle tunnels showing the deep cutting between the two. The signal is the Newcastle down distant, electrically operated as it was so far from the home signal to which it applied, at the other end of the tunnel.

Newcastle station on 7 January 1964 looking towards Stoke. The diesel multiple-unit (later Class 104) has arrived from Stoke on a short working and will soon depart whence it came. The guard is bringing the tail lamp from what had been the rear of the unit to what will now become the rear. Despite these trains having electric tail lamps, at this time the oil tail lamp was still an obligatory requirement so that signalmen and others could ensure trains were complete. The B4 headcode was part of a short-lived scheme in use at the time to identify trains, in this case signifying multiple units on the route from Manchester to Birmingham and branches, of which to line to Newcastle and Silverdale was one. (Martin R Connop-Price - Authors Collection)

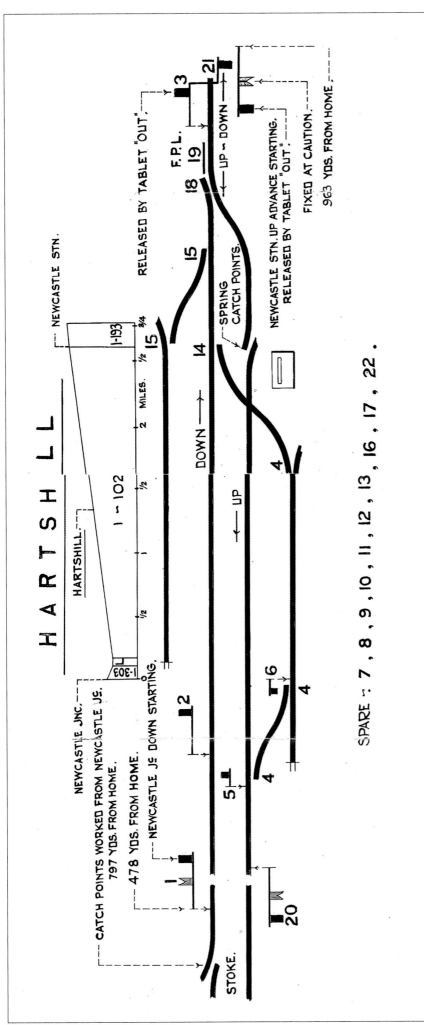

HARTSHILL

NEWCASTLE STN.

RELEASED BY TABLET "OUT."

F.P.L.

UP - DOWN

NEWCASTLE STN. UP ADVANCE STARTING.
RELEASED BY TABLET "OUT."

FIXED AT CAUTION.

963 YDS. FROM HOME.

SPRING CATCH POINTS.

HARTSHILL.

1-193

1 ~ 102

¾

½ 15 MILES. 2 2

½ ½ 1 ½

DOWN →

← UP

1-303

NEWCASTLE JNC.

CATCH POINTS WORKED FROM NEWCASTLE JC.
797 YDS. FROM HOME.

478 YDS. FROM HOME.

NEWCASTLE JC DOWN STARTING.

STOKE.

SPARE :- 7 , 8 , 9 , 10 , 11 , 12 , 13 , 16 , 17 , 22 .

Hartshill were reconstructed, at a total cost of £4,825.

The Audley line passenger services ceased altogether on 27 April 1931 with Madeley Road station, where traffic had always been sparse, closed the same day. The section of line between Silverdale and Market Drayton, along with the Audley line, was singled as and from 7 October 1934, with a passing loops at Pipe Gate on the Market Drayton line and at Leycett and Diglake (Audley) on the Audley line. The junction with the Audley line was moved back to Silverdale from where the two tracks westwards were worked as parallel single lines until their separation west of Keele at the site of the former Keele Junction. Electric token working was introduced on both the Market Drayton and Audley lines, despite the latter no longer carrying passenger traffic. These new and revised works were inspected by Colonel A C Trench and Major G R S Wilson on behalf of the Ministry of Transport on 18 June 1935, although with no passenger traffic the inspection did not cover the Audley line. With the exception of a wire worked set of points at Market Drayton Silverdale Junction, the former military gentlemen were happy with the arrangements.

Closure of the Knutton Forge in 1931 was followed by the failure of several other nearby mining operations that used the adjacent sidings and a mine loading stage on the down side of the line. Extensive re-modelling of the layout was inevitable and about 1938 Knutton Forge Junction was taken out of use and the Pool Dam branch extended as a single line to join the main line at Ketleys Siding, north of the former junction. The signal box here had originally been called Gordon's Sidings, but the name was changed in about 1908, to reflect J H Ketley & Company taking over the operations hereabouts formerly undertaken by W F Gordon. The signal box dated from November 1882 and the sidings were extended to cater for Ketley's traffic in January 1908. As the junction still faced Silverdale, a loop was provided to enable engines of trains from the Newcastle direction to run round their trains before proceeding to Pool Dam.

The 'Stoke-on-Trent Control Area Local Trip & Shunting Engine Working' for the period commencing 26 September 1938 has a number of diagrams covering workings on the lines under discussion. Trip No.7, diagrammed for a class 4 2-6-4 tank engine, after working the 7.34am passenger to Market Drayton (it was not unusual for trip engines to work the odd passenger train) and the 8.40am back, made a short trip to Bucknall and then went engine and brake van to Brampton

Left. **NSR signal box diagram for Hartshill showing the relationship of the signals and points and the numbers of the levers operating them.**

A thin line between the hour and minute figures indicates p.m.

189

STOKE-ON-TRENT, NEWCASTLE,
HARECASTLE (VIA AUDLEY) AND MARKET DRAYTON.

Week Days.

																B																		
Stoke-on-Trent ....dep.	5 32	6 50	7 10	7 40	8 2	8 39	8 50		9 15	10 8	10 43	11 15	11 52	12 25	12 45	1 8	1 13	1 40	2 12	2 50		3 4	4 15	4 55	5 12
Newcastle { Station	5 40	6 55	7 15	7 45	8 9	8 43	8 57		9 21	10 48	11 20	11 57		12 30	12 50	1 15	1 18	1 45	2 17	2 55		3 14	4 30	5 0	5 17
{ Liverpool Rd. H.														12 33			1 18	1 49				3 18			
Silverdale { Crown St. Halt ...	5 44													12 38				1 54	2 22			3 25			
{ Station	5 58	7 3	7 22		8 16		9 6		9 28	10 55	11 27			12 41	12 56	1 25		1K57	2 25	3 2		3 27	4 36	5S06	5 24
Keele	6 1	7 7	7 26		8 21		9 10		9 32	10 59	11 31			12 45	1 0			2 1	2 29	3 7			4 41	5S011	5 28
Leycett	6 11		7 31							11 3				12 49				2H44	2 33				4 46		
Halmerend	6 16		7 37							11 8				12 55				2 48	2 38				4 51		
Audley & Bignall End......			7 44							11 14									2 42				4 56		
Alsager Road			7 53							11 22									2 50				5 4		
Harecastle ....arr.			8 0							11 33									3 2				5 9		
Madeley Road ....dep.					8 27		9 16	9 38			11 37					1 6			3 15					5 54	
Pipe Gate............					8 36		9 25	9 46			11 44					1 12			3 21					5 41	
Norton-in-Hales......					8 43		9 34	9 53			11 51					1 18			3 28					5 49	
Market Drayton......arr.					8 50		9 41	10 0			11 58					1 25			3 35					6 0	
Tern Hill ....arr.								10 20								1 46			5 55					7 21	
Hodnet								10 26								1 52			6 0					7 29	
Peplow								10 31								1 57			6 8					7 35	
Wellington								10 48								2 20			6 29					7 55	
Shrewsbury								11 18								3 5			7 35					9 8	

Notes in columns: Weds. only. — Saturdays only. — Saturdays only. — Saturdays only. — Saturdays excepted. — Saturdays excepted. — Sats. only. — Commences June 4th. — Saturdays excepted. — Saturdays excepted.

Week Days—continued. | Sundays.

Stoke-on-Trent ....dep.	5 28	5 32		6 4	6 35	6 54	7 40	8 10	8 20	9 18	10 2	10 37	11 15		8 15	9 5	2 30	3 4 25	5 0	6 42		7 10	8 15	10 47
Newcastle { Station	5 35	5 38		6 9	6 40	6 59	7 45	8 15	8 25	9 23	10 7	10 42	11 30		8 20	9 10	2 35	4 30	5 5	6 47		7 15	8 20	10 52
{ Liverpool Rd. H.		5 42									10 11													
Silverdale { Crown St. Halt ...		5 49		6 13							10 18													
{ Station	5 41	5 50		6 16	6S046		7 52	8 22		9 30	10 21	10 48	11 27		9 17	3 44		5 13	6 546			7 22	
Keele	5 45			6 20			7 56	8 26		9 34	10 28	10 52	11 31		9 21	2 48		5 16	6 592			7 26	
Leycett								8 30		9 38	10 38	10 56											
Halmerend								8 35		9 43	10 35	11 1											
Audley & Bignall End...								8 39				11 6											
Alsager Road								8 46				11 14											
Harecastle ....arr.								8 54				11 21											
Madeley Road ....dep.	5 51							8 5			11 37				9 28	3 55		5 23	7 6			7 30	
Pipe Gate............	5 57							8 15			11 43				9 35	3 3		5 30	7 13			7 35	
Norton-in-Hales......	6 3							8 22			11 49				9 48	3 10		5 45	7 20			7 47	
Market Drayton......arr.	6 10							8 33			11 56				9 50	3 17		5 55	7 30			7 52	
Tern Hill ....arr.	7 21														11 41								
Hodnet	7 29														11 48								
Peplow	7 35														11 54								
Wellington	7 55														12 16								
Shrewsbury	9 8														3 3								

Notes: Sats. only. — Saturdays excepted. — Saturdays excepted. — Saturdays excepted. — Saturdays only. — Saturdays excepted. — Saturdays only. — Also runs Dec. 24th 1926, and April 14th, 1927. — Commences May 8, 1927. — Not after May 1st, 1927. — Runs September 26th, 1926, and commencing May 1st, 1927. — Commences June 5th, 1927.

Week Days.

Shrewsbury ....dep.						6 58	9 10	11 25										
Wellington						7 20	9 50	11 40										
Peplow						7 48	10 6	12 1										
Hodnet						7 55	10 12	12 7										
Tern Hill						8 2	10 18	12 13										
Market Drayton ......dep.						8 26	10 34	12 22		1J18	1E50	2 55						
Norton-in-Hales......						8 34	10 40	12 28		1J24	1E56	3 1						
Pipe Gate............						8 43	10 46	12 34		1J30	2E 2	3 7						
Madeley Road......						8 52	10 52	G		1J36	2E 8	3 14						
Harecastle............dep.					8 23					1 50	2 10							
Alsager Road					8 27					4	2 23							
Audley & Bignall End......					8 36					2 13	2 23							
Halmerend	6 26				8 41				1 10	2 18	2 28	3 0						
Leycett	6 31				8 47				1 15	2 24	2 39							
Keele	6 35			8 8	8 51	9 0	10 58		12 45	1 19	2 29	2E15	2 43	5 10	3 20			
Silverdale { Station	5 33			8 11	8 55	9 5	11 2		12 49	1 23	2 34	2 18	2 54	5 17		4 55		
{ Crown St. Halt	5 35		6 43	7 21	8 14					1 26			2 58	3 21				
Newcastle { Liverpool Rd. H.	5 39		6 46	7 25						1 30								
{ Station	5 41	6 40	6 48	7 28	7 54	8 20	8 50	9 2	9 12	10 25	11 8	12 15	12 55	1 33	1 47	1 53	2 41	2 26	3 5	3 24	3 14	4 10	4 40
Stoke-on-Trent ....arr.	5 43	6 45	6 56	7 35	8 4	8 27	8 56	9 9	9 19	10 30	11 15	12 20	1 2	1 44	1 52	2 1	2 51	2 36	3 15	3 38	4 18	4 51

Notes: Saturdays only. — Saturdays only. — Saturdays excepted. — Sats. excepted. — Saturdays only. — Saturdays only. — Saturdays excepted. — Weds. excepted. — Saturdays excepted.

Week Days—continued. | Sundays.

Shrewsbury ....dep.	2 30				5 10				7 45	5 5								
Wellington	3 35				5 50				8 10	5 40								
Peplow	3 51				6 8				9 25	6 0								
Hodnet	3 57				6 17				9 30	6 8								
Tern Hill	4 3				6 25				9 36	6 17								
Market Drayton ......dep.	4 20				6 45		9 2		10 20	6 45	8 36							
Norton-in-Hales......	4 27				6 51		9 8		10 25	6 51	8 42							
Pipe Gate............	4 36				7 0		9 15		10 34	7 0	8 49							
Madeley Road......	4 42				7 13		9 21		10 44	7 15								
Harecastle............dep.	4 40	5S028	5 41							8 45	9 0							
Alsager Road	4 44	5S032	5 45							8 49	9 4							
Audley & Bignall End......	4 53	5S041	5 54				10 5	10 47		8 56	9 11							
Halmerend	4 58	5S045	6 0				10 10	10 51		9 1	9 16							
Leycett	5 3	5S058	6 7							9 7	9 22							
Keele	4 49	5 3	5S058	6 12	6 55		7 21	9 27	10 11	10 57		10 50	7 22	9 7	9 11	9 26		
Silverdale { Station	4 54	5 10		6 17	6 53		7 25	9 33	10 18	11 1		10 55	7 26	9 13	9 16	9 30		
{ Crown St. Halt										11 7								
Newcastle { Liverpool Rd. H.										11 13								
{ Station	5 0	5 18	5 25	6 10	6 23	7 8	7 37	7 31	8 30	9 38	10 24	11 18	8 30	11 14	5 0	7 32	8 30	9 10	9 23	9 36
Stoke-on-Trent ....arr.	5 11	5 26	5 31	6 18	6 33	7 17	7 17	7 38	8 35	9 47	10 32	11 25	8 35	10 4	5 67	7 39	8 36	9 26	9 33	9 43

Notes: Saturdays only. — Saturdays excepted. — Saturdays excepted. — Saturdays only. — Saturdays only. — Saturdays excepted. — Also runs Dec. 21th 1926, and April 14th, 1927. — Saturdays excepted. — Runs on September 26th, 1926, and commencing May 1st, 1927. — Not after April 24th, 1927. — Commences May 1st, 1927. — Saturdays excepted.

A—Arrives Newcastle at 4.23 p.m.

B—Will not run on Saturdays after May 28th, 1927.

E—Will not apply November 6th, 1926, to January 29th, 1927, inclusive.

G—Calls by signal to pick up passengers on notice being given at the station, and to set down on notice being given to the guard at Pipe Gate.

H—Arrives Leycett 2.14 p.m

J—Runs November 6th, 1926, to January 29th, 1927, inclusive.

K—Departs Silverdale 2.5 p.m.

S—Saturdays excepted.

SO—Saturdays only.

LMS Public Timetable for the branch, including the Audley line, for the period 30 September 1926 to June 1927.

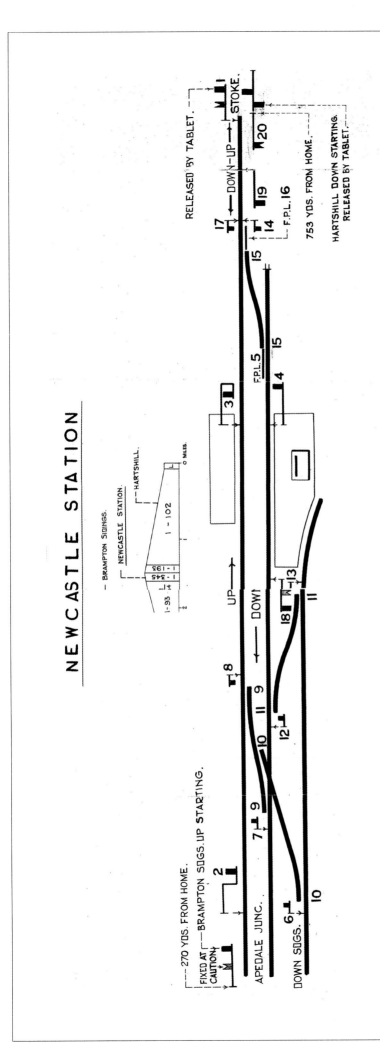

NEWCASTLE STATION

Left. **BR signal box diagram for Newcastle, little altered from NSR times. Notice that the Hartshill down and the Newcastle up starting signals could only be released and placed in the clear position, after the electric tablet for the single line section had been withdrawn at whichever end a train was to enter the section. Thus, for example, if a tablet had been withdrawn by the signalman at Newcastle, his opposite number at Hartshill, as well as not being able to withdraw another tablet, would not be able to clear his starting signal. This represented a second safety feature, to ensure that two trains were not on the single line section running in opposite directions at the same time. FPL stands for a facing point lock; where turnouts were facing the direction from which trains normally travelled, it was standard practice to provide for an arrangement such that two separate lever movements were required by the signalman to change the direction of the points, thus providing a safety measure in addition to the normal interlocking against inadvertent operation. As both platform lines at Newcastle could be used for trains departing towards Stoke, this is the reason for an FPL at turnout 15.**

Sidings. After shunting there it went back to Stoke taking any traffic with it, and on Saturdays only worked the 2.35pm goods and mineral to Market Drayton, coming back at 5.56pm. The day was completed banking trains between Stoke and Caverswall on the line to Derby. Trip No.8 was booked for a class 3 2-6-2 tank engine which, after a passenger job to Kidsgrove and then Blythe Bridge, went to shunt the sidings at Apedale and, excepting Saturdays (Trip 7 did that day) later worked the same train to and from Market Drayton. Trip No.14 was another job for a class 3 tank engine; after shunting the north end of Stoke yard during the night, it worked a train to and from Leycett, shunting Hartshill sidings en-route. This one too, completed its day assisting trains up the bank from Stoke to Caverswall. Trip No.22, a class 4 tank engine this time, was employed literally all over the place, but made a journey to and from Newcastle and Silverdale early in the morning, returning from the latter place with the 8.3am passenger train to Stoke. Trip No.40, yet another class 3 2-6-2 tank, went to Market Drayton on the 12.45pm from Stoke, coupled to the train engine. It returned at 3.45pm after shunting there, picking up and dropping off as necessary, along with any shunting that might be required at Silverdale and Brampton Sidings en-route to Stoke. Trip No.46, a 2-6-4 tank, worked a goods and mineral to Market Drayton, departing Stoke at 5am and returning at 6.50am, to arrive Stoke at 8.10am; it then worked empties to Silverdale returning with loads, before setting off for Tutbury. Trip No.56, diagrammed for a class 4 0-6-0 tender engine, made an afternoon trip to and from Apedale between its other duties, while Trip No.57, another class 4 tank engine, left Stoke at 11 20am for Knutton Forge, Pool Dam and Silverdale; it was not back at Stoke until 4 37pm after which it went to attend to the needs of the Cheadle branch.

The above were all Stoke diagrams, but there were some worked from Alsager shed too. Trip No.81, booked for another class 4 tender engine, among its other multifarious duties made a trip from Alsager via the Audley line to Silverdale at 3.45pm, except on Saturdays, returning at 5.10pm. On Saturdays this job was covered by Trip No.82, with a class 3 tank engine. Trip No.86, a class 4 tender engine again, although largely employed between Alsager and stations on the Audley line, made a brief foray to Silverdale arriving at 11.55 am and departing at 12.30pm. Engines on these jobs would carry a target displaying the Trip number on the front and rear lamp irons so that signalmen and shunting staff could identify them, as several might be at the same place at the same time.

The predominance of the Stanier class 3 2-6-2 tank engines is a reflection of Stoke's dissatisfaction with them. They were poor machines, unsuitable for the local passenger workings and were not powerful enough to keep the schedules on some of the sharply timed trains, particularly on the Loop Line through Hanley and the Pottery towns. They had been allocated to Stoke for passenger work, but were soon found deficient and, as nobody else wanted them, they had to be employed somewhere! They were, it has to be added, inadequate substitutes for the NSR engines they were supposed to replace! The men would have much preferred the engines they had been brought up on, and had recently been parted from, or an LMS 'Standard Freight', as the ubiquitous Class 4 0-6-0 tender engines were known, or even perhaps, a 3F six-coupled Jinty tank. Additional passenger trains were operated during the Second World War and afterwards from Silverdale to the Royal Ordnance Factory at Swynnerton. A new branch, just over a mile long, was opened on 3 August 1941 to serve this factory. It diverged from the former NSR line from Stone to Norton Bridge at Swynnerton Junction and ran to a new four platform station called Cold Meece. At the height of operations, during 1943-45, there were 15 arrivals and 15 departures on weekdays including three trains from Silverdale and Newcastle with corresponding return trains. All arrivals and departures coincided with the start and finish of each shift.

A view from the level crossing at Brampton, looking towards Newcastle on 10 April 1966, only a few weeks after this section had closed completely but before dismantling took place. Newcastle station can be seen in the distance, and notice the additional down running line on the right. Between this point and Newcastle station the route was formerly part of the Newcastle-under-Lyme Junction Canal.

The extreme Silverdale end of Brampton Sidings in September 1961, with the Liverpool Road Halt platforms just visible in front of the bridge taking the Liverpool Road over the railway. The PMT bus garage, referred to in the text, is the large building to the far left. (Martin R Connop-Price - Authors Collection)

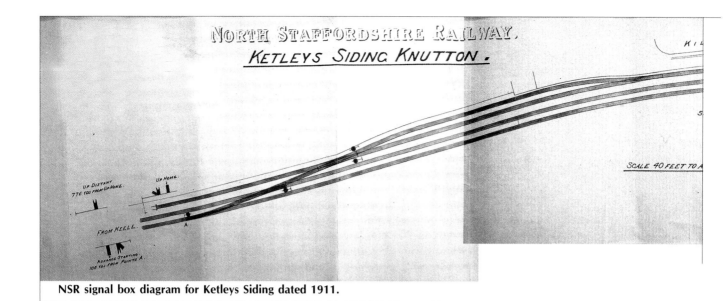

Up Distant
776 Yds from Up Home.

Up Home.

SCALE 40 FEET TO A

FROM KEELE.

A

ADVANCED STARTING
106 YDS FROM POINTS A.

NSR signal box diagram for Ketleys Siding dated 1911.

During the LMS regime the character of Newcastle station changed again. Apart from the fillip of extra wartime traffic the pace of the station was less intense than in NSR days. The miners trains had ceased, the bustle of the rail motors was no more and passenger trains no longer traversed the Audley Line. Following the demise of the electric trams in 1928, motor transport had taken hold and Newcastle had become a wayside station on a rural branch line to Market Drayton.

British Railways and Closure
The LMS era came to an end on 31 December 1947 when this huge commercial undertaking was vested in the British Transport Commission. The railway facilities at Newcastle were now nationalised and operated by The Railway Executive, trading as British Railways (BR) London Midland Region (LMR). The Market Drayton Branch suffered an early casualty by losing the halt at Silverdale Crown Street, closed on 7 June 1949. In September 1953 a loop siding to serve a long loading dock belonging to the Hartshill Brick & Tile

Company was taken out of use. It had been provided under an agreement dated 29 January 1872 and took the form of a loop on the down side of the line from Stoke just prior to the entrance to the first of the two Newcastle tunnels. There was also a loop on the up side at this location for general goods traffic.

A study of Bradshaw for the period 6 October to 2 November 1952 reveals that the Sunday passenger services had ceased. Weekday departures from Newcastle in the up direction were as follows:

7.21am   Through train to Birmingham

Empty wagon train on the Pool Dam branch heading towards Knutton on 2 April 1965, crossing the Silverdale Road by the interesting oblique cast iron girder bridge. The engine is another of Stoke's BR Class 2 2-6-0s, 78017; they were a familiar sight on the branch in its last few years. (Martin R Connop-Price - Authors Collection)

120

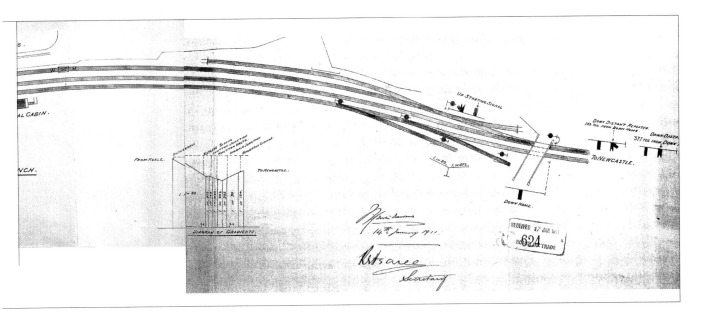

ex-Silverdale
7.52am Through train to Birmingham ex-Silverdale
8.50am (SX) Stoke only ex-Newcastle
9.15am Stoke only ex-Market Drayton
12.54pm Stoke only ex-Market Drayton
2.21pm (SO) Stoke only ex-Market Drayton
4.17pm (SX) Through train to Birmingham ex-Newcastle
7.39pm Through train to Stafford ex-Market Drayton

Down trains were as follows:
7.43am Market Drayton ex-Stoke

8.41am (SX) Terminating train from Stoke
9.11am Market Drayton ex-Stoke
12.47pm (SO) Market Drayton ex-Stoke
5.5pm Market Drayton ex-Stoke
6.41pm Silverdale ex-Birmingham
SX = Saturdays excepted
SO = Saturdays only

It was all a far cry from NSR days. By this time the standard formation for the three weekday Market Drayton trains (four on Saturdays) normally comprised a rake of three LMS metal-bodied non-corridor stock. They gave a very solid,

comfortable and quiet ride nothing at all like the noisy rattling and banging of modern day 'Pacer' diesel multiple units which we now frequently are forced to endure. A happy memory for one of the authors is accompanying his father on business trips from Newcastle to Birmingham, using the through trains, to be left at Wolverhampton Low Level to get a taste of GWR engines with their brass plates and copper capped chimneys. Happy days! Passenger trains from Stoke to Market Drayton continued until 1956 when the decision was taken to close all stations beyond Silverdale

The up platform at Liverpool Road Halt in about 1958. While it might beggar belief that trains still stopped here when this picture was taken, but stop they did, as one of the authors can testify as he used it on a regular basis! The wagons are loaded with scrap for a merchant using the land adjacent to the goods yard. The scrap continued to run for another ten years or so, indeed it was to be the last remaining traffic on the section from Apedale Junction after the line had been severed between Stoke and Newcastle.

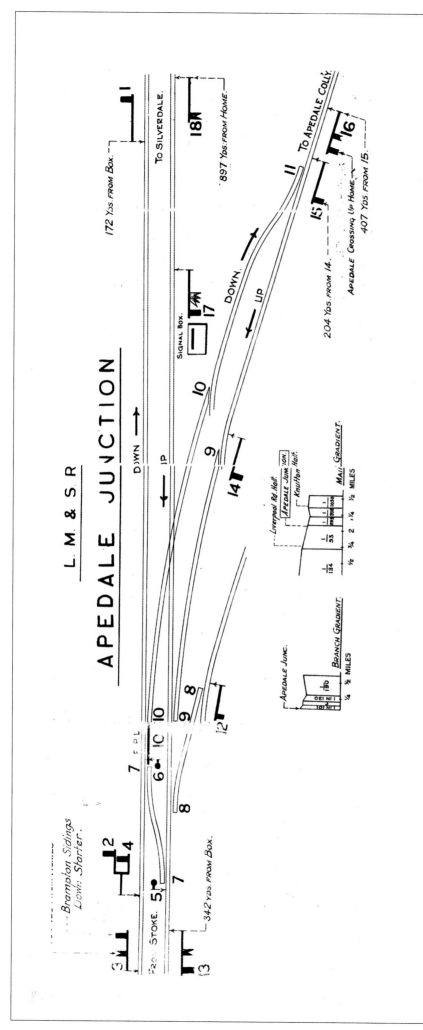

L. M. & S. R.

APEDALE JUNCTION

Left. BR signal box diagram for Apedale Junction. As with the other BR diagrams illustrated, this would be little different from what would have existed in NSR times.

because of poor patronage – Keele, Pipe Gate and Norton-in-Hales. The last regular passenger train left Market Drayton at 7.00pm for Stoke on Saturday 5 May 1956 with four coaches behind Stanier 2-6-4 tank 42671. Market Drayton Station remained open for the service on the former GWR route from Nantwich to Wellington, the trains running to and from Crewe. This route also closed for local passenger traffic as from 9 September 1963 and completely from 1 May 1967.

The curtailment of passenger trains between Silverdale and Market Drayton was not surprising. The Potteries Motor Traction Company Limited (PMT) as successor to the PET had long since established regular bus services to Pipe Gate and Market Drayton, while Madeley and Woore were served by Crosville Motor Services. In 1955 a new cafeteria called 'The Four in Hand' was opened at the PMT garage on the Liverpool Road just north of Newcastle. The name recalled the hey-day of the stage coaches and on summer Saturdays it was buzzing with activity as the long distance motor coaches stopped to allow their passengers to refresh themselves. We recall the visiting coach fleets of Royal Blue, Standerwick, Yelloway, Ribble, Midland Red and the smart white coated PMT senior coach drivers. This activity was in marked contrast to that at the Liverpool Road Halt which abutted the northern boundary of the garage. The halt, so bravely created to counter electric tramway competition, now saw only three trains on weekdays, two up and one down, with an extra train each way on Saturdays and nothing at all on Sundays. However, a strong fight was maintained by BR in North Staffordshire throughout the 1950s to retain summer holiday traffic, especially during the Potteries Wakes Weeks in August when many closed stations were reopened to accommodate specials to Blackpool, North Wales and elsewhere. Newcastle and Silverdale, which remained open for normal traffic at this time, had their fair share of these additional trains. There were other specials too. One of the authors can recall a school trip from Newcastle to London in 1954. After the closure of the branch to regular passenger trains beyond Silverdale, specials still ran through Market Drayton to Tern Hill for the air display at RAF Tern Hill on Battle of Britain Day. These specials continued until 1964, after which the annual air displays were discontinued. The last passenger train carrying workers from the ROF Factory at Swynnerton for Newcastle and Silverdale left Cold Meece at 5.0pm on 28 February 1958

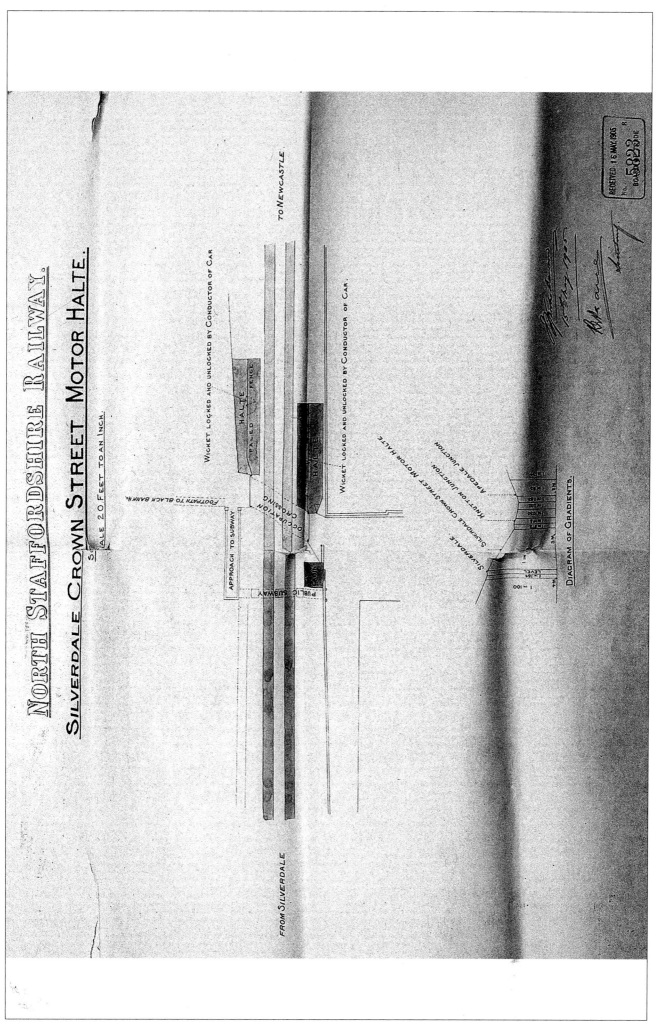

NORTH STAFFORDSHIRE RAILWAY.

SILVERDALE CROWN STREET MOTOR HALTE.

Scale 20 Feet to an Inch.

FOOTPATH TO BLACK BANK

APPROACH TO SUBWAY

PUBLIC SUBWAY

BANK

OCCUPATION CROSSING

FROM SILVERDALE

TO NEWCASTLE

HALTE
PALED FENCE

WICKET LOCKED AND UNLOCKED BY CONDUCTOR OF CAR.

HALTE

WICKET LOCKED AND UNLOCKED BY CONDUCTOR OF CAR.

SILVERDALE CROWN STREET MOTOR HALTE.

KNUTTON JUNCTION

APEDALE JUNCTION

SILVERDALE.

DIAGRAM OF GRADIENTS.

1 IN 100

LEVEL

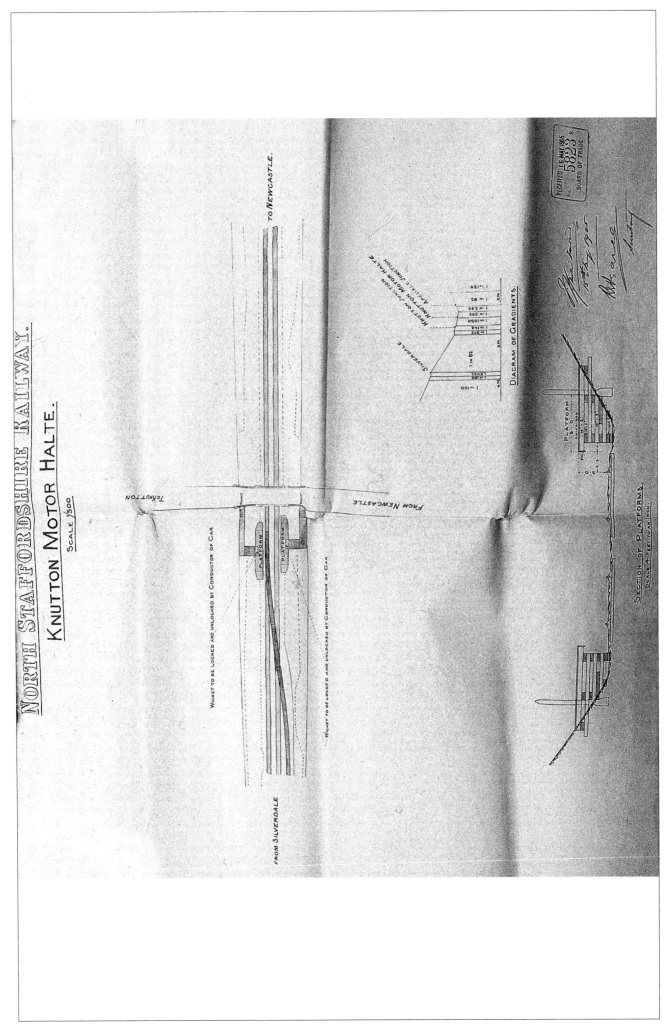

North Staffordshire Railway.

Knutton Motor Halte.

Scale 1/500

To Newcastle.

To Knutton

From Newcastle

From Silverdale

Wicket to be locked and unlocked by Conductor of Car

Wicket to be re-locked and unlocked by Conductor of Car

Diagram of Gradients.

Knutton Junction

Knutton Motor Halte

Apedale Junction

Silverdale

1 in 134
1 in 82
1 in 293
1 in 202
1 in 1050
1 in 164
1 in 972
1 in 82
Level
1 in 185
1 in 100

Section of Platforms.
Scale 4 Feet to an Inch

Platform 6.0
Platform 6.0

RECEIVED 16 MAY 1905
5823
BOARD OF TRADE

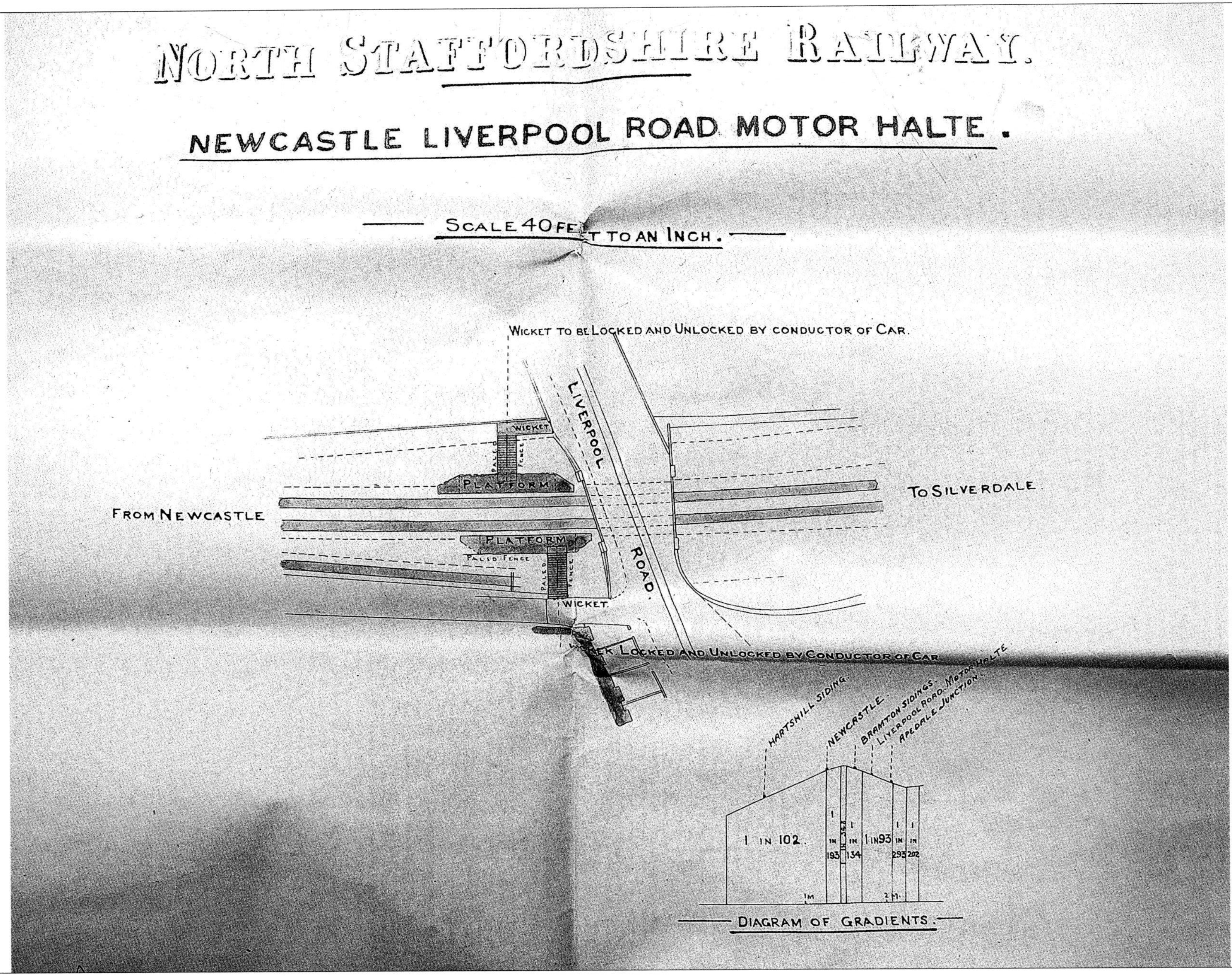

NORTH STAFFORDSHIRE RAILWAY.

NEWCASTLE LIVERPOOL ROAD MOTOR HALTE.

— SCALE 40 FEET TO AN INCH. —

TO SILVERDALE.

WICKET TO BE LOCKED AND UNLOCKED BY CONDUCTOR OF CAR.

LIVERPOOL ROAD.

WICKET TO BE LOCKED AND UNLOCKED BY CONDUCTOR OF CAR.

WICKET

FENCE

PLATFORM

PLATFORM

PALED FENCE

WICKET

PALED FENCE

FROM NEWCASTLE

DIAGRAM OF GRADIENTS.

1 IN 102.

1 IN 193

1 IN 93

1 IN 111

1 IN 354

258200

HARTSHILL SIDING

NEWCASTLE

BRATTON SIDINGS

LIVERPOOL ROAD MOTOR

PRACRIE ROAD JUNCTION

North Staffordshire Railway.

Brampton Level Crossing.

WICKET TO BE LOCKED AND UNLOCKED BY CONDUCTOR OF CAR

TO NEWCASTLE.

LEVEL CROSSING

LEVEL CROSSING

FROM SILVERDALE

WICKET TO BE LOCKED AND UNLOCKED BY CONDUCTOR OF CAR

SCALE 40 FEET TO AN INCH

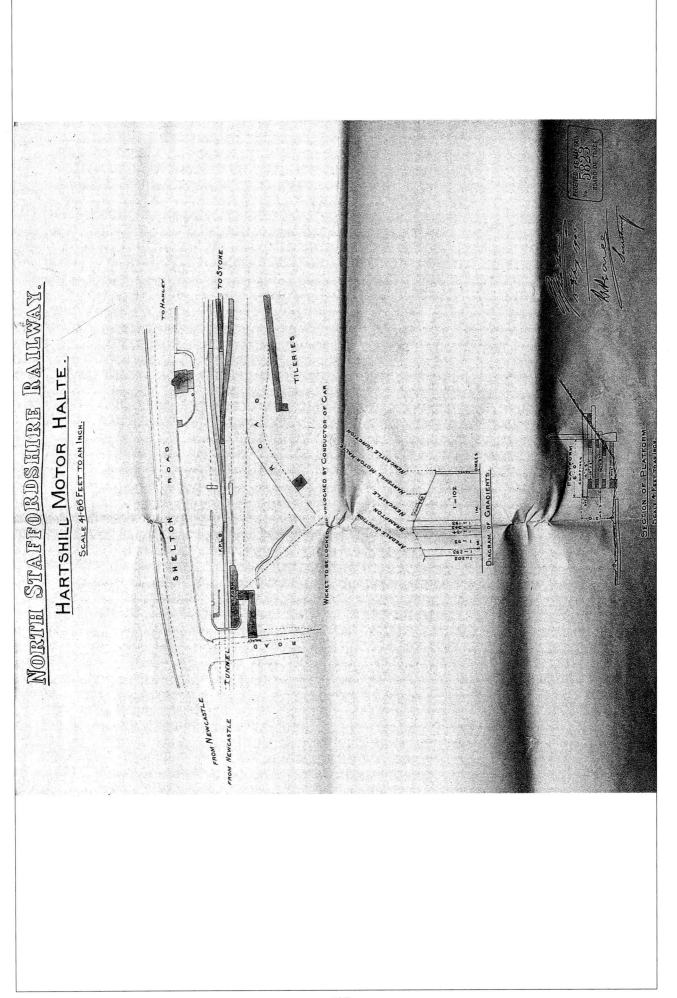

North Staffordshire Railway.

Hartshill Motor Halte.

Scale 41·66 Feet to an Inch.

Diagram of Gradients.

Section of Platform.
Scale 1 Feet to an Inch.

Apedale Junction on 9 August 1966 with the Apedale branch curving away to the right. The signal box here was one of very few remaining on the former NSR system to the early McKenzie & Holland design with a hip roof.

behind Stanier 2-6-4 tank 42665, but still the truncated service to Silverdale soldiered on.

On 1 October 1960 the LMR published an Appendix to the Working Timetable for its Western Lines which included an interesting reference to the Pool Dam branch, worth quoting in full:

Level Crossings – Drivers and Guards working on this branch must bring their trains to a stand at each crossing, which must not be fouled until the train is called forward by the Handsignalman who must accompany all trains over the branch. Except as shown below, trains are not allowed to work between the hours of sunset and sunrise.

Trains requiring to work at the S.P.D. Ltd. siding may be allowed to proceed to that siding during the hours of darkness. A Handsignalman must be stationed at the Level Crossing adjacent to S.P.D. Ltd. siding to warn users and must remain at the crossing until the train has completed work at the siding.

Drivers of Trains from the Pool Bam branch must not pass the Stop and await instructions board, situated on the Pool Dam side of the points leading to the down sidings neck, until permission is received from the Shunter or Guard, who, before giving such permission, must ascertain that no movement is being made in the sidings.

The points in the Pool Dam branch leading to the down sidings neck must be set for the neck except when it is necessary for a movement to or from the Pool Dam direction to be made over them, in which case Trainmen or Shunters must, immediately the movement has passed over the points,

re-set them for the neck and clip and padlock them in that position.

The maximum permitted speed on the branch was 30 mph except through the junction at Ketleys Sidings where speed had to be reduced to 15 mph. Drivers had to whistle when one mile distant from Blackfriars Level Crossing, Shelton Wharf Level Crossing and Brook Lane Pool Dam Level Crossing.

Reverting to the Market Drayton branch, where the maximum permitted speed was 45 mph, a new connection was made to the ex-LNWR main line at Madeley and became known as the Madeley Chord. It opened on 18 June 1962 and was laid on an embankment constructed some 90 years earlier but which had never carried any track. It was part of the NSR plans to counter the proposals for other railways to penetrate this part of North Staffordshire as outlined in Chapter Two. The chord connection was put in to facilitate alternative routing of freight trains following the closure of marshalling yards at Chatterley and Alsager, and the concentration of this activity at Basford Hall south of Crewe. As a result of this, Newcastle witnessed more through freight trains hauled by larger locomotives than the long-familiar LMS 4F 0-6-0s and tank engines. Stanier Black Five 4-6-0s and 8F 2-8-0s came to the fore, together with Ivatt Class 4 2-6-0s and BR Standard Class 4 2-6-0s and Class 5 4-6-0s.

The *Evening Sentinel* for 27 March 1963 covered the implications of the

Beeching Report, *The Reshaping of British Railways*, insofar as North Staffordshire was concerned. There were six photographs of stations to be closed including Newcastle. For those lines covered by this book the newspaper reported: *The Stoke-Newcastle-Silverdale branch line, which until 1956 continued to Market Drayton, is used by workers at the Wedgwood factory at Barlaston. An estimate of daily passenger traffic is 200 each way. Stations named for closure are Newcastle, Liverpool-Road Halt and Silverdale.*

This rationalisation also saw the effective closure of the Audley line. Prior to this, some mineral traffic to and from Silverdale and Holditch Collieries was routed via Alsager and Audley. The final weekday service passenger service from Newcastle was as follows:

Up Trains
7.19am (SX) Barlaston & Tittensor ex-Silverdale
7.33am (SO) Birmingham ex-Silverdale
7.52am (SX) Stone ex-Silverdale
8.50am Birmingham ex-Newcastle
4.20pm (SX) Stoke ex-Newcastle
Down Trains
6.52am (SO) Silverdale ex-Stafford
8.35am Terminating train ex-Stafford
3.55pm (SX) Terminating train ex-Stoke
5.10pm (FSX) Silverdale ex-Stoke
5.18pm (FO) Silverdale ex-Stoke
6.25pm Silverdale ex-Birmingham
Notice that most of the trains were extensions of other services, and not branch line trains as such. The terminating trains went back to Stoke as empty stock.

The final passenger service was operated by diesel multiple units which were first introduced on the line on 3 March 1958. They were based at Cockshute, a new purpose-built depot adjacent to the junction of the line at Stoke Newcastle Junction. Newcastle had become a mere shadow of its former self. The passenger service ended completely on 2 March 1964. Goods traffic continued for a further two years but subsidence was causing problems in the Newcastle tunnels, and we have already seen not only the problems associated with their original construction, but also the expensive remedial work the LMS had undertaken in 1930 and 1931. As a result, the decision was taken to close the branch as a through route, retaining only the section between Brampton Sidings and Madeley Chord, and henceforth operating it from Crewe, rather than Stoke. The closure took place on and from 8 March 1966; after this, the only access to Brampton Sidings, the Apedale branch for Holditch Colliery, the Pool Dam branch and Silverdale Colliery, which between them constituted the sole remaining traffic, was via reversal at Madeley Chord. However, it is interesting to note that the section between Madeley Chord and

Market Drayton was not taken out of use until May 1967. While the track had been left in place, it is extremely doubtful if any traffic used the section after it ceased to be a through route from Newcastle. In the period 13-19 May 1967, a stop block was provided at Madeley Chord, 750 yards on the Pipe Gate side of the loop points, and the junction at Market Drayton was clipped and padlocked out of use.

Brampton Sidings signal box was taken out of use in the period 16-22 September 1967, the line beyond Apedale Junction becoming a siding. Apedale Junction signal box and associated signalling were removed the following week. Thereafter, the line from Silverdale to Brampton, along with the Apedale branch, as described in Chapter Three, was worked as a siding under the 'one engine in steam, or two or more engines coupled together', regulations. At the same time the Pool Dam branch was taken out of use with Ketleys Siding signal box being abolished and all the signals and points removed. The connections to the Pool Dam branch were left in place, clipped and padlocked, as it had been agreed that the track would be recovered by BR with direct labour using rail transport. However, the official date of closure for the Pool Dam branch was 7 October 1967. So, the first railway to arrive in Newcastle was the last to go – 117 years of railway activity was at an

end.

It is worthwhile saying a little more about the closure of the Pool Dam branch, as it was both prolonged and of some interest. First of all mention should be made of a new siding connection for SPD Limited, a distribution company with a warehouse and distribution centre on part of the site of the Knutton Forge. A trailing connection was provided for trains heading for Pool Dam, at a point near to the former Knutton Forge Junction, the arrangements coming into use in December 1958 with invited guests for the official opening conveyed into the new premises in a diesel multiple unit. It did not, however, last very long, and was removed in October 1964, the agreement being terminated in July. The Newcastle Gas Works had ceased using rail transport early in 1961, which left the coal landsale wharf at Pool Dam, by this date operated by the Silverdale Co-op, and a wagon load general goods facility at the Brook Lane wharf. Discussions with a view to closing the branch commenced in late 1964, when it was established that BR was still paying rent to Sneyd Estates under the 999 year lease of the SNuLR dated 29 November 1860. The whole thing got very messy when it was realised that the lease only covered the line as far as Pool Dam. The remainder of the line to Brook Lane Wharf, the Canal Extension Railway, was not part of the railway lease but

Crossing Pool Dam; the shunter is acting as flag man for road vehicles. A structural steel contractor and merchant had workshops at the Brook Lane Wharf, hence these wagons being returned to Corby steelworks (note lettering on the wagons); they would have arrived earlier loaded with steel sections. (Martin R Connop-Price - Authors Collection)

was instead concluded under a much earlier lease from the Newcastle-under-Lyme Canal Company. By this time the canal had long been closed but it had been leased to the NSR. The lease thus passed, to the LMS but when the British Transport Commission was disbanded, the remaining canal interests had not passed to BR, but rather to the British Waterways Board (BWB). It was therefore, concluded that in fact this section of the branch belonged to the BWB and not BR! The British Railways Board (BRB) Solicitor advised that while it was possible to close the branch in its entirety, the BRB would be legally obliged to leave it in place, and maintain the original section in a form in which it could be used at any time, under the two leases! Negotiations were therefore entered into with both Sneyd Estates and the BWB, although the latter proved extremely difficult to pin down. Eventually agreement was reached with Sneyd Estates to surrender the lease of the portion of the line between the junction at Knutton and Pool Dam. This cost £9,000, the land reverting to the estate, and there was a £498 per annum reduction in the rental. The BWB eventually agreed to the closure of its portion of the line, with BR recovering the redundant materials. There was some good news for BR, as it was able to sell for £7,000 some land that it actually owned at Pool Dam and Brook Lane

wharf. It would appear that some time later both the BWB and Sneyd Estates disposed of their land, initially at least, to Newcastle Borough Council. The landsale coal traffic for the Silverdale Co-op was transferred to Silverdale goods yard.

Mention has been made in Chapter Three of closure of the line between Silverdale and Holditch Colliery via Apedale Junction, for which again, one assumes, an arrangement had to be made with Sneyd Estates, regarding the rental paid for the section between Silverdale and the former Knutton Forge Junction. The line onwards to Madeley Chord remained open to serve Silverdale colliery, until this pit closed in May 1996. The track however, was left *in situ* and only recently (2009) has agreement been reached for Network Rail to remove it!

The same Pool Dam branch train on 7 November 1964 hauled by BR Class 2 2-6-0 78056. The train is between Blackfriars Road and Pool Dam on the Canal Extension Railway, heading for Knutton. (Martin R Connop-Price - Authors Collection)

Freight train passing Liverpool Road on 29 July 1964 heading towards Silverdale hauled by 3F 0-6-0T 47596, and in all probability destined for the Pool Dam branch. The engine has steam brakes and is not equipped with vacuum train brakes, so the train would have been completely unbraked, such that the guard would have to pin down individual wagon brakes prior to descending steep gradients. The headcode of one lamp over the left-hand buffer confirms a train without continuous automatic brakes. (Martin R Connop-Price - Authors Collection)

Silverdale Colliery with the locomotive SILVERDALE No.11, built by Peckett of Bristol in 1911, shunting in the colliery yard on 2 September 1964. This locomotive would have been a familiar sight working Silverdale coal traffic to and from Pool Dam over the NSR and later LMS, from when it was built until some time during the Second World War when the operation of private trains ceased. Always kept in lovely external condition, as is obvious from this photograph, it had a long life and was not scrapped until November 1966. The wagons on the skyline are on the site of the original NSR line from Silverdale to Leycett, as described in Chapter Two.

Appendices

APPENDIX I
BOARD OF TRADE RETURNS
NORTH STAFFORDSHIRE RAILWAY 1879-1912

YEAR	PASSENGERS	£
1879	4,712,976	143,082
1880	4,904,342	153,276
1881	5,058,585	153,078
1882	5,688,461	159,514
1883	6,056,166	165,368
1884	6,047,515	167,655
1885	5,902,848	164,932
1886	5,917,077	164,883
1887	5,920,822	168,550
1888	5,995,873	166,553
1889	6,386,956	173,210
1890	6,860,498	184,734
1891	7,015,888	191,697
1892	7,185,042	192,808
1893	7,018,620	189,434
1894	7,065,778	191,560
1895	7,257,470	194,215
1896	7,527,526	202,240
1897	7,700,412	206,154
1898	8,057,228	213,510
1899	8,314,719	220,207
1900	7,563,771	216,758
1901	7,121,402	214,547
1902	7,021,505	214,730
1903	6,937,791	214,198
1904	6,648,497	210,145
1905	6,528,906	209,431
1906	6,592,370	213,631
1907	6,792,015	219,280
1908	6,485,174	220,348
1909	6,566,493	211,925
1910	7,064,178	220,616
1911	7,001,301	222,696
1912	6,536,188	213,085

£ = GROSS RECEIPTS
The number of passengers shown is exclusive of season ticket
holders but the gross receipts include season ticket revenue.

When they were built, as described in the text, the MCCI Yorkshire Engine Company of Sheffield locomotives for use at Apedale did not have cabs. However, as can be seen on the photograph earlier in the book, they did later have them fitted. This is APEDALE, Yorkshire number 1276 of 1915, in the maker's official guise prior to delivery and bestowing of its name. These were quite large locomotives with 16in diameter cylinders and Haycock design fireboxes - notice that the top of the firebox is level with the top of the saddle tank. The design was based on the earlier locomotives at Apedale built by Manning Wardle. However, at the time the new engines were ordered, one of the MCCI directors, Sir Fredrick J Jones Bt, was also a director of the Yorkshire Engine Company, and this may have had a bearing on why the order went to Sheffield. Nevertheless, it should be noted that as it was war time, the Ministry of Munitions would have been involved as both Yorkshire and the MCCI were Controlled Establishments under the various Munitions of War Acts.

APPENDIX II INDUSTRIAL LOCOMOTIVES

APEDALE IRONWORKS AND COLLIERIES

CHESTERTON (formerly KNUTTON)	0-6-0ST	IC	13 x 18	MW	317/1870
KNUTTON (formerly KEELE)	0-4-0ST	OC	13 x 18	MW	471/1874
PEPLOW	0-4-0ST	OC	13 x 18	MW	503/1875
AUDLEY	0-6-0ST	IC	13 x 18	MW	542/1875
BURLEY (formerly APEDALE)	0-6-0ST	IC	13 x 18	MW	222/1866
PODMORE	0-6-0ST	IC	13 x 18	MW	870/1882
		Rebuilt	14 x 18		1900
APEDALE	0-6-0ST	IC	16 x 22	MW	1367/1897
NEWCASTLE (formerly APEDALE)	0-6-0ST	IC	13 x 18	MW	1462/1899
NEWCASTLE	0-6-0ST	IC	13 x 18	MW	1532/1901
HALMEREND	0-6-0ST	IC	16 x 22	YE	1275/1915
APEDALE	0-6-0ST	IC	16 x 22	YE	1276/1915
KNUTTON	0-6-0ST	IC	16 x 22	YE	1356/1917

APEDALE SLAG & TAR MACADAM CO. LTD., APEDALE

AUDLEY	0-6-0ST	IC	13 x 18	MW	542/1875
SLAGDALE	0-4-0ST	OC	12 x 18	WB	2574/1937

EFFRA (SALES) LTD., GENERAL ENGINEERS, APEDALE

	4wDM		65/85hp	MR	5752/1939

JOHN PRICE & SON, CONTRACTORS, CONSTRUCTION OF HOLDITCH COLLIERY BRANCH

DAN-Y-GRAIG	0-6-0ST	IC	13 x 20	MW	835/1882

HOLDITCH COLLIERY

CANNOCK WOOD	0-6-0ST	OC	13 x 20	FW	318/1876
		Rebuilt		SIS	1931
WALMER	0-4-0ST	OC	14 x 22	SIS	2/1910
		Rebuilt		SIS	1930
LIONEL	0-4-0ST	OC	14 x 22	AB	871/1900
		Rebuilt		SIS	
WINWICK	0-6-0T	OC	16 x 24	HC	1418/1923
No. 17	0-6-0ST	OC	16 x 24	WB	2818/1945
	4wVBT	VCG	6¾ x 9	S	9534/1952
BOWOOD	0-6-0ST	OC	16 x 24	AB	1113/1907
CORNIST	0-6-0T	OC	17 x 24	HC	1503/1923
		Rebuilt		NCB	1963
ARTHUR LEIGHTON	0-6-0ST	IC	18 x 26	HC	1754/1943
DILHORNE No. 3	0-6-0ST	IC	18 x 26	WB	2787/1945
		Repaired		WB	8355/1953
HEM HEATH 3D	0-6-0DM		208hp	WB	3119/1956
HEM HEATH 4D	0-6-0DM		208hp	WB	3134/1958
No. 13D	6wDH		272hp	TH	181V/1967
HOLDITCH No. 1 (formerly 8D)	0-6-0DH		400hp	HE	7018/1971
HOLDITCH No. 2 (formerly 1D)	0-6-0DH		325hp	HE	6663/1969

KNUTTON IRONWORKS AND FORGE

KNUTTON	0-4-0ST	OC	14 x 22	AB	882/1900

SILVERDALE IRONWORKS AND COLLIERIES

				TW	162/1859
B9C (formerly JUDITH, originally SILVERDALE)	0-6-0ST	IC	13 x 18	MW	169/1865
APEDALE	0-6-0ST	IC	13 X 18	MW	222/1866
B8C (formerly ALICE, originally CHESTERTON)	0-6-0ST	IC	13 x 18	MW	247/1868
B10C (formerly AGNES, originally NEWCASTLE)	0-6-0ST	IC	13 x 18	MW	254/1868
KNUTTON (formerly KEELE)	0-4-0ST	OC	13 x 18	MW	471/1874
PEPLOW	0-4-0ST	OC	13 x 18	MW	503/1875
SILVERDALE No. 11	0-6-0ST	IC	14 x 20	P	1274/1912
No. 12 FORWARD (formerly EVELYN)	0-6-0ST	IC	13 x 20	HC	542/1900
WALMER	0-4-0ST	OC	14 x 22	SIS	2/1910
		Rebuilt		SIS	1930
DOLLY	0-4-0ST	OC	14 x 20	YE	470/1891
		Rebuilt Hartley Etruria 1905 and CW			1930
No. 17	0-6-0ST	OC	16 x 24	WB	2818/1945
	4wVBT	VCG	6¾ x 9	S	9535/1952
HESKETH	0-6-0ST	IC	14 x 20	P	1068/1905
HEM HEATH No. 1	0-6-0ST	OC	16 x 24	WB	3077/1955
HEM HEATH 3D	0-6-0DM		208hp	WB	3119/1956
HEM HEATH 4D	0-6-0DM		208hp	WB	3134/1958
	4wDM		88hp	RH	321730/1952

3' 0" GAUGE LOCOMOTIVES USED AT THE COKE OVENS:

APE	0-4-0			LILL	1877
TIGER	0-4-0			LILL	1877
	0-4-0VBT	G		CHAPLIN	1860-70

ABBREVIATIONS
DH	DIESEL HYDRAULIC LOCOMOTIVE
DM	DIESEL MECHANICAL LOCOMOTIVE
hp	HORSE POWER
G	GEARED TRANSMISSION
IC	INSIDE CYLINDERS: diameter x stroke in inches
OC	OUTSIDE CYLINDERS: diameter x stroke in inches
ST	SADDLE TANK ENGINE
T	SIDE TANK ENGINE
VCG	VERTICAL CYLINDERS – GEARED TRANSMISSION
VBT	VERTICAL BOILER TANK ENGINE

LOCOMOTIVE MANUFACTURERS
AB	ANDREW BARCLAY SONS & CO. LTD., CALEDONIA WORKS, KILMARNOCK
CHAPLIN	ALEXANDER CHAPLIN & CO. LTD., CRANSTONHILL WORKS, GLASGOW
CW	COWLISHAW WALKER & CO. LTD., ENGINEERS, BIDDULPH
FW	FOX, WALKER & CO., ATLAS ENGINE WORKS, BRISTOL
HC	HUDSWELL, CLARKE & CO. LTD., RAILWAY FOUNDRY, LEEDS
HE	HUNSLET ENGINE CO. LTD., LEEDS
LILL	LILLESHALL CO. LTD., OAKENGATES
MR	MOTOR RAIL LTD., SIMPLEX WORKS, BEDFORD
MW	MANNING, WARDLE & CO. LTD., BOYNE ENGINE WORKS, LEEDS
NCB	NATIONAL COAL BOARD, AREA CENTRAL WORKSHOPS, TRENTHAM
P	PECKETT & SONS LTD., ATLAS LOCOMOTIVE WORKS, BRISTOL
RH	RUSTON & HORNSBY LTD., LINCOLN
S	SENTINEL (SHREWSBURY) LTD., SHREWSBURY
SIS	SHELTON IRON STEEL & COAL CO. LTD., STOKE-ON-TRENT
TH	THOMAS HILL (ROTHERHAM) LTD., VANGUARD WORKS, KILNHURST
TW	THORNEWILL & WARHAM, BURTON-ON-TRENT
WB	W.G. BAGNALL LTD., CASTLE ENGINE WORKS, STAFFORD
YE	YORKSHIRE ENGINE CO. LTD., MEADOW HALL WORKS, SHEFFIELD

APPENDIX III
TRAIN MOVEMENTS AT NEWCASTLE STATION
TUESDAY, 13 JULY 1915

am

4.55	EMPTY STOCK ARRIVES FROM APEDALE FOR MIDLAND, COAL, COKE & IRON COMPANY'S (MCCI) PRIVATE WORKMEN'S TRAIN
5.02	PASSENGER TRAIN FROM STOKE DEPARTS FOR LEYCETT CALLING AT KNUTTON, SILVERDALE CROWN STREET, SILVERDALE AND KEELE
5.05	MCCI WORKMEN'S TRAIN DEPARTS FOR APEDALE CALLING AT BRAMPTON, LIVERPOOL ROAD AND KNUTTON GATE
5.35	PASSENGER TRAIN ARRIVES FROM STOKE AND TERMINATES HERE
5.40	PASSENGER TRAIN ORIGINATING HERE DEPARTS FOR STOKE
5.50	ORDINARY GOODS TRAIN FROM STOKE TO SILVERDALE PASSES THROUGH
6.09	PASSENGER TRAIN FROM LEYCETT TERMINATES HERE
6.10	ORDINARY GOODS TRAIN ARRIVES, STOKE TO BRAMPTON, AND SHUNTS AS REQUIRED
6.25	RAIL MOTOR ARRIVES FROM STOKE AND TERMINATES HERE
6.33	PASSENGER TRAIN ORIGINATING HERE DEPARTS FOR STOKE CALLING AT HARTSHILL & BASFORD
6.42	ORDINARY GOODS TRAIN, STOKE TO APEDALE, PASSES THROUGH
6.45	ORDINARY GOODS TRAIN FROM STOKE DEPARTS FOR BRAMPTON
6.50	RAIL MOTOR RETURNS TO STOKE
7.10	ORDINARY GOODS TRAIN, STOKE TO MARKET DRAYTON, PASSES THROUGH
7.23	PASSENGER TRAIN ARRIVES FROM STOKE AND TERMINATES HERE
7.39	PASSENGER TRAIN FROM STOKE DEPARTS FOR HARECASTLE CALLING AT SILVERDALE, KEELE, LEYCETT, HALMEREND, AUDLEY AND ALSAGER ROAD
7.40	PASSENGER TRAIN ORIGINATING HERE DEPARTS FOR STOKE
7.58	PASSENGER TRAIN ARRIVES FROM STOKE AND TERMINATES HERE
8.10	PASSENGER TRAIN ORIGINATING HERE DEPARTS FOR STOKE
8.12	ORDINARY GOODS TRAIN, BRAMPTON TO NEWCASTLE JUNCTION (THENCE 9.30am CLIFF VALE TO CREWE) PASSES THROUGH
8.20	PASSENGER ARRIVES FROM STOKE AND TERMINATES HERE
8.30	PASSENGER TRAIN ORIGINATING HERE DEPARTS FOR STOKE
8.40	GREAT WESTERN GOODS TRAIN FROM SHREWSBURY DEPARTS FOR STOKE – THIS TRAIN ARRIVED BRAMPTON AT 8.30am
8.56	PASSENGER TRAIN ARRIVES FROM STOKE AND TERMINATES HERE
9.03	PASSENGER TRAIN ORIGINATING HERE DEPARTS FOR STOKE
9.10	PASSENGER TRAIN FROM MARKET DRAYTON DEPARTS FOR STOKE – DOES NOT CONVEY HORSES OR PRIVATE CARRIAGES EXCEPTING FROM MARKET DRAYTON OR BEYOND FOR STOKE OR BEYOND
9.25	MCCI PRIVATE GOODS TRAIN FROM APEDALE ARRIVES AT MARSH WHARF
9.26	PASSENGER TRAIN FROM STOKE DEPARTS FOR MARKET DRAYTON CALLING AT SILVERDALE, KEELE, MADELEY ROAD, PIPE GATE AND NORTON-IN-HALES – ENGINE SHUNTS AS REQUIRED AT MARKET DRAYTON
9.40	ORDINARY MINERAL TRAIN FROM STOKE TO APEDALE DEPARTS
9.42	PASSENGER TRAIN FROM HARECASTLE DEPARTS FOR STOKE – THIS TRAIN WAS WORKED BY ENGINE AND MEN OFF THE 8.0am WHEELOCK TO HARECASTLE TRAIN
9.55	MCCI PRIVATE GOODS TRAIN DEPARTS MARSH WHARF FOR APEDALE
10.15	ORDINARY MINERAL TRAIN FROM SILVERDALE TO STOKE DEPARTS
10.25	PASSENGER TRAIN ARRIVES FROM STOKE AND TERMINATES HERE
10.30	PASSENGER TRAIN ORIGINATING HERE DEPARTS FOR STOKE
10.38	GREAT WESTERN GOODS TRAIN, STOKE TO COLEHAM, PASSES THROUGH
10.52	ORDINARY MINERAL TRAIN, APEDALE TO NORTON BRIDGE, PASSES THROUGH
10.55	ORDINARY GOODS TRAIN FROM MARKET DRAYTON ARRIVES AND SHUNTS AS REQUIRED
11.05	ORDINARY GOODS TRAIN FROM MARKET DRAYTON DEPARTS FOR STOKE – THIS TRAIN CONVEYS FROM MARKET DRAYTON WAGONS FOR GREAT NORTHERN ROUTE TO CONNECT AT NEWCASTLE JUNCTION WITH THE 2.25pm CHADDESDEN TRAIN
11.20	ORDINARY GOODS TRAIN FROM STOKE TO DIGLAKE ARRIVES AND SHUNTS AS REQUIRED DEPARTING BRAMPTON AT 11.43am
11.41	PASSENGER TRAIN FROM STOKE DEPARTS FOR HARECASTLE CALLING AT SILVERDALE, KEELE, LEYCETT, HALMEREND AND AUDLEY AND ALSAGER ROAD
11.52	ORDINARY GOODS TRAIN, STOKE TO SILVERDALE, PASSES THROUGH
11.55	RAIL MOTOR ARRIVES FROM STOKE AND TERMINATES HERE
12.00	RAIL MOTOR DEPARTS FOR STONE CALLING AT STOKE, WHIELDON ROAD, MOUNT PLEASANT, SIDEWAY, TRENTHAM AND BARLASTON

pm

12.32	PASSENGER TRAIN ARRIVES FROM STOKE AND TERMINATES HERE
12.38	PASSENGER TRAIN ORIGINATING HERE DEPARTS FOR STOKE
12.50	ORDINARY GOODS TRAIN, STOKE TO APEDALE, DEPARTS
1.01	PASSENGER TRAIN FROM STOKE DEPARTS FOR MARKET DRAYTON CALLING AT SILVERDALE, KEELE, MADELEY ROAD, PIPE GATE AND NORTON-IN-HALES
1.01	PASSENGER TRAIN FROM MARKET DRAYTON DEPARTS FOR STOKE – DOES NOT CONVEY HORSE BOXES OR PRIVATE CARRIAGES EXCEPTING FROM MARKET DRAYTON OR BEYOND FOR STOKE OR BEYOND
1.20	RAIL MOTOR FROM STOKE DEPARTS FOR LEYCETT CALLING AT BRAMPTON, LIVERPOOL ROAD, KNUTTON, SILVERDALE CROWN STREET, SILVERDALE AND KEELE
1.35	PASSENGER TRAIN ARRIVES FROM STOKE AND TERMINATES HERE
1.53	ORDINARY GOODS TRAIN, STOKE TO MARKET DRAYTON, ARRIVES AND SHUNTS AS REQUIRED DEPARTING BRAMPTON SIDING AT 2.10pm AND THEN SHUNTS AS REQUIRED AT SILVERDALE, KEELE, PIPE GATE AND NORTON-IN-HALES – CONVEYS TRANSHIP ROAD VANS
1.55	PASSENGER TRAIN ORIGINATING HERE DEPARTS FOR STOKE
2.05	ORDINARY GOODS TRAIN, PRATTS SIDINGS TO LEYCETT, ARRIVES
2.10	ORINARY GOODS TRAIN FOR LEYCETT DEPARTS, SHUNTING AT SILVERDALE AND KEELE AS REQUIRED – DOES NOT RUN BEYOND SILVERDALE IF TRAFFIC IS LIGHT
2.32	PASSENGER TRAIN ARRIVES FROM STOKE AND TERMINATES HERE
2.37	PASSENGER TRAIN FROM HARECASTLE DEPARTS FOR STOKE
2.52	PASSENGER TRAIN ORIGINATING HERE DEPARTS FOR STOKE
2.58	ORDINARY GOODS TRAIN, APEDALE TO STOKE, PASSES THROUGH
3.05	ORDINARY GOODS TRAIN, NEWCASTLE JUNCTION TO BRAMPTON, PASSES THROUGH
3.13	RAIL MOTOR ARRIVES FROM LEYCETT AND TERMINATES HERE
3.15	PASSENGER TRAIN ARRIVES FROM STOKE AND TERMINATES HERE
3.17	MCCI WORKMEN'S TRAIN ARRIVES FROM APEDALE AND TERMINATES HERE
3.25	MCCI EMPTY STOCK DEPARTS FOR APEDALE
3.35	ORDINARY GOOS TRAIN, BRAMPTON TO NEWCASTLE JUNCTION, DEPARTS – PROCEEDS TO PRATTS SIDINGS IF REQUIRED
3.40	ORDINARY MINERAL TRAIN, DIGLAKE TO STOKE, PASSES THROUGH
3.50	PASSENGER TRAIN ORIGINATING HERE DEPARTS FOR STOKE
4.04	PASSENGER TRAIN FROM STOKE DEPARTS FOR HARECASTLE CALLING AT SILVERDALE, KEELE, LEYCETT, HALMEREND, AUDLEY AND ALSAGER ROAD
4.15	RAIL MOTOR ORIGINATING HERE DEPARTS FOR STOKE
4.25	ORDINARY MINERAL TRAIN, STOKE TO APEDALE, PASSES THROUGH
4.56	PASSENGER TRAIN FROM MARKET DRAYTON DEPARTS FOR STOKE
5.01	PASSENGER TRAIN FROM STOKE DEPARTS FOR MARKET DRAYTON CALLING AT SILVERDALE, KEELE, MADELEY ROAD, PIPE GATE AND NORTON-IN-HALES
5.15	PASSENGER TRAIN FROM STOKE TERMINATES HERE
5.20	PASSENGER TRAIN ORIGINATING HERE DEPARTS FOR STOKE
5.26	RAIL MOTOR FROM TRENTHAM PARK DEPARTS FOR BRAMPTON
5.38	RAIL MOTOR FROM BRAMPTON DEPARTS FOR TRENTHAM PARK CALLING AT HARTSHILL & BASFORD, STOKE, WHIELDON ROAD, MOUNT PLEASANT, SIDEWAY AND TRENTHAM

BIBLIOGRAPHY

BAKER, Allan C.

An Illustrated History of Stoke and North Staffordshire's Railways, Irwell Press, 2000

Holditch Colliery, The Industrial Locomotive 28 & 29, 1983

Industrial Locomotives of North Staffordshire, Industrial Railway Society, 1997

Madeley & Leycett Collieries, The Industrial Railway Record 161, 2000

Silverdale Colliery, The Industrial Locomotive 31 & 34, 1983/4

The Iron, Steel and Coal Industry in North Staffordshire, Irwell Press, 2003

The Potteries Loop Line, Trent Valley Publications, 1986

BRIGGS, John

Newcastle under Lyme 1173-1973, North Staffordshire Polytechnic, 1973

CHRISTIANSEN, Rex and MILLER R W

The North Staffordshire Railway, David & Charles, 1971

DEAN, Richard

Map – Canals of North Staffordshire, M & M Baldwin, 1997

DIBDIN, H G

Tramways in the Potteries and North Staffordshire, The Tramway Review 26 and 27, 1959/60

FELL, Mike G

Memories of the Market Drayton Branch, North Staffordshire Railway Study Group Journal 15, 2004

The North Stafford Argentinas, The Journal of the Stephenson Locomotive Society 812, 2001

HADFIELD, Charles

The Canals of the West Midlands, David & Charles, 1966

HOLLICK, Dr. J R

The Workings of the Locomotives and Trains of Private Firms over the North Staffordshire Railway, Private publication

HOPKINS, Ken

North Staffordshire Locomotives, Trent Valley Publications, 1986

LESTER, C R

The Stoke to Market Drayton Line, The Oakwood Press, 1983 & 2001

LINDSAY, Jean

The Trent & Mersey Canal, David & Charles, 1979

MANIFOLD

The North Staffordshire Railway, Henstock, 1952

PHILLIPS, John

Phillips Inland Navigation 1805, David & Charles reprint, 1970

PRIESTLEY, Joseph

Priestley's Navigable Rivers and Canals 1831, David & Charles reprint, 1969

We have also consulted the Victoria History of the County of Stafford Vol. VIII published by the University of London in 1963 and NSR, LMS and BR Working Timetables, Appendices to Working Timetables and other official documents. Reference has also been made to various issues of the Locomotive Magazine, The Railway Magazine, Railway World and to the following issues of the Journal of the Stephenson Locomotive Society: 278, 286, 306, 309, 311, 312, 313, 317, 322 and 335. These were published between 1948 and 1953 and contain extensive notes on the North Staffordshire Locomotives.

The engine in this view, seen when newly delivered, is almost certainly the Silverdale Company locomotive given the name NEWCASTLE very soon after the photograph was taken. Like all the early Silverdale locomotives it was built by Manning Wardle & Company of Leeds (No 254 of 1868), and later named AGNES, reputedly after a member of the Stanier family; a daughter perhaps. After the Butterley Company took over the Silverdale lease it was given the designation B10C, but probably reverted to AGNES after the lease was terminated in 1903. Unlikely to have been used as a locomotive after about 1911, parts of its frames, cylinders and motion, along with parts from the sister engine SILVERDALE (manning Wardle 169/1865), were used in about 1920 to construct a stationary winding engine which survived at the colliery until about 1979.

Manning Wardle locomotives were also favoured at Apedale, and this is another of them, NEWCASTLE (No1532 of 1901), a photograph taken when the engine was quite new. The engine stands on the Apedale & Podmore Hall Railway, a line connecting the operations at Apedale with those at Halmerend, identified by the line of poplar trees in the background at Miry Wood, as the line left the Apedale site for Halmerend.